CAROLINGIAN CHRONICLES

CAROLINGIAN CHRONICLES

Royal Frankish Annals and Nithard's *Histories*

Translated by
Bernhard Walter Scholz
with
Barbara Rogers

Ann Arbor Paperbacks
THE UNIVERSITY OF MICHIGAN PRESS

First edition as an Ann Arbor Paperback 1972

ISBN 0-472-06186-0
Published in the United States of America by
The University of Michigan Press
Manufactured in the United States of America

1991 1990 6 5

Preface

The annals of the Carolingian court and Nithard's history of the wars among the sons of Louis the Pious tell the story of a century of Carolingian history (741–843). These works are perhaps less elegant than Einhard's *Life of Charlemagne* and certainly less familiar to the student of medieval history. But we have no more comprehensive or more detailed record of this formative period in the making of the West. Not less significantly the *Royal Frankish Annals* and Nithard's *Histories* are two conspicuous examples of medieval historiography. Thus, they are worthy of wider notice, especially at a time when historical thought and method in the Middle Ages are attracting an increasing number of readers.

If my interest in medieval historians goes back some years to three remarkable medievalists at the Julius-Maximilians-Universität in Würzburg, the late Michael Seidlmayer, Karl Bosl (now at Munich), and Otto Meyer, the translation of these two chronicles—using the term in its broader sense—was actually begun while I was teaching courses in historiography and early medieval history. Changing Carolingian Latin into readable modern English is no mean challenge, as I now know, and this book would not be what it is without the aid of others. I am much indebted to Dr. Barbara Rogers, who discovered some of the idiomatic possibilities of the texts in English translation; to Dr. Joseph Mahoney, who read the Introduction and cheerfully remedied patent oversights; to the Reverend Dr. William Scott Morton, who reviewed the whole of the manuscript and, at an early stage, made a number of valuable suggestions, leaving behind some echoes of sermons on sin and damnation from the pulpit of the Kirk; and to Mrs. Rosalind Tsai, who drew recognizable maps from my crude drafts. Of course, I remain ultimately responsible for the translations and for the introductory and annotative materials. Finally, I am grateful to my wife for her tact and sustaining good sense.

BERNHARD WALTER SCHOLZ

Seton Hall University
South Orange, New Jersey

Contents

MAPS

SHORT TITLES AND ABBREVIATIONS

Abel-Simson	S. Abel, *Jahrbücher des fränkischen Reiches unter Karl dem Grossen,* I, rev. B. Simson, II by B. Simson. Leipzig, 1888, 1883.
BML	J. F. Boehmer, *Regesta Imperii: Die Regesten des Kaiserreichs unter den ersten Karolingern,* rev. E. Mühlbacher, 2d ed. J. Lechner. Innsbruck, 1908.
Einhard	*Einhardi vita Caroli Magni,* 6th ed. O. Holder-Egger. MGH, *SrG.* Hanover/Leipzig, 1907.
Kurze	*Annales regni Francorum 741-829,* ed. F. Kurze. MGH, *SrG.* Hanover, 1895.
Lauer	P. Lauer, ed. and tr., *Nithard: Histoire des fils de Louis le Pieux. Les Classiques de l'histoire de France au moyen âge.* Paris, 1926.
Lot/Halphen	F. Lot and L. Halphen, *Le règne de Charles le Chauve.* Paris, 1909.
LP	*Le Liber Pontificalis,* ed. L. Duchesne, 2 vols. *Bibliothèque des Écoles françaises d'Athènes et de Rome.* Paris, 1886–92.
Meyer	G. Meyer von Knonau, *Über Nithards vier Bücher Geschichten: Der Bruderkrieg der Söhne Ludwigs des Frommen und sein Geschichtsschreiber.* Leipzig, 1866.

MGH	Monumenta Germaniae historica.
Cap.	*Legum sectio* II: *Capitularia regum Francorum,* 2 vols., ed. A. Boretius and others. Hanover, 1883–90.
EE	*Epistolae,* 8 vols., ed. P. Ewald, L. M. Hartmann, E. Dümmler, E. Perels, E. Caspar, and others. Berlin, 1887–1939.
PL	*Poetae latini medii aevi: Poetae latini aevi Carolini,* 4 vols., ed. E. Dümmler, L. Traube, P. von Winterfeld, K. Strecker. Berlin, 1880–1923.
SrG	*Scriptores rerum Germanicarum in usum scholarum ex monumentis Germaniae historicis recusi.* Hanover, 1840 ff.
SS	*Scriptores,* 32 vols. Hanover/Leipzig, 1826–1928.
Müller	*Nithardi historiarum libri IV,* 3d ed. E. Müller, MGH, *SrG.* Hanover/Leipzig, 1907.
NA	*Neues Archiv der Gesellschaft für ältere deutsche Geschichtskunde*
O	Original version of the *Royal Frankish Annals.*
PL	J. P. Migne, *Patrologiae cursus completus. . . .* Series Latina, 217 vols. Paris, 1844–55.
R	Revised version of the *Royal Frankish Annals.*
RFA	*Royal Frankish Annals.*
Simson	B. Simson, *Jahrbücher des fränkischen Reichs unter Ludwig dem Frommen.* 2 vols. Leipzig, 1874–76.
Thegan	*Thegani vita Hludowici imperatoris.* MGH, *SS,* II, 590–604.
VH	*Anonymi vita Hludowici imperatoris.* MGH, *SS,* II, 607–48.

Introduction

One of the perennial obsessions of medieval authors was the suspicion that the past was superior to the present. In the preface to his *Life of Charlemagne*, Einhard of Seligenstadt expressed the fear that his work might offend the minds of those who despise everything modern. Yet he managed to overcome his scruples because he also knew of many "who do not consider everything done today as unworthy of mention and deserving to be given over to silence and oblivion." The vigorous government of the Carolingians and the regeneration of society in their time were indeed a great impulse to historical writing. Charles Martel, Pepin, and Charlemagne and his descendants provided great deeds for the historian. These rulers also dispensed patronage, and their reform of the Church provided a measure of literacy and learning; as a consequence, the number of historical works was large and their variety considerable.[1] Charlemagne himself collected historical poems written in the vernacular, which Einhard called the "barbarous and age-old songs that sing the deeds and battles of the ancient kings." Paul the Deacon wrote the history of his Lombard people, a sort of tribal history *(origo gentis)* in the manner of Gregory of Tours's history of the Franks or Bede's history of the Anglo-Saxons. Freculph of Lisieux and Ado of Vienne followed a familiar pattern of historical literature in their world chronicles. Einhard wrote his celebrated secular biography, the *Life of Charlemagne.* Alcuin was one of many contemporaries who paid homage to the saints by composing their lives. Ermoldus Nigellus recorded the varying fortunes of Louis the Pious in a Latin poetical history, and a monk of St.-Wandrille wrote the history of his monastery, in the tradition of the *Liber Pontificalis*, centered on the lives of its abbots.

The most unassuming works of history written during this age were the Carolingian annals, yet in the *Royal Frankish Annals* they become the most important narrative of this time: the story of the growth and flowering of the empire. Other works are almost impossible to classify; this is true of Nithard's *Histories*, also called the *History of the Sons of Louis the Pious*, the report of an eyewitness on the internal conflicts which tore the Frankish empire apart. Together, the *Royal Frankish Annals* and Nithard's *Histories* provide a record, contemporary and official, of Carolingian history from the death of Charles Martel to the Treaty of Verdun. Their significance both as sources of the Carolingian age and as examples of medieval historiography has been long recognized. Not surprisingly, much French and German élan and subtlety have gone into the analysis of these works and their authors. The debate on textual problems, value, and viewpoints will certainly go on. But from the studies of these men and a fresh reading of the texts a relatively clear and reliable picture emerges of who these writers were and of what they wished and were able to do.

THE ROYAL FRANKISH ANNALS

The *Royal Frankish Annals* (*Annales regni Francorum,* as they have been called since Ranke) covers the period from 741 to 829. Although the oldest manuscript of the RFA was found in the monastery of Lorsch near Worms, Ranke saw that these annals had not been written there but at the royal court.[2] Of their character and significance M. L. W. Laistner has said:

> The *Royal Annals* provide the reader with a brief, unadorned narrative; but being restricted in scope, they leave him in the dark on many topics connected with the political, diplomatic, and military history with which they deal. Nor must one expect

analysis of motives or a deeper understanding of cause and effect in a plain annalistic record of events. Nevertheless the *Royal Annals* must be regarded as the most important single source for the reign of Charlemagne, and must form the basis of any historical reconstruction of that momentous era in European history.[3]

During the Carolingian age annals appeared simultaneously in many places, the result of man's ancient urge to give form to his collective memory.[4] Egyptian and Babylonian rulers had kept annual records, and in Roman days the lists of the consuls had given rise to a similar form of rudimentary historiography. In the centuries when Christian missionaries were carrying the Gospel into the West, the Easter tables provided room for annual entries on the events of the year. Anglo-Saxon monks were apparently the first to record on these lunar calendars noteworthy occurrences around them, and Anglo-Saxon missionaries brought the Easter tables and their casual notations to the Continent. One monastery, then, copied from another, frequently borrowing not only the dates of Easter but the events noted on the margins. Before long the historical records were copied and continued for their own sake and expanded into major works of history by consulting and using other sources of information. Their diversity, varying degree of accuracy, and uncertain relationship to each other make them a difficult source to use. Students of the Carolingian annals have been struck, for example, by the similarity of phrases, which seem to suggest a complicated interdependence; they have assumed that some surviving annals are based on lost works, and with some luck they have even discovered works very similar to those whose existence they had suspected, as was the case with the *Annals of Salzburg* or the *Annals of Metz.* But it has also been made clear more recently that the similarities in many cases may have been due simply to the fact that the language of the annalists was limited and conventional.[5] The earliest continental annals had their origins in monasteries, but soon annals were composed which looked upon the events of their age with a broader view and from a more central perspective; this is particularly true of the *Royal Frankish Annals.*

Among the learned activities which Charlemagne and his court inspired and promoted was the writing of history. Not only was the

Frankish king interested, as his biographer reveals, in St. Augustine's theology of history,[6] but he made an effort to preserve records on which the history of his rule could be based. The RFA mentions his archives; he ordered the preservation of his laws, and the compilation in the *Codex Carolinus* of papal and Byzantine letters addressed to himself and his father and grandfather. He probably had the *Liber Pontificalis* copied at his court and apparently gave his approval when Paul the Deacon wrote the *Deeds of the Bishops of Metz,* in which the history of the Carolingian house is given special attention. Whether he ordered the writing of the RFA remains uncertain. But it seems at least likely that Charlemagne encouraged the composition of this work as a record for posterity and an aide-mémoire to the officers of his government.[7]

That the RFA has an official character was convincingly argued by Leopold von Ranke more than a century ago. The historian noted two striking features in the first part (741–95), written evidently by a single author: first, a tendency to keep silent on great disasters in the field and on internal troubles, such as the conspiracies which arose from time to time, and second, his intimate knowledge of the affairs which he chose to record. No monk living in the seclusion of the cloister could have been so well informed on matters of politics and diplomacy. Ranke suggested a comparison of the RFA with the monastic annals of this period. The annals written in monasteries report only the most striking events and then note only their most general features. The first author of the RFA, however, tells in terse and precise terms not only about military campaigns but about the make-up of the armies, their commanders, and the purpose and nature of the individual military actions. He is also well versed in the diplomatic negotiations of the court. No one who was not close to Charlemagne's council could give such detailed information about the operations against Benevento and Bavaria. The combination of these two elements, good information and great reservation, convinced Ranke that the work was an official compilation. Ranke thought that the author was a cleric well acquainted with public affairs and perhaps officially commissioned to do this work. He compiled his notes at the court in a rough style, since he wrote before the palace school helped polish the Latin of the Frankish clergy; he was a man of the old ways, but he rose above himself because he witnessed and commemorated momentous events.[8]

Ranke's view of the RFA as an official work has now been generally accepted. But its official character does not mean that every single word was examined and approved or that the annals were in any way conceived to have a secret character. On the contrary, their purpose was obviously to influence public opinion and to convey to posterity the Carolingian version of Carolingian history.[9] It was an old custom by the time of Charlemagne, as Smaragdus, the reforming abbot of St.-Mihiel, points out, for the ruler to authorize an official record of his reign. The relatives of Pepin commissioned such a record; Charles the Bald carried with him the annals composed by Prudentius,[10] and Alfred the Great inspired the writings of annals later in the ninth century.[11] Considerations of politics and public opinion occasionally influenced the nature of the information revealed or concealed by the RFA. A Byzantine offer of the imperial title made in 798 has been omitted, obviously for political reasons, since the well-informed annalist could not have been unaware of this extraordinary proposal.[12] The propagandistic character of the work persuaded at least one scholar that more reliable and detailed court annals existed at one time. This hypothesis, however, cannot be upheld, since later annals, in particular the important ninth-century *Annals of St. Bertin,* resume the story in 829, the very year in which the RFA ends.[13]

Even a casual reading of the RFA suggests that more than one author had a hand in this work. Its composite nature is betrayed both by the manuscripts and by its language and style. Friedrich Kurze, who has published the best critical edition of the RFA, attempted to clarify the problem of authorship by an examination of the manuscripts. The results of his effort were unsatisfactory, and more recently scholars have again fallen back on an examination of the linguistic and stylistic peculiarities of the work. It seems certain now that the first author compiled the RFA between 787 and 793 on the basis of older annals and the continuations of Fredegar, and then followed them with contemporary events. The personality of the first author remains an insoluble problem. None of the names suggested, such as Arno, bishop of Salzburg, or Riculf, archbishop of Mainz, have found general acceptance, nor has the thesis that the fall of Duke Tassilo of

Bavaria in 788 led to the composition of the annals. The author was probably a member of the royal chapel; he shows familiarity with the language of documents and of the law and made use of official records and notations. Ranke proposed that Angilram of Metz, archchaplain from 784 to 791, inspired the writing of the RFA; it was Angilram who prevailed on Paul the Deacon to write the *Deeds of the Bishops of Metz* and on Donatus to compose a *Life of St. Trudo.* Several authors can be assumed if the work was compiled in the royal chapel, as Monod has pointed out, and the archchaplains would have done no more than supervise the work. The theory of multiple authorship would explain the fact that changes in style do not coincide with the archchaplains' years of death.[14]

The second part of the RFA comprises the years 795 to 807. The entries during these years are obviously contemporaneous with the events, but there is no agreement about the exact year in which authors changed. Different dates, all within the period from 792 to 795, have been suggested. Monod would ascribe the confusion of the annals during these years to the fact that Charles's favorite palace at Worms burned down in 790 and that only in 794 did Aix-la-Chapelle become the new residence of the court. The annals between 795 and 807 are more personal; the narrative remains simple, but the language reveals the author's classical training. Again, the identity of the writer is a mystery and authorship by several members of the chapel is a possibility.[15]

The third part of the RFA begins with the year 808 and extends to the last entries in 829. These annals are also contemporaneous. Their language is characterized by more skillful sentence construction, more extensive use of participles and connectives, a larger vocabulary, a stronger influence of classical models, and an occasional tendency toward bombast. This section of the RFA can be subdivided after the annal for 820. It seems that in the last part, from 818 to 829, the influence of the archchaplain Hilduin, abbot of St.-Denis, is unmistakable; he may have had the cooperation of Helisachar, abbot of St. Maximin in Trier and of other monasteries and chancellor of Louis the Pious (808–19); in any case the composition of these annals in the royal chapel is almost a certainty.[16]

Among the different men who have been suggested as authors of the RFA, the name of Einhard is obviously of special interest. F.

Kurze assumed that Einhard wrote the annals from 796 to 819, and B. Simson believed that he could detect Einhard's pen in the annals from 809 to 829. But none of the arguments for ascribing any part of the RFA to the author of the *Life of Charlemagne* has been very convincing. There are similarities in the language of the RFA and in that of the *Life of Charlemagne.* But this is explained by the fact that Einhard knew and used the RFA. The style and the language of the third part of the RFA eliminate Einhard as a possible author. There is a similarity between Einhard's Latin and that of the second part of the RFA, but this is because literary skills improved during the Carolingian Renaissance to the benefit of the authors of both works. The first to claim Einhard as the author of the RFA was Odilo of St.-Médard in his *Translatio S. Sebastiani.* He names Einhard as the author of a work which he entitles *Gesta Caesarum Karoli Magni et filii Hludowici* and which, according to Odilo, has a reference to the translation of St. Sebastian by Hilduin, abbot of St.-Denis. This translation is, indeed, mentioned in the RFA under the year 826; and the *Gesta Caesarum* is obviously identical with the RFA. Odilo's erroneous belief that Einhard was its author probably resulted from the fact that in his, as in most medieval manuscripts, the RFA is preceded by Einhard's *Life of Charlemagne.*[17]

Einhard's relationship to the RFA has been a particular problem with regard to a group of manuscripts of the RFA containing a version of the RFA which has been revised in style and contents. Ranke and others considered Einhard as the author of these revised annals;[18] they appear in print as *Annales qui dicuntur Einhardi.*[19] The revision originally was believed to have been undertaken shortly after 801. But then H. Bloch demonstrated that there are stylistic revisions up to 812, although no change in the material recorded was made after 801. At the present time the consensus among students of the RFA seems to be that the revision was carried out after Charlemagne's death in 814 but before 817; Einhard's *Life of Charlemagne*, which reveals that its author knew the revised RFA, was written after 817. The language of the revised version is similar to that of the third part of the RFA. The revisor apparently belonged to the same court circle as the authors of the RFA, but wished to give the work a form more in keeping with the new style. As far as content is concerned, the revisor attempts to supplement the information of the original RFA by drawing on other sources that were accessible to him at the court. But a different point of view is evident in the revised version; most strikingly, it relates failures and disasters which the original annalist had been careful to omit, for example, the famous debacle of Charles's army at Roncesvalles in 778 which later inspired the *Chanson de Roland.* The revisor adds personal, geographical, and other details, as a comparison of the very first annal in its original and revised forms shows. He is also more inclined to make conjectures and to probe the motivations of the actors. He injects a new element into the RFA by attempting to present Charlemagne as the central figure, who alone plans, decides, and acts. Although he shows a great attachment to the deceased emperor, the revisor betrays that he was further in time from the actual events than the annalists. Apart from Einhard other persons have been suspected of revising the RFA, but no really convincing arguments have been put forward for any one individual.[20]

The authors of the RFA note only the bare outlines of the world in which they live. Military actions, diplomatic missions, and major political events attract their attention first; yet, in their barren record we catch a glimpse of the universe—physical, social, and spiritual—in which the writers breathed and thought.

It is a world in which nature presents a forbidding challenge to man, raising barriers around him and beating down his ambitions. The changes of the season determine the rhythm of life. Summer is the time of action, and campaigns begin when the horses can feed off the land and come to a sudden halt when heavy rains cause rivers to flood. In winter the king settles down in his palace, leaving the annalist little to report. Minor variations in the climate spell disaster. Animals and men are killed by severe cold or by pestilence resulting from mild weather and excessive humidity. Expeditions into foreign lands end with military success and yet lead to calamity when disease carries off the men and horses of the victor. Hail and lack of sunshine spoil the harvest and sour the wine. Famine stays the king's hand and forces him to postpone a campaign. Lightning strikes men and burns villages. Earthquakes cause mountains to tumble on top of cities, and eclipses inspire wonder and apprehension.

While nature threatens man with its spasmodic violence, divinity intervenes mysteriously: a large block of earth is moved without human support; ominous lights appear in the sky at night; a woman for two years abstains from all food except the bread of the Eucharist; a trace of the blood of Christ is found, and the discovery moves the pope to journey from Rome to Mantua; the relics of the saints miraculously heal the sick; the army of Charlemagne when suffering from thirst is marvelously relieved, like the Hebrews in the desert, by a sudden flow of water in a brook; the heathens are unable to burn a church because St. Boniface foretold that it would be proof against fire; and a picture of the Virgin and the infant Christ unaccountably shines with unusual brightness. Although the annalists record the intervention of the supernatural, divine activity is not presented as the immediate cause of political events. Rather it appears as a reminder that the natural order is forever maintained by the divine will and subject to sudden dispensation: the Lord of history ordains the happenings among men. But human decisions and drives—the lofty resolutions of the Frankish monarch and the beastly instincts of the Saxons—and stubborn circumstance cause change and thus make the history which the annalists record.

The annalists live in a world of villages and manors, of camps and castles, of few roads and fixed routes, where the Lombards can keep a single messenger or an entire army from passing across the Alps, and of uncertain frontiers which are difficult to protect. It is a world of simple and unpredictable technology. The Saxon siege machines do more damage to their operators than to the enemy; the gift of an organ from the emperor of Constantinople deserves an entry in the annals of the realm, and an organ-builder from the East is escorted to Aix-la-Chapelle by the treasurer of the emperor. Traveling is hazardous and slow; three men set out for the court of Harun al-Rashid in Bagdad, but only one survives to return after four years. Yet the intrepid main actor of the RFA, the Frankish king, seems as oblivious of physical obstacles as he is impatient with political opponents. In one year he builds two bridges over the Elbe and fortifies one of them by bulwarks of wood and earth at both ends; with a movable bridge of pontoons connected by anchors and ropes he makes the Danube passable. He attempts to construct a canal between Altmühl and Rednitz which would allow him to travel by ship from the Rhine into the Danube. On the coast of the North Sea he builds a fleet and restores a lighthouse. The Danish king Godofrid plans a protective rampart which is to connect the coast of the Baltic with that of the North Sea. These are interesting efforts but they cannot conceal that ambitions and designs far outstripped technical knowledge and expertise. The technological innovations which are made during these centuries naturally escape the attention of the annalists; they know nothing of the new plough, the harness, the crank, inventions which before long were to revolutionize the European economy, but are fascinated, as the ancients would have been, by a water clock, a marvel from the East, which at the completion of the hour makes a cymbal ring and has twelve tiny horsemen step out of little windows. Craftsmen and merchants are considered a great asset; the provision of builders and bricklayers by the archbishop of Grado is a reason for a diplomatic complaint; the merchants of Reric on the Baltic are resettled by the Danish king in his own kingdom because of the taxes which their town pays. Although this is not a narrow world—the king and his commanders range over the lands from the Ebro to the Elbe and from Schleswig to Salerno—it is a world of poor communication, where the exchange of ambassadors takes years and rumors determine or delay political action.

Since the economic resources are limited, social relations are tense and brutal. Warfare and violence rake Carolingian society. The king embarks on at least one large military campaign a year; his failure to do so he fears might be interpreted as a sign of weakness. Military expeditions aim at the conquest of hostile strongholds and the pacification of provinces, but are regularly accompanied by savage punitive actions designed to ravage and destroy the fields and villages of the enemy. The frontiers of the vast kingdom are fluid and quickly overrun by elusive bands of Saxons, Basques, or Saracens which vanish into their forests or out to the seas before the cumbersome Frankish host appears. Even within the borders of the kingdom, the hold of the Carolingian ruler is precarious; revolt, conspiracy, and sullen opposition force the king into costly and time-consuming operations which frequently end with nothing more than feigned submission. Violence flares where the royal might is a distant menace; the king's emissary is slain and his missionary martyred while preaching the Gospel. Moorish and Viking pirates haunt the coasts, burn villages, seize booty, and carry away the inhabitants, leaving only the old and infirm behind. The Frankish ruler counters the violence of his subjects and enemies with brutal force; rebellious nobles are tonsured and locked up in monasteries; conspirators against the king are blinded or hanged on gibbets; multitudes are slain in battle, and the annalists report proudly the massacres wreaked on foreign tribes; over four thousand Saxon nobles are executed at Verden in 785; countless numbers are forcibly baptized; and entire populations are removed from their homelands and resettled in new regions.

The society of which the annalists write consists of the nobles and the people, *primores* and *populus*, but it is only the former who have a voice in determining the course of affairs. They are the large landowners and feudal warriors who are bound to their lord by bonds of personal loyalty. The RFA refers specifically to the act of homage by which a vassal places his hands in those of the king and becomes the king's man, and to the oath of fidelity sworn on the bodies of the saints. On important issues of the day—a foreign campaign, an expedition to Rome, the trial of a vassal—the king seeks the counsel of his vassals at special meetings or at the annual general assembly of the Franks. Foreign relations and military actions are the major, almost the exclusive, interest of the annalists. This is due in part to the old tradition of political history as first popularized by Thucydides, but it is also a result of the virtual absence from the Carolingian scene of properly organized governmental institutions about which the annalists might have written. The king is the government, an absolute monarch, the supreme commander, the chief legislator, the highest court of appeal. He derives his power from God and is bound to keep the peace on earth and to help his people to be saved in heaven. His despotism is restrained by his scanty resources rather than by the ethics of his political ideology.

There is no central government but only the royal household, and the functions of the officers of the court are primarily domestic. The RFA mentions the officials of the court—the chancellor, the chaplain, the treasurer, the notary, the chamberlain, the seneschal, the marshal, the master of the cupbearers, the master of the doorkeepers. They act as advisers, ambassadors, and military commanders of the king but do not head branches of a central government. The official most frequently mentioned in the RFA is the count, the king's representative who exercises full public authority in one of the several hundred counties into which the realm of the Carolingians is divided.

More prestigious and powerful are the positions of the counts or wardens of the marches along the frontiers of the empire or the special posts of command given from time to time to the *missi* of the Frankish king. The most important of these offices are held by relatives of the royal family. An incident which the RFA relates in the revised part of the annals under the year 782 indicates that kinship gives a man higher prestige than any official rank or position. The chamberlain Adalgis, the marshal Gailo, and the count of the palace Worad are defeated by the Saxons because they do not go into battle with a Frankish host under the command of the king's kinsman Theodoric for fear that he would receive all the credit for victory. The king's personal appearance is still the most effective and often the only way of enforcing the royal will, and this is another explanation for the king's ceaseless journeyings through his realm. The Carolingians, under the influence of their clerical advisers, attempt to replace the Merovingian notion that the kingdom is simply the monarch's personal property by the idea that king and community are bound together by mutual obligations. The kings continue to divide the kingdom among their heirs, however, just as they split their booty and distribute their spoils.

Filling the king's treasury, preserved apparently in the royal bedchamber and guarded by the chamberlain, is one of the unadmitted objectives of Carolingian foreign policy. The incessant conflicts of the Carolingians with their neighbors are a means to provide the king with sufficient funds to reward his vassals and to compensate for the meager resources and inadequate revenues of his kingdom. Tributes, gifts, and booty are therefore constant themes of the RFA. The Saxons have to present three hundred horses every year; Charlemagne carries away the gold and silver stored in the Saxon sanctuary called the Irminsul; he captures the treasure of the Lombard king Desiderius. Duke Eric of Friuli takes the treasure of the Avars, which has been accumulated by centuries of conquest and pillage and is stored in their central fortress, the "ring," and Charlemagne shares it with his vassals and the pope. Similarly, the spoils after the defeat of Ljudovit, duke of Lower Pannonia, are avidly seized and carried home.

The RFA usually fails to reveal the underlying objectives of campaigns and diplomatic missions, but it indicates the direction and the changing thrust of Carolingian foreign policy. In the beginning Pepin and Charles have their hands tied because they are forced to subjugate independently minded powers within the borders of the kingdom, in particular the dukes of Alamannia (742), Aquitaine (742–69), and Bavaria (743–88). These conflicts end with the seizure and submission of the rebels. The annalists make no attempt to determine the deeper causes of these revolts. They are most explicit in the case of Tassilo, duke of Bavaria, who is charged with wickedness, breach of oaths and promises, inconstancy, mendacity, disobedience, treachery, desertion, an attempt on the king's men, lèse majesté, with inciting the Huns against the Frankish king, and with permitting his wife Liutberga, a daughter of deposed King Desiderius of Lombardy, to set him against the Franks. His crime is not that he sought autonomy for his tribe but that he broke his oath of loyalty and deserted his lord.

The alliance of the Frankish kings with the papacy involves the Franks in the affairs of northern Italy, and the ensuing destruction of the Lombard kingdom results in the first great expansion of the Carolingian realm. The annalists describe the conflict from a narrow, self-righteous point of view as a struggle for the pope and the rights of St. Peter and against a wicked and oath-breaking tyrant and his arrogance and oppression. Next, the Saxon war consumes the energy of the Frankish king for more than two decades, ending in the permanent subjugation of the Saxons. Whereas Pepin conducts only occasional retaliatory raids against the pagan Saxon tribes (743, 744, 747, 758), Charles presses the war by annual campaigns (772–85), numerous battles, calculated brutalities, and the systematic depredation of Saxon territory. Charlemagne's determination and at the same time his sense of frustration are indicated by the revisor of the RFA when he writes that the king "decided to attack the treacherous and treaty-breaking tribe of the Saxons and to persist in this war until they were either defeated and forced to accept the Christian religion or entirely exterminated." Although this author is writing long after the Saxons have become part of the Carolingian empire, he does not trust them and maintains, under the year 785, that "the stubborn treachery of the Saxons quieted down for a few years, mainly because they could not find convenient opportunities for revolt." In 793 the Saxons, in fact, rebel again, and even the almost continuous presence of the king and his army between 793 and 799 does not entirely root out all opposition; as late as 804 the emperor has recourse to deportation and resettlement. Whereas the revisor of the RFA explains the bloody campaigns against the Saxons primarily as a consequence of their rebellion, their inroads into Frankish territory, and their stubborn treachery and perfidy, the original annalist sees the conflict above all as a war between Christians and pagans. One of the first acts of Charlemagne in Saxony is the destruction of the Irminsul, the heathen sanctuary; three times Frankish exploits and victories are accompanied by miracles; and phrases like "by the will of God," "with the help of God," "God frustrated their intentions," and "How much the power of God worked against them for the salvation of the Christians, nobody can tell," seem to indicate that to this annalist the Saxon campaign is almost a holy war to increase the kingdom of God.

The conquest of the lands between the Rhine and the Elbe involves the Carolingians with the eastern and northern neighbors of the Saxons. Charles considers the Elbe and the Saale as his eastern frontier and builds castles along these rivers, but the presence of Frankish power easily leads to Frankish interference in the affairs of the Slavs living on the eastern banks of the Elbe and the Saale. Deep inroads into Slavonic territory, like the attack on the Bohemians in 805, however, remain exceptional. The Slavs appear in the RFA for the first time in 780, but from then on Wilzi, Sorbs, Smeldingi, Linones, and especially the Obodrites are of continued interest to the annalists (782, 789, 806, 810, 811, 812, 815, 816, 817, 819, 821, 822, 823, 826). Charles plays the petty Slavonic chieftains against each other and punishes the attacks of the Slavs by expeditions beyond the Elbe, devastating the land and leaving only after hostages have been given. In this way the Slavs are compelled to recognize Frankish overlordship; they remain a potential threat to the Franks because they tend to ally themselves with their northern neighbors, the Danes. The annalists reveal no sympathy or understanding for the interests of these tribes. If the Franks wage war on them it is for breach of faith, or, if the people have at no time been subject to the Franks, because of their arrogance and hatred.

The Danes move within range of the annalists for the first time in 782 when their king Sigifrid sends ambassadors and the Saxon Widukind seeks refuge with them. Their relations with Franks and Slavs and their unending internal squabbles receive much attention in the RFA between 804 and 829. The annalists note that the Vikings infest the North Sea in 800 and are ravaging the Frankish coast in 810 and 820. In later years the RFA is extremely well informed on Danish affairs. The author knows, for example, about their exploits against Scotland and Ireland. Perhaps his information stems from the Frankish ambassadors sent to the Danish kings in 823, Counts Theothari and Hruodmund, who "carefully studied the dispute with the sons of Godofrid as well as the condition of the whole kingdom of the Norsemen and informed the emperor of all they could find out in these lands," or from Archbishop Ebbo of Reims, "who had gone to preach in the land of the Danes, on the counsel of the emperor and with the approval of the Roman pontiff, and had baptized many converts to the faith during the previous summer." The initial point at issue between Franks and Danes is apparently the question of Saxon fugitives. Later, the factions battling for the Danish throne seek outside support, and Charlemagne sponsors the cause of Heriold, who is baptized in 826 and given a base in Frisia for any emergency that might arise. The Danish kings are represented as haughty and foolhardy potentates who fail to recognize the power and majesty of the Frankish emperor, and references abound to "the mad king," "the arrogance and pride of the Danish king," his being "inflated with the vain hope of victory," his "hypocrisy" and "empty talk." But the concern with the Danes during these years indicates that the authors of the RFA were not only writing with all the frontiers of the wide empire in mind but perceived that the Norsemen constituted a growing threat in their time.

While the annalists frequently complain about the stubborn resistance of Saxons and Slavs, they are equally dissatisfied with the conduct of Basques and Bretons in the west. The Basques inflict a stinging defeat on the Frankish army in 778 in which many officers of the court are killed. The original annalist keeps silent on this episode; the revisor is frank but blames the disaster on "the unfavorable terrain and the unequal method of fighting" and considers the Franks superior to the Basques in arms and valor. Here again the charge of the annalists is that of "customary recklessness," "insolence," and "treachery." The Bretons rebel repeatedly (786, 799, 811, 818, 822, 824, 825), and the revisor as well as the later annalists similarly charge them with "fickleness," "treacherous spirit peculiar to the nation," "senseless obstinacy," and speak of the "arrogance of this faithless tribe," whose opposition, however, quickly collapses under the fierce blows of Frankish counts. Central and southern Italy, in particular the duchies of Spoleto and Benevento, enter the Frankish sphere of influence with the destruction of the Lombard kingdom in 774—and with Charlemagne's growing imperial ambitions. While the dukes of Spoleto are usually Franks appointed by the king, the dukes of Benevento retain a measure of independence but pay tribute. With the exception of the annal for 787 in the original version of the RFA, the affairs of central and southern Italy appear to be of marginal interest to the annalists. In any case, they appear to be of less significance than matters pertaining to Danes or Slavs.

The expansion of the empire and the growing prestige of its ruler bring the Franks into contact with the more distant powers of their world. In 777 a Moslem embassy from Spain is noted for the first time in the RFA; it is followed by a campaign which takes the emperor across the Ebro to Saragossa. Spanish affairs receive much attention between 797 and 828. Repeatedly peace is made with the emirs of Cordova and subsequently broken again. The Frankish kings concentrate their efforts on the areas of Pamplona and Saragossa and create the Spanish March in what later becomes the kingdom of Navarre and the county of Barcelona. But even at the end of the period covered by the RFA the Spanish March is not entirely secured, as the revolt of 827, the ravages of Abumarvan, the failure of the Frankish army, and the punishment of its commanders indicate. In the meantime the Franks are compelled to fight the Moslems on a much more uncertain front, the islands of the Mediterranean—Sardinia, Corsica, the Balearics—and the coasts of Italy which suffer from constant raids of Moslem pirates. The Christians repeatedly suffer severe losses. At one time eight merchant ships are sunk on their way from Corsica to Italy, and at another five hundred prisoners are discovered with a defeated Moslem force. They strike out, however, against the pirates from Italian ports, and Frankish counts fight the Moslems in Sardinia, Corsica, the Balearics, and even in North Africa.

Charles's conflicts with the Umayyard emir of Cordova make him an ally of the Abbasid caliph of Bagdad, the celebrated Harun al-Rashid. The RFA records two embassies sent by Charlemagne to Bagdad and two missions in return from the caliph (797–807).

Harun's emissaries carry presents which include an elephant, a clock, and a beautiful tent. Harun al-Rashid even cedes certain rights of the Holy Places in Palestine to Charlemagne. The embassy from the oriental ruler—called the "king of Persia" by the annalists—and his exotic gifts receive much attention in the RFA and seem to confirm in the authors' minds their lofty notion of Charlemagne's place in the world.

For a period of about twenty years (797–817) the RFA gives evidence of close diplomatic relations between Francia and Constantinople. As in the case of Harun al-Rashid the annalists take note of the Byzantine emperor first as the donator of expensive and unwonted presents; in the year 757 the emperor sends an organ to Pepin the Short. The next encounter recorded by the RFA is less friendly; Emperor Constantine V orders his Sicilian governor to attack the Beneventan allies of Charlemagne. He is enraged "because he had been denied the king's daughter," a piece of information contained only in the original version of the RFA. The issues which divide the Frankish and the Byzantine emperors are vaguely identified by the annalists as "the Dalmatian question," the position of Venice, or the role of the archbishop of Grado. The sensitive problem of Charles's imperial title receives only implicit attention. After Venice has been restored to the Byzantines in 810, however, the Greek ambassadors at Aix-la-Chapelle "acclaimed him according to their custom, that is in Greek, and called him Emperor and Basileus." Although there is actual military conflict between Franks and Greeks in the years 806 to 810, the authors of the RFA refer to the Byzantines with respect, note the honorable treatment of Frankish emissaries, and record with interest events in the Byzantine world which have no bearing on the affairs of the West. The hostile and abusive tone which the annalists frequently affect when dealing with the opponents of the Franks is conspicuously absent in their description of Byzantine-Frankish relations.

Two powers complicate the relations between the Franks and the Byzantines in the course of the last ten years covered by the RFA. First the duke of Lower Pannonia, Ljudovit, revolts against Carolingian rule, and the Franks attack him on many campaigns. After Ljudovit's timely death in 823 the Franks encounter a new foe in the Bulgars, whose emissaries appear before Emperor Louis the Pious for the first time in 824. At issue is the border between Franks and

Bulgars and the control of the Slavonic tribes living along the Danube in Dacia and in neighboring territories. That the Franks are fighting the Bulgars deep in the Balkans by the time the annalists discontinue the official annals of the realm is a measure of the expansion which the Carolingian empire undergoes over the nine decades of Carolingian history recorded by the RFA.

The RFA assigns a special significance to the contacts between the Frankish kings and the Roman popes. The name of a pope, Zacharias, first appears in the RFA under the year 749, an error for 750, in connection with the famous question of Pepin the Short addressed to the pope: whether the man with the name of king or the one who had the power should rule in Francia. The RFA then becomes the history of the alliance between the Carolingians and the papacy. Under the year 753 it records the unprecedented journey of a pope, Stephen II, across the Alps to Francia; under 754 the anointing of Pepin and his sons by the pope; under 755 the first campaign against the Lombard Aistulf "to seek justice for the blessed apostle Peter"; and under 756 the donation of the exarchate of Ravenna and the Pentapolis to the pope. For the years 773 and 774 the RFA records the renewed intervention of the Frankish king in Italy, stressing the invitation and request of the pope, and the destruction of the Lombard kingdom. In 781 two sons of Charlemagne are crowned kings by the pope. In recording these events the annalists leave no doubt that the pope is the petitioner but at the same time the indispensable mediator of grace when he consecrates kings and princes.

The true nature of Charlemagne's relationship with the pope is revealed by later events. The pope threatens the emissaries of Tassilo of Bavaria "with the sword of his anathema" if they should break fealty to Charlemagne and thus supports with his spiritual power the policy of the Frankish king; the king, on the other hand, when faced with the problem of the Adoptionist heresy, tries the heretical bishop twice before his own synod, relegating the pope and his representatives to a supporting role (792, 794). Councils are convoked and ecclesiastical legislation is initiated by the king and emperor. The pope upon his consecration sends to the emperor the keys of the tomb of St. Peter and the banner of the city of Rome. Popes announce their election to the emperor and have to be confirmed by him; in 827 Pope Gregory is not ordained "until the emperor's ambassadors had come to Rome and examined the character of the election by the people." The annalists record the imperial coronation of both Charlemagne and his son Louis the Pious by the pope, but they are obviously far removed from giving these acts a meaning even remotely similar to later papal interpretations. Instead, there seems to be much implicit criticism of the popes, although the language remains reverential throughout and the charges are reported as hearsay. In 799 Pope Leo III is saved from the fury of his Roman enemies by the agents of the king, but he is forced to purge himself publicly from all charges leveled against him. The emperor is displeased when the pope is reported to be responsible for the execution of some of his opponents (815). He examines carefully and by his own ambassadors the pope's blinding and decapitation of two papal officials whose crime is reported to have been that they always acted loyally toward the emperor's son Lothair, king of Italy. The annalist notes this charge as well as the pope's vigorous defense of the murderers and on another occasion claims that Roman affairs have been "confused due to the wickedness of several popes." As a result the RFA leaves the impression that the annalists think of the emperor very much in terms of the Christian Roman emperors whose foes are guilty of lèse majesté. The emperor is "the Lord's steward," *Dei dispensator,* holding his power from God and responsible alone to the Lord, but assisted in matters divine by a revered and prayerful Roman pope.

Such was the world of the Carolingians as observed and recorded by the nameless royal Frankish annalists, or rather a small part of that world, since the authors in the style of annalists remained indifferent to the complexities of personality and social life. It is a picture of the Carolingian world as viewed by a particular class of men. Although the annalists were men of greatly diverse mind and ability, they shared some common traits. The task, after all, for which they were called required peculiar talents and a special station in society. They were literate men in an age of illiteracy and thus more enlightened than most in their rough environment. They were members of the clergy or had at least attended monastic schools, which would have fostered in them, as it did in Alcuin and Einhard, a deep concern with the religious life and the current issues of theology. As writers they were obviously influenced by the language and thought of the Bible and easily borrowed the polished phrases of classical authors.

In spite of their ecclesiastical garb their spirituality was superficial, superstitious, and legalistic, and their devotion to the pope tempered by their loyalty to the king. They were the king's men first, just as were the secular vassals, and cherished above everything the bond which personal fidelity tended to create between lord and faithful followers. They were probably men of aristocratic descent who shared the values and prejudices of their class; who served the king not only as priests and scribes but as emissaries and administrators; who would not wield a sword themselves but appreciated a good bout with plenty of blood and piles of spoils; who were proud of being Franks and contemptuous of their faithless enemies; who knew the court and its intrigues and competed with their peers for the honors and offices dispensed by royal bounty. They were men of limited sophistication who did not usually foresee the consequences of the acts they recorded, but they were also the men who supported Charlemagne's vision of empire and made possible its short-lived realization and the regeneration of Carolingian society.

Regardless of its authors' limitations, the RFA became an important source of information about the Carolingian age and, judging by the number of surviving manuscripts, for centuries was thought to deserve reading and copying.[21] Among the immediate users of the RFA were Einhard in his *Life of Charlemagne* and Nithard in his *Histories*, Poeta Saxo, and the biographers of Louis the Pious.[22] The RFA also served as a direct or indirect source for the other annalistic works of the ninth century, e.g., the *Annales Mettenses Priores* (678–831).[23]

In the revised version the RFA was continued in the ninth century. A copy which contained minor additions for the years 741 to 829 was extended into the *Annales Bertiniani*, named after the location of the first manuscript. The first writer who added to the annals was a native of Belgian Gaul and loyal follower of Emperor Louis the Pious. From 835 on, Prudentius, chaplain of Louis the Pious and later bishop of Troyes (843/46–61), continued these annals. While he wrote at first as the annalist of the empire and with sympathy for the emperor, he identified himself after 840 with the interests of Charles the Bald and the western part of the Carolingian empire. After 853 his attitude towards Charles became more critical and reflected the resolve of the French episcopacy to guide and direct the king. It was, therefore, only natural that after Prudentius' death Hincmar, archbishop of Reims, the most important statesman in the realm of Charles the Bald, took it upon himself to record the events of the kingdom until his death in 882.[24] The *Annales Xantenses* (790–873), whose main author, Gerward, was librarian in the palace of Aix-la-Chapelle and Einhard's successor as supervisor of building, for the years 797–811 incorporates an abridged version of the RFA.[25] The *Annales Fuldenses* (714–902), a source well informed on affairs in the eastern part of the empire, made extensive use of the RFA for the years 771–827. Like the *Annales Bertiniani,* it reflects some sort of official interest or inspiration, perhaps on the part of the archbishop of Mainz.[26] This threefold continuation of the RFA is a fitting symbol of the fate which struck Charlemagne's realm and eventually caused the official annalists to keep their silence.

Nithard's *Histories*

Nithard's *Histories* is the most important source for the wars among the sons of Louis the Pious, which set the stage for the dissolution of the empire. It provides the only evidence for many episodes between the old emperor's death in June 840 and the treaty of Verdun in August 843, which set the seal on the partition. Nithard attached himself to the emperor's youngest son, whose birth in 823 and investment with part of the empire a few years later had been the root of the conflicts between Louis the Pious and his three older sons in the 830's. For this reason, Nithard's work records the fraternal wars from Charles's and a western point of view and with obvious bias against Lothair. Nonetheless, in scope, in depth, in detail of information, Nithard far surpasses the other historians of the dying empire, such as Prudentius, the annalist of St.-Bertin, who shared Nithard's bias in favor of Charles; Rudolf, the annalist of Fulda, who from a partisan of Lothair gradually changed into a supporter of Louis, or the nameless annalist of Xanten, who favored Lothair but recorded little of relevance about him during these years.[27]

Nithard's *Histories* is not only a significant source of information for a crucial event in the history of medieval Europe but an interesting and rather unusual piece of historical literature. It is contemporary, self-contained, and programmatic history, i.e., Nithard relates the events of his own time and experience, he limits himself to a specific and well-defined theme, and he frankly admits that he writes to prove a point and to forestall a different interpretation. Nithard wrote in this fashion apparently without following a literary model. Tacitus in his *Histories*, however, had written contemporary history. Similarly, Sallust, whom Nithard may have read, in his *Catiline* and *Jugurthine War* had written the histories of significant and self-contained episodes. Hardly a historian, on the other hand, had ever admitted partisanship as candidly before; instead, every writer claimed with Tacitus to be "unmoved . . . by either hatred or partiality." But the open profession of a point of view seems appealing today and did not prevent an upright man from writing an honest work. A further peculiar feature of Nithard's *Histories* is that the author was a layman—"for a long time the last layman to write history, without literary ambition, but with lucidity, insight, and honesty."[28] Like Einhard, also a layman, Nithard benefited from the reform of education and revival of learning in the days of Charlemagne, which improved Latin style, inspired a deeper interest in the knowledge of classical and Christian antiquity, gathered the native memories of the past, and introduced the historical tradition of Anglo-Saxon England. A wide-ranging, realistic, personal, and unparochial historiography was the result; Nithard was an important exponent of this.

Some knowledge of Nithard's family and public life can be gathered from his work. He was a grandson of Charlemagne, his mother being Bertha, the emperor's daughter by Hildegard. His father was the poet Angilbert, nicknamed "Homer" at Charlemagne's court, who received the abbey of St.-Riquier near Amiens and died shortly after his emperor.[29] The illicit relations between Angilbert and Bertha, which produced another son, Hartnid, and may have given rise to the tale of Einhard and Emma, occurred in the 790's, and Nithard thus must have been in his forties when he lived through the fraternal wars.[30] Although Nithard led the life of a soldier and held high public office, he was obviously a man of some learning. His position as Charles's official historian, his careful tracking of a comet which appeared in the winter of 841–42, his biblical quotations and Virgilian reminiscences indicate the breadth of his scholarship.[31] Why Nithard took the side of the young Charles cannot be explained, but he looked upon him as a ruler appointed by God.[32] In the fall of 840 Charles sent Nithard and another count, Adalgar, as his envoys from Bourges to make peace with Lothair. Because the envoys refused to defect from their lord they lost the fiefs which they had received from Louis the Pious. The author participated in the fratricidal battle of Fontenoy on June 25, 841, and was able to lend crucial support to Adalgar. On October 18, 841, he was in Charles's headquarters at St.-Cloud near Paris, writing his record of the battle. In 842 the historian was chosen as one of twelve magnates representing the western half of the empire to consult with twelve nobles of the eastern half about the proposed division of the entire realm between Louis and Charles.[33]

Little is known about Nithard beyond the data which he provides in his work. Like his father he became lay abbot of the monastery of St.-Riquier or Centulum, apparently in 843. He died in a battle against the Normans on May 15, 845.[34] An epitaph by the monk Mico notes his wisdom and fortitude and bemoans his brief tenure of office and death by the sword.[35] Hariulf's chronicle of St.-Riquier records that Nithard was first buried in the abbey next to his father but after the latter's translation in the eleventh century was placed in Angilbert's sarcophagus. At that time the head wound of which he died could still be seen.[36]

Nithard, as he informs the reader in the preface to the first of his four books, wrote his work at the request of his lord, Charles the Bald, who asked him, before occupying the city of Châlons in May 841, to record the events of their time. Although the author accepted the task as an honor and an obligation which he owed to his lord, he was wary of the difficulties and of possible mistakes. He wondered whether he would have sufficient leisure in such troublesome times; whether he could apply the attention and care necessary and convey the proper meaning of events.[37] At the beginning of the third book Nithard revealed that he would have preferred to end with the second, since he was ashamed of what he had to record about his Frankish people. What alone impelled him to go on was the fear that someone else might produce an improper version of the history of his times.[38] The concern which Nithard voices here indicates the nature of the work: it was an official, partisan piece of history, intended to explain to posterity what Charles and his followers considered the cause and meaning of the fraternal wars. Nithard's main theme was Lothair's unjust persecution of Charles and his party. In Book I he tells why Lothair pursued Charles and his brother Louis after their father's death; in the rest of the work he describes "with how much vigor and zeal" Lothair tried to execute his resolution.[39] Nithard's *Histories* thus consists of two distinct parts: one book of history in the customary sense and three books of contemporary history, the former covering the years from 814 to the death of Louis the Pious in 840, the latter from the summer of 840 to the spring of 843.

The summary in Book I of the events from the death of Charlemagne to that of Louis the Pious is a concise and necessary prologue to Nithard's topic. It is a more lucid and purposeful survey of the period than the biographies of Louis the Pious and has been called "the best guide to find a way out of the confusions of that time." In the welter of conflicting loyalties and uncertain alliances, Nithard clearly discerned the opposing principles: the unity of the whole versus the autonomy of the parts.[40] The story in Book I is selective; some important events are omitted because they did not seem relevant to Nithard's topic, but even here Nithard is often the only source of essential detail. He alone, for example, reports that Louis the Pious made his illegitimate brothers companions of his table and that it was Bertmund, prefect of the province of Lyons, who blinded Bernard in 818. Since the first book was written from memory and some of the events had occurred more than two decades earlier, Nithard makes some minor mistakes. He fails to mention the widows, orphans, and churches who received a share of Charlemagne's treasure when it was divided after the emperor's death. He erroneously maintains that Charles was held captive with his father at Soissons in the summer of 833, that Pepin met Louis the Pious in St.-Denis instead of Quierzy, that Lothair was told to go to Italy in 834, that Judith's captors in Italy suddenly became her liberators. He underestimates the profound excitement caused by the meeting of the brothers Lothair and Louis at Trent in 838. He is confused in his chronology and refers to Bernard's revolt before the division of the empire in 817, although it was this event which caused the nephew to rise against the emperor; Judith purged herself of charges of adultery in 831 and not in 834; Louis the Pious died at age sixty-two and not sixty-four; he was emperor for twenty-six years and nine months, not twenty-seven years and six months.

The degree of Nithard's objectivity can best be established by an examination of the first book, where only in rare cases is his record the sole source for an event. Nithard proclaims himself a partisan of Charles the Bald at the beginning of his work and his prejudices affect his history. He is silent when the facts might hurt Charles or Louis the Pious; he does not mention Charles's total exclusion at the partition of 833 nor the humiliating act of public penance performed by Louis the Pious at Soissons in October 833.[41] He places Lothair in the worst light, plays down the position of co-emperor which he was given in 817, calls him a breaker of oaths and promises, and makes much of the judgment which Lothair had to pronounce on his own followers when Louis the Pious regained the upper hand over his rebellious son in 831. Lothair is pictured as the lone instigator of the revolt of 830 when, in fact, his presence in Italy at its outbreak precluded his participation; he was, of course, the natural rallying point for all who were disturbed by Judith's influence and the emperor's misgovernment. Nithard permits himself an obvious misrepresentation of the facts when he portrays Counts Hugo and Mathfrid as invidious intriguers, although they opposed Judith solely because they wished to preserve the unity of the empire. On the other hand, he records the granting of Aquitaine to Charles as an incident of no significance when in reality it was highly unfair, made Pepin an open enemy of the empire, and constituted a threat also to the other brothers. Pope Gregory IV appears as a tool of the conspirators in 833, but Nithard neglects to report that the pope had a genuine interest in the unity and peace of the empire and did not savor the sad role he was forced to play in Lothair's service. The two other brothers of Charles, Louis and Pepin, are also treated unfairly on occasion: Louis' contribution to his father's restoration in 831 and 834 is not sufficiently noted; Nithard exaggerates when he claims that both Louis and Pepin strove for precedence over each other, when their real concern was simply the retention of their respective portions of the empire; the historian looks upon Louis as an inveterate troublemaker when Louis revolted against being deprived of territories he had controlled for many years. In spite of the fact that Nithard viewed events from Charles's perspective, he was not a mindless partisan; his prejudices are those of his environment, the court of Louis the Pious with its hostility to the older sons. This climate, however, did not demoralize the historian, as it did the emotional and deceptive author of the life of Louis the Pious. Nithard believed that Charles's mother Judith had committed adultery with Duke Bernard of Septimania, but was hardly in a position to say so in his book; he nevertheless records the charge and does not dispute its validity. He candidly criticized the same Bernard for abusing his authority, although the man was one of Judith's and Charles's most loyal followers, and toward the end of his work he charges that his lord married the niece of the influential Adalhard "because he believed that with Adalhard he could win a large part of the people for himself."[42]

The three last books of Nithard's *Histories* confirm the impression that the author, though a fervent partisan of Charles and an opponent of the empire, recorded the events of his time with honesty and objectivity. These three books are devoted to the political moves and military campaigns, the diplomatic missions and shifting alliances, the drafts for a division of the empire and the growing weariness of the people, which eventually resulted in the treaty of Verdun.[43] Book II was apparently written from memory, but in Books III and IV Nithard let little time elapse between the event and his record.[44] Charles remains in the center of things throughout the work, but in the later parts a change of method is noticeable. Apparently, Nithard took less pleasure in his task as the war dragged on; in the preface to his last book he not only welcomed a respite from the labor of writing but contemplated a complete withdrawal from the burden of public affairs. Only the prospect that he might dispel the haze of error to the benefit of future generations made him go on. Increasingly, the unity of his theme is disregarded and digressions creep in. Earlier in the work any digression was related to the fate of his hero, as in the story of the royal vestments and insignia which arrived unexpectedly at Troyes on Easter 841.[45] In his last two books, however, the author talks about the weather, a comet, his family, or the war games performed by the soldiers when the forces of Louis and Charles united in 842.[46] In the very last book Nithard's style almost resembles that of the monastic chronicler. Without definite plan and employing awkward connectives, he strings together events in which his hero is involved, but also describes the society of the Saxons, the invasion of the Saracens, an earthquake, and a lunar eclipse.[47] Want and disease and natural disasters abound in the last chapters and induce pessimistic reflections on the selfish and bestial actions of men which provoke the judgment of God.[48] As he started his work with a eulogy to Charlemagne, Nithard ends with a nostalgic glance back at the reign of his grandfather when men were righteous and walked the ways of the Lord and peace and prosperity filled the realm of the Franks.[49] In the later books Lothair emerges again as indecisive, treacherous, and cowardly, Louis on the other hand, as a man of nobility and magnanimity. In both cases Nithard's assessment of the character of the man is generally confirmed by other contemporary sources. Only in his portrait of Charles does Nithard find no corroboration. The later history of his reign reveals Charles II as a spineless coward, greedy, crafty, "timid as a rabbit," in the words of a contemporary, but ruthless enough to have his own son, Carloman, blinded. In Nithard's *Histories* this *novellus Sennacherib* cannot be found; instead Charles, who was in fact a gifted and well-educated man, appears as a cautious diplomat, a resolute leader, a masterly strategist, a humble and charitable prince, almost a martyr. The contrast is striking. Nithard was describing a youth between the ages of seventeen and twenty, however, and his judgment may have been affected not so much by the spirit of party as by the hopes and expectations of a guide and teacher. That he was not an uncritical panegyrist his frank revelation of Charles's failures and defeats makes abundantly clear.[50]

If Nithard was willing to provide an accurate picture of the events of his time, he was also in an excellent position to do so. Only in connection with the battle of Fontenoy does he mention his personal involvement in military action, but he evidently advised and aided Charles in many campaigns of these years. His detailed reports on marches and expeditions, their beginnings and ends, routes and obstacles, on the prevailing weather and the motives and purposes of his lord admit no other conclusion.[51] Similarly, his intimate knowledge of delicate negotiations and deliberations at court, and of the aims and objectives of the main actors, leaves no doubt that he was close to the center of power and belonged to the innermost council of Charles and perhaps previously of Louis the Pious. He knows about the fears which troubled the doting father when Charles was born and of the consultations concerning Charles's future place and safety when the old emperor's days were drawing to an end; he is aware of the rivalries between certain Frankish noblemen as to who was to exercise the greatest influence over Lothair.[52]

Nithard also relied on written evidence; he probably was familiar with Einhard's *Life of Charlemagne*, the *Royal Frankish Annals*, and the *History of the Lombards* by Paul the Deacon. He certainly used numerous documents.[53] He presents verbatim accounts of the speeches made to their troops by Charles and Louis at Strasbourg in February 842 and of the verdict pronounced by the clergy assembled at Aix-la-Chapelle in March of the same year on the partition of Lothair's share of the empire, and he preserves the German and French texts of the Strasbourg Oaths.[54] In many passages of his work it is obvious that Nithard was using texts of treaties, mandates, letters, and protocols or aide-mémoires and notes which he himself had made on the spot while involved in the business of war and diplomacy. The description of his own and Adalgar's embassy to Lothair, of the treaty of Charles and Lothair at Orléans in the fall of 840, the promises of Bernard of Septimania, Lothair's complaint and Charles's response at Christmas 841, the deliberations of the war council at Attigny, the joint resolution of Charles and Louis after their meeting in the spring of 841 and their mandates to Lothair, the negotiations about the division of the empire before the truce of Ansilla, the truce of Ansilla, all argue heavy reliance on documentary evidence. Similarly, in the first book, the circumscription of the areas assigned to Charles, Lothair's oath to protect Charles, the promise of Louis the Pious in 830 to improve his government, the conditions of peace between Louis and Lothair at Blois in 834, and the last admonitions of Louis the Pious to his son Lothair seem to be derived from written sources.[55]

While Nithard's role as an eyewitness and his reliance on official records inspire confidence in the trustworthiness of his history, his language and style show a marked decline from the high level of literary art in the days of the Carolingian Renaissance. Grammatical errors are rare in the *Histories*, although the author on occasion uses a subjunctive where one would expect an indicative, an adverb instead of an adjective, or a dependent clause instead of an accusative with infinitive, but obscurities and infelicities are more frequent. Nithard's language is artless and unaffected by the influence of ancient historiography; it resembles Alcuin's Latin although it does not imitate the language of the Bible.[56] If Nithard's style sometimes seems pedestrian and repetitious, it must be remembered that his work was that of a soldier and statesman, composed between diplomatic missions and military campaigns. But because Nithard's writing is unsophisticated, he was probably not widely read. The anonymous author of the life of Louis the Pious was familiar with the *Histories;* Mico, who composed Nithard's epitaph, may have known it; Hucbald of St.-Amand in his *Vita Lebuini* copies Nithard's passage on the three classes in Saxon society; excerpts found their way into a manuscript which Abbot Gervinus took from Gorze to St.-Riquier and from which Hariulf extracted his information on Nithard; the thirteenth-century author of a *Historia regum Francorum* refers to Nithard as one of his sources but gives no evidence of really having read him.[57] Nithard's *Histories* consequently survived only in a single tenth-century manuscript of the monastery of St.-Médard in Soissons, of which the monks of St.-Victor in Paris made a copy in the fifteenth century.[58]

Wherever Nithard feels deeply or is personally involved, he can nevertheless write with passion and arouse interest and sympathy, as in the mournful reflections on his grandfather at the beginning and end of the book or in his lively description of the war games conducted by the soldiers of Charles and Louis. By beginning his book with a chapter on Charlemagne, whose work the fraternal wars were to undo, Nithard reveals historical insight as well as a sense of literary artistry.[59] With a few phrases he is able to sum up a complex situation, as when Lothair's bedraggled forces defeated Louis' army in 834 just when the emperor had triumphed over the rebellious son: "The small number of Lothair's men," Nithard says, "put them at a great disadvantage, but at least they moved as one man. Wido's large army made him and his men secure but quarrelsome and disorganized"; or when he speaks of Charlemagne's "tempered severity with which he subdued the fierce and iron hearts of Franks and barbarians."[60]

The simple, direct style mirrors the mind of the author. Nithard's *Histories* is the work of a Frankish noble, a royal vassal engaged in war, administration, and politics and embracing the ideals of his class. Nithard was ready with a light heart to risk his life rather than betray the king and desert his cause; he let Lothair deprive him of the fiefs which Louis the Pious had conferred on him rather than break his oath and join the new emperor, and he likened to slaves those who preferred disloyalty and defection to the temporary loss of their property.[61] To Nithard the supreme wickedness, so it seems, was the breach of one's faith and the flouting of public order and lawful authority. Religion plays a minor role in his writings; they speak the language of the layman, a rare voice in those days. He sees the hand of God move the fortunes of man and decide the battle of Fontenoy in favor of Louis and Charles, but only on two occasions is he bold enough to suggest that divinity supported his hero's cause by a direct miraculous intervention.[62] Although he fought the party which carried the banner of unity and thus helped to destroy the empire of Charlemagne, he was pained by the rising anarchy, the growing autonomy of the nobles, the ever more daring attacks of Vikings and Saracens, the collapse of internal order, and the spreading evidence of want and poverty. He thus shared the pessimism and sense of impending disaster voiced by the poets who supported the party of unity and empire.[63] His stand for the independence of the parts and against the unity of the whole may strike us as perfidious today. It was probably justified in Nithard's mind not only by the idea of personal loyalty to his lord but by a sense of realism. "The natural and inevitable effect of immoderate greatness," as Edward Gibbon said of Rome, is the decline and fall of empires.

THE TRANSLATION

The translation of the RFA and of Nithard's *Histories* is based on the latest critical editions by F. Kurze and P. Lauer, respectively. These are now considered the standard texts, and their readings or emendations of the manuscripts have been generally followed.

The Latin of the RFA is relatively simple, sometimes archaic and, because of the repetition of the same phrases and formulae, often stereotyped. There is, of course, no unity of style since various authors worked on it and many different sources were mined. But the language of the annalists offers few problems for the translator. Nithard, on the other hand, writes a more difficult Latin, with sometimes long and involved sentences and fuzzy adverbial phrases, which can raise real problems for his readers. This syntactical complexity is compounded by obscurities resulting from the manuscript tradition. Thus, it is easier for the translator to stay close to the text of the RFA than to Nithard's.

A word must be said on the problem of the revised version of the RFA. This is essentially a revision in style. How the revisor modified the original may be seen from a comparison of the annal for the year 749, a famous passage of the RFA:

Original

Burghardus Wirzeburgenses episcopus et Folradus capellanus missi fuerunt ad Zachariam papam, interrogando de regibus in Francia, qui illis temporibus non habentes regalem potestatem, si bene fuisset an non.

Et Zacharias papa mandavit Pippino, ut melius esset illum regem vocari, qui potestatem haberet, quam illum, qui sine regali potestate manebat; ut non conturbaretur ordo, per auctoritatem apostolicam iussit Pippinum regem fieri.

Revision

Burchardus Wirziburgensis episcopus et Folradus presbyter capellanus missi sunt Roman ad Zachariam papam, ut consulerent pontificem de causa regum, qui illo tempore fuerunt in Francia, qui nomen tantum regis, sed nullam potestatem regiam habuerunt; per quos praedictus pontifex mandavit, melius esse illum vocari regem, apud quem summa potestatis consisteret; dataque auctoritate sui iussit Pippinum regem constitui.

It is impossible to reproduce these stylistic revisions in English unless the text of the revised version were to be published with the original. A complete translation of the revision was made, but it seemed advisable to print only those passages which are different from the original not only in style but in content. The revisor occasionally added to, omitted from, and modified in substance the text of the original. His omissions are indicated in the notes, as are phrases and short sentences which he chose to add. Major additions are presented here—indented and marked by R (for revision)—right in the text of the translation. This technique may possibly arouse the wrath of some critics. But the different views of the revisor or the conspicuous omissions of the original annalist seem to provide a worthwhile glimpse into the minds of these authors. This insight would have been lost had the additions all been buried in the notes.

The notes, needless to say, owe much to the French and German scholars, Simson, Mühlbacher, Böhmer, Meyer von Knonau, Lot,

Halphen, and others whose works established a solid factual record of Carolingian history, and to the editors of our texts, especially Kurze, Müller, and Lauer. The names of living authorities on Carolingian history have been largely omitted here, because the annotation had to be minimal, not because of indifference.

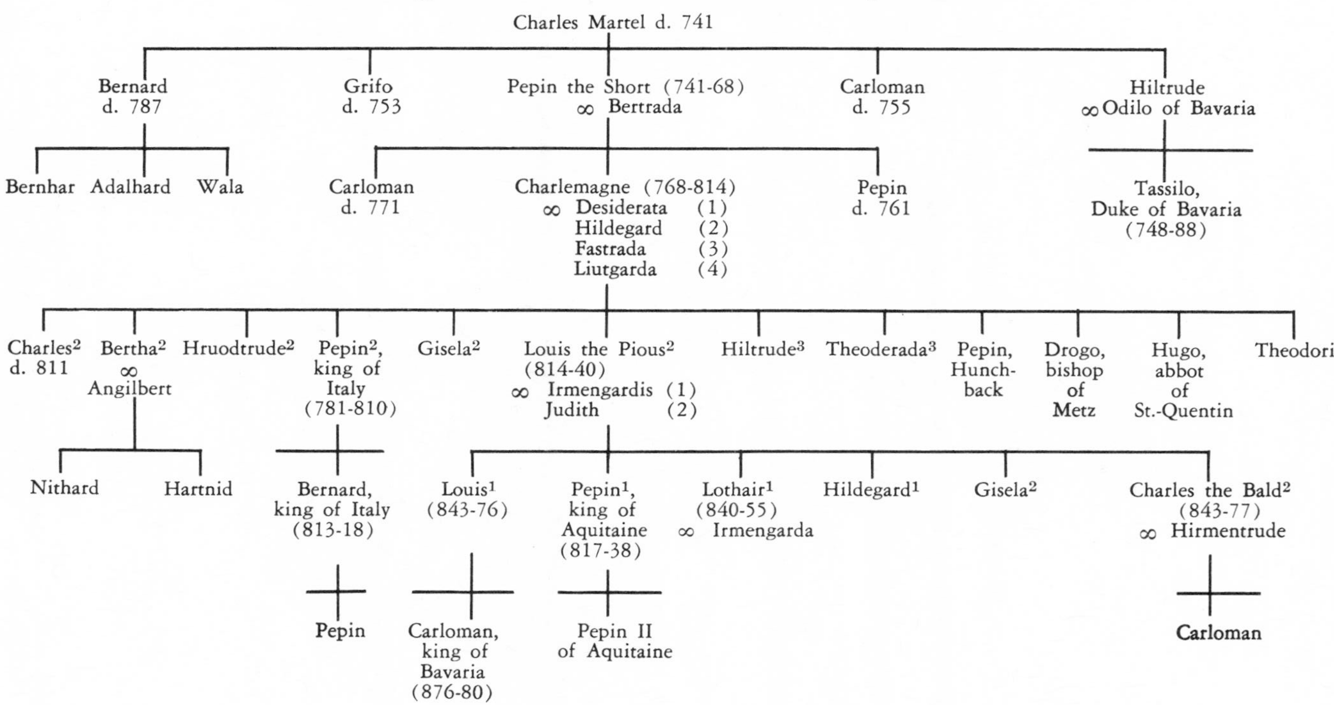
Charlemagne's Kinsmen and Descendants in *Carolingian Chronicles*
Charles Martel d. 741
Bernard d. 787
Grifo d. 753
Pepin the Short (741-68) ∞ Bertrada
Carloman d. 755
Hiltrude ∞ Odilo of Bavaria
Bernhar
Adalhard
Wala
Carloman d. 771
Charlemagne (768-814) ∞ Desiderata (1) Hildegard (2) Fastrada (3) Liutgarda (4)
Pepin d. 761
Tassilo, Duke of Bavaria (748-88)
Charles[2] d. 811
Bertha[2] ∞ Angilbert
Hruodtrude[2]
Pepin[2], king of Italy (781-810)
Gisela[2]
Louis the Pious[2] (814-40) ∞ Irmengardis (1) Judith (2)
Hiltrude[3]
Theoderada[3]
Pepin, Hunch-back
Drogo, bishop of Metz
Hugo, abbot of St.-Quentin
Theodoric
Nithard
Hartnid
Bernard, king of Italy (813-18)
Louis[1] (843-76)
Pepin[1], king of Aquitaine (817-38)
Lothair[1] (840-55) ∞ Irmengarda
Hildegard[1]
Gisela[2]
Charles the Bald[2] (843-77) ∞ Hirmentrude
Pepin
Carloman, king of Bavaria (876-80)
Pepin II of Aquitaine
Carloman

ROYAL FRANKISH ANNALS

(741-829)

741

Charles, mayor of the palace, died.

R He left three sons as heirs, Carloman, Pepin, and Grifo. Grifo, the youngest of them, had a mother named Swanahilde, a niece of Odilo, duke of the Bavarians.[1] By her malicious counsel she aroused in him such high hopes of possessing the whole kingdom[2] that he at once occupied the city of Laon and declared war on his brothers. Carloman and Pepin quickly gathered an army, besieged Laon, and captured Grifo. And from then on they applied themselves to restoring order in the kingdom and to recovering the provinces[3] which had fallen away from the Franks after their father's death. To make sure everything was safe at home while they were abroad, Carloman took Grifo and held him at Neufchâteau in the Ardennes Mountains, where Grifo is said to have remained in custody until Carloman left for Rome.[4]

742

Carloman and Pepin, mayors of the palace, then led an army against Hunald, duke of the Aquitanians, and took the castle of Loches. On this campaign they divided the kingdom of the Franks among themselves at Vieux Poitiers.[1] Carloman laid waste Alamannia that year, too.[2]

743

Carloman and Pepin then started a war against Odilo,[1] duke of the Bavarians.[2] That year Carloman advanced alone into Saxony. By treaty, he got possession of the castle called Hohenseeburg and made Theodoric the Saxon submit.[3]

744

Again Carloman and Pepin invaded Saxony, and Theodoric the Saxon was captured a second time.[1]

745

Carloman then confessed to his brother Pepin that he wished to retire from the world. They undertook no campaign that year, but both made preparations, Carloman for his journey and Pepin for his brother's departure with gifts and honors.[1]

746

Carloman proceeded to Rome, took the tonsure, and built a monastery in honor of St. Sylvester on Mount Soratte.[1] There he remained for a while and then moved to St. Benedict's at Monte Cassino, where he became a monk.[2]

R Carloman departed for Rome. He gave up the glory of this world, changed his garb, and on Mount Soratte built a monastery in honor of St. Sylvester. Here, as they say, St. Sylvester once lived in secret at the time of the persecution under Emperor Constantine. Carloman stayed for a while but then wisely decided to leave this place. To serve his God he passed on to the monastery of St. Benedict near the castle of Cassino in the province of Samnium. And there he received the monastic habit.

747

Grifo fled to Saxony,[1] and Pepin entered Saxony through Thuringia, going as far as the River Meissau near Schöningen. Grifo joined the Saxons on the River Oker near Ohrum.[2]

R Grifo, Carloman's and Pepin's brother, did not want to be under the thumb of his brother Pepin, although he held an honorable place. He gathered a handful of men and fled to Saxony. In

Saxony he raised an army of natives and positioned himself on the River Oker near Ohrum. But Pepin marched through Thuringia with the Frankish host, entered Saxony in spite of his brother's machinations, and positioned himself on the River Meissau near Schöningen. Nevertheless, there was no battle between them; instead, they separated after making a treaty.

748

Fleeing from Saxony Grifo came to Bavaria, subdued the duchy, and captured Hiltrude and Tassilo. Suidger came to Grifo's aid. When Pepin heard this, he hurried with his army to Bavaria, overcame all those mentioned above, took Grifo and Lantfrid away with him, and by his grace installed Tassilo as duke of the Bavarians. He sent Grifo to Neustria and gave him twelve counties.[1] From Neustria Grifo fled again into Gascony and went to Waifar, duke of the Aquitanians.[2]

749

Bishop Burchard of Würzburg and the chaplain Fulrad were sent to Pope Zacharias to inquire whether it was good or not that the kings of the Franks should wield no royal power, as was the case at that time. Pope Zacharias instructed Pepin that it was better to call him king who had the royal power than the one who did not. To avoid turning the country upside down, he commanded by virtue of his apostolic authority that Pepin should be made king.[1]

750

Pepin was elected king according to the custom of the Franks, anointed by the hand of Archbishop Boniface of saintly memory, and raised to the kingship by the Franks in the city of Soissons. But Childerich, who was falsely called king, was tonsured and sent into a monastery.[1]

753

Pepin marched into Saxony, and Bishop Hildegar was killed[1] by the Saxons in the castle called Iburg.[2] In spite of this Pepin had the victory and came as far as Rehme.[3] On his return from his campaign he was informed that his brother Grifo, who had fled into Gascony, had been killed.[4]

That year Pope Stephen came to Francia, seeking aid and support for the rights of St. Peter. Carloman, monk and brother of King Pepin, came to Francia also, under orders from his abbot, hoping to interfere with the granting of the pope's request.

R That year Pope Stephen came to King Pepin at the villa called Quierzy advising the king that he defend the pope and the Roman Church against the aggression of the Lombards. Carloman, brother of the king and already a monk, also came on the order of his abbot to oppose the requests the Roman pontiff was making of his brother. But it is believed that he did this unwillingly and only because he dared not slight the orders of his abbot; nor did the abbot dare to defy the command of the Lombard king who had ordered him to do this.[5]

754

Pope Stephen confirmed Pepin as king by holy anointing and with him he anointed as kings his two sons, the Lords Charles and Carloman.[1] The Lord Archbishop Boniface, who was spreading the word of God in Frisia, became a martyr of Christ while preaching.[2]

755

King Pepin, on papal invitation, embarked on a campaign into Italy to seek justice for the blessed apostle Peter. Aistulf, the king of the Lombards, who refused this justice, moved into the Lombard Cluses[1] and marched against King Pepin and the Franks. They began the war. By God's help and the intercession of the blessed apostle Peter, Pepin with his Franks had the victory.[2]

In the same year Pope Stephen was taken back to the Holy See by the emissaries of the Lord King Pepin, Fulrad and his companions.[3] When King Aistulf was surrounded in the city of Pavia, he promised to respect the rights of St. Peter. Then King Pepin, after obtaining forty hostages and confirming the treaty by oaths, returned to Francia.

The monk Carloman, however, remained sick at Vienne with Queen Bertrada; he languished for many days and died in peace.

R On the order of the king his body was taken to the monastery of St. Benedict, where Carloman had received the monastic habit.[4]

Italy on the Eve of Carolingian Intervention

756

When King Pepin saw that Aistulf, king of the Lombards, was not true to his word, which he had previously given regarding the rights of St. Peter, he made another expedition into Italy, besieged Pavia, surrounded Aistulf, and made even more sure that the rights of St. Peter would be preserved, as Aistulf had promised before. In addition, he conquered Ravenna with the Pentapolis and the whole exarchate and handed it over to St. Peter.[1] When King Pepin returned, the villainous king Aistulf wanted to go back on what he had promised before, desert his hostages, and break his oaths. But one day, when he went hunting, he was smitten by the judgment of God and ended his days.

R He fell from his horse while hunting. And the ailment which he contracted from this accident[2] brought an end to his life within a few days.[3]

Why and how King Desiderius was raised to the kingship we shall report later.[4]

757

Emperor Constantine sent King Pepin among other presents an organ which was taken to Francia. King Pepin held his assembly with the Franks at Compiègne.[1] Tassilo, duke of the Bavarians, came there, commended himself into vassalage with his hands, and swore innumerable oaths. Touching the relics of the saints, he promised fealty to King Pepin and his sons Charles and Carloman, behaving honestly and faithfully, in accordance with the law and as a vassal should to his lords. Tassilo thus swore on the bodies of St. Dionysius, Rusticus, Eleutherius, St. Germanus, and St. Martin that he would remain faithful all his life, as he had promised by oaths. His magnates swore this with him also, as was said above and elsewhere.

758

King Pepin went into Saxony and took the strongholds of the Saxons at Sythen by storm. And he inflicted bloody defeats on the Saxon people. They then promised Pepin to obey all his orders and to present as gifts at his assembly up to three hundred horses every year. And the date changed to

759

A son was born to King Pepin, to whom the king gave his own name, so that he was called Pepin like his father. He lived for two years and died in his third.[1]

In this year he celebrated Christmas at Longlier and Easter at Jupille,[2] and the date changed to

760

When King Pepin saw that Waifar, duke of the Aquitanians, in his lands did not grant even the least of their rights to the churches in Francia, he decided with the Franks to conduct a campaign in order to obtain these rights in Aquitaine.

R Waifar, duke of Aquitaine, wanted to retain power over the properties of churches that were in the hands of King Pepin and was unwilling to return it to the pastors of these venerable places. He disdained to hear the king himself in these matters when the king warned him through his envoys. By his defiance Waifar goaded the king into making war on him.

He advanced as far as the place called Tedoad.[1] When Waifar saw that, he sent his emissaries Otbert and Dadin and handed over to King Pepin the hostages Adalgar and Either as assurance that he would return everything the king demanded in ecclesiastical disputes.

R By these acts he appeased the king, who had been furious with him, so that Pepin stopped the war at once. When he had received hostages, as assurance that the promises would be kept, the king broke off his campaign and went home.

Pepin celebrated Christmas at Quierzy and Easter. And the date changed to

761

Waifar, duke of the Aquitanians, showed little regard for his hostages and his oaths, and in order to revenge himself sent an army against King Pepin, which marched as far as the city of Chalon. While the king held his assembly at the villa called Düren, he was informed that Waifar had lied in everything. Again King Pepin, together with his first-born son Charles,[1] set out on a campaign into that region and captured many castles, the names of which are Bourbon, Chantelle, and Clermont. These he took in battle, and in Auvergne he obtained by treaty many other castles, which submitted to his authority. He went as far as Limoges, devastating this province because of Duke Waifar's slights.

R On this campaign the king was accompanied by his first-born son Charles, who was given supreme rule over the whole empire after his father's death.

He celebrated Christmas at the villa of Quierzy and also Easter. And the date changed to

762

For a third time King Pepin launched a campaign into Aquitaine and he took the city of Bourges and the castle of Thouars.[1] He celebrated Christmas at the villa of Gentilly[2] and Easter, too. And the date changed to

763

King Pepin held his assembly at Nevers and conducted a fourth campaign against Aquitaine. There Tassilo brushed aside his oaths and all his promises and sneaked away on a wicked pretext, disregarding all the good things which King Pepin, his uncle, had done for him. Taking himself off, with lying excuses, he went to Bavaria and never again wanted to see the king face to face.[1] On his further campaign through Aquitaine King Pepin went as far as Cahors. After laying waste Aquitaine he returned by Limoges to Francia.

The winter was hard, and King Pepin celebrated Christmas at the villa of Longlier and Easter, too. And the date changed to

764

King Pepin then held his assembly at Worms and launched no further campaign but remained in Francia and occupied himself with the matter of Waifar and Tassilo.[1] He celebrated Christmas at his villa of Quierzy and also Easter. And the date changed to

765

King Pepin then held his assembly at Attigny and launched no further campaign.[1] He celebrated Christmas at the villa of Aachen and also Easter.[2] And the date changed to

Orléans
Auxerre
R. Loire
Angers
Tours
Sels
Doué
Loches
Thouars
Duasdives
Nevers
Autun
Chasseneuil
Vieux Poitiers
Argenton
Bourges
Chantelle
Clermont
Limoges
Ally
Turenne
Saintes
AUVERGNE
Angoulême
Fronsac
PERIGORD
LE GEVAUDAN
Cahors
Peyrusse
R. Garonne
R. Tarn
Albi
Arles
Toulouse
GASCONY
Narbonne
100
Miles

Aquitaine

766

King Pepin made a campaign into Aquitaine and held his assembly at Orléans. He restored the castle of Argenton,[1] which Waifar had previously destroyed. When he had rebuilt this castle, King Pepin installed Franks there to hold Aquitaine and also garrisoned a Frankish detachment at Bourges.

He celebrated Christmas at Samoussy and Easter at Gentilly.[2] And the date changed to

767

The Lord King Pepin then held a great council at Gentilly with Romans and Greeks about the Holy Trinity and the images of the saints.[1] Afterward, he continued his march through Aquitaine into Narbonne and conquered Toulouse as well as Albi and Gevaudan.[2] Returning home safely, he celebrated Easter at the city of Vienne.

In August of the same year he marched for the second time into Aquitaine and came as far as Bourges. There he held an assembly in camp with all the Franks as was the custom. Continuing his march from here, he proceeded as far as the Garonne, captured many rocks and caves, and the castles of Ally, Turenne, and Peyrusse, and returned to Bourges.[3] There the death of Pope Paul was announced to him, and there he celebrated Christmas. And the date changed to

768

The Lord King Pepin launched a campaign and captured Remistagnus. He came as far as the city of Saintes, and taking Waifar's mother, sister, and nieces prisoner, he pushed on to the Garonne. From there he continued to Mons, where Herwig came with the duke's other sister. Having returned safely from Mons, he celebrated Easter in the castle of Sels.[1] Setting off again on his campaign, he arrived with the Lady Queen Bertrada at the city of Saintes. Here he left the queen with her retinue and entered Perigord. When Waifar had been killed,[2] Pepin returned in triumph to Saintes.

While delaying there for a few days he fell sick. He passed through Tours on his way home, prayed at St. Martin's, and reached St.-Denis. There he died on September 24.[3]

The Lords Charles and Carloman were raised to the kingship; the Lord Charles on October 9 at Noyon and Carloman at Soissons.

The glorious Lord King Charles[4] celebrated Christmas at the villa of Aachen and Easter at Rouen. And the date changed to

769

The glorious Lord King Charles went campaigning in Aquitaine because Hunald wished to make the whole of Gascony and Aquitaine renew the war.[1] By the help of God Hunald's hostile designs were thwarted with the support of only a few Franks. On this same campaign the great king joined his brother at Duasdives.[2] From there Carloman suddenly set out to return to Francia. The most gracious Lord King Charles went to the city of Angoulême, where he commandeered a number of Franks with tools and equipment. He took them with him to the River Dordogne and there built the castle of Fronsac.[3] From there he sent his messengers to Lupo the Gascon in search of Hunald and his wife.

R These two brothers had succeeded their father and divided the kingdom between themselves. The province of Aquitaine, which had been allotted to the older brother, King Charles, had been up in arms ever since the hostilities of the past war.[4] A certain Hunald who wanted to be king incited the people of the province to new ventures. Against this man King Charles, to whom the province had been allotted,[5] marched with his army. But since he received no assistance from his brother, who was kept from giving it by the crooked counsel of his magnates, Charles only had a talk with him at Duasdives. While his brother returned to his kingdom, Charles marched to the city of Angoulême in Aquitaine and from there, with troops gathered from all sides, pursued Hunald on his flight and almost caught him. But Hunald went free because he knew the places where he could hide from the king's army. He slipped out of Aquitaine and made his way into Gascony, where he thought he would be safe.[6] At that time Lupus was duke of the Gascons, and Hunald did not hesitate to put himself under his wing. To Lupus the king sent envoys, commanding him to hand over the fugitive and letting him know, if he did not listen to orders, that he would make war on Gascony and not leave before he had made an end to his defiance. Lupus was frightened by the king's threats and promptly surrendered Hunald and his wife, promising to do everything that he was told to do.

While he was staying at Fronsac with his Franks, Hunald was delivered with his wife. When Hunald had been handed over and the castle constructed, Charles returned to Francia.

He celebrated Christmas at the villa of Düren and Easter in the royal town of Liège. And the date changed to

770

The Lord King Charles held an assembly at the city of Worms, and Carloman and Queen Bertrada met at Seltz. In the same year the Lady Queen Bertrada traveled through Bavaria to Italy.

R But Bertrada, the mother of the kings, after a talk with her younger son Carloman at Seltz, traveled to Italy in the interest of peace. She settled the business for which she went there, and after prayers at the threshold of the holy apostles in Rome, returned to her sons in Gaul.[1]

The Lord King Charles celebrated Christmas at the city of Mainz and Easter at Herstal.[2] And the date changed to

771

The Lord King Charles held an assembly at Valenciennes. In the same year King Carloman died at the villa of Samoussy on December 4. The Lord King Charles came to the villa of Corbény, as did Archbishop Wilchar[1] and Fulrad, the chaplain, with the other bishops and priests, Counts Warin and Adalhard and the other magnates who had been Carloman's men. But Carloman's wife with a few Franks departed for Italy.

R The king, however, bore patiently with their departure for Italy, although it was needless.

The noble and glorious King Charles celebrated Christmas at the villa of Attigny and Easter at the villa of Herstal. And the date changed to

772

The most gracious Lord King Charles then held an assembly at Worms.[1] From Worms he marched first into Saxony. Capturing the castle of Eresburg,[2] he proceeded as far as the Irminsul, destroyed this idol and carried away the gold and silver which he found. A great drought occurred so that there was no water in the place where the Irminsul stood. The glorious king wished to remain there two or three days in order to destroy the temple completely, but they had no water. Suddenly at noon, through the grace of God, while the army rested and nobody knew what was happening, so much water poured forth in a stream that the whole army had enough. Then the great king came to the River Weser. Here he held a parley with the Saxons, obtained twelve hostages, and returned to Francia.

He celebrated Christmas at Herstal and Easter, too. And the date changed to

773

The Lord King Charles then went to the villa of Thionville to spend the winter there. To Thionville came an emissary of the Lord Pope Hadrian by the name of Peter, who had traveled by sea to Marseilles and from there by land to the Lord King Charles. He came to invite the glorious king and his Franks, to help the Church against King Desiderius and the Lombards for the sake of God's service and the rights of St. Peter.

R Hadrian could no longer bear the insolence of King Desiderius and the oppression of the Lombards. He resolved to send an embassy to Charles, king of the Franks, and ask him to render aid to him and the Romans against the Lombards.

The pope's emissary came by sea because the Lombards had closed the roads to the Romans. Then the noble Lord King Charles deliberated with the Franks what he should do. After it had been decided that all should be done as the pope's emissary had requested, through the word of the Lord Pope Hadrian, the glorious king held a general assembly with the Franks at the city of Geneva.[1] There the Lord King divided his army. He himself went on by way of Mont Cenis and sent his uncle Bernard[2] with his other vassals through the Great St. Bernard Pass. When the two armies united at the Cluses, Desiderius on his part moved to confront the Lord King Charles. Then the Lord King Charles with his Franks laid out his camp in this mountain valley and sent a detachment of his men through the mountains. When Desiderius' realized what was going on, he withdrew from the Cluses. The Lord King Charles and his Franks entered Italy by the help of the

Lord and the intercession of St. Peter, the blessed apostle, bringing his entire army through the valley without loss or disorder. He came as far as the city of Pavia, surrounded Desiderius, and besieged the city.[3]

The Lord Charles celebrated Christmas there in his camp, and he celebrated Easter in Rome.[4] While he went to Rome during this year to defend God's Holy Roman Church at the invitation of the supreme pontiff, the borderland against the Saxons was exposed and not secured by any treaty. The Saxons, however, fell upon the neighboring Frankish lands with a large army and advanced as far as the castle of Büraburg. The inhabitants of the borderland were terrified when they saw this and retreated into the castle. When the Saxons in their savagery began to burn the houses outside, they came upon a church at Fritzlar which Boniface of saintly memory, the most recent martyr, had consecrated and which he had said prophetically would never be burnt by fire. The Saxons began to attack this church with great determination, trying one way or another to burn it. While this was going on, there appeared to some Christians in the castle and also to some heathens in the army two young men on white horses who protected the church from fire. Because of them the pagans could not set the church on fire or damage it, either inside or outside. Terror-stricken by the intervention of divine might they turned to flight, although nobody pursued them. Afterward one of these Saxons was found dead beside the church. He was squatting on the ground and holding tinder and wood in his hands as if he had meant to blow on his fuel and set the church on fire.[5] And the date changed to

774

On his return from Rome the Lord King Charles came again to Pavia and captured the city and Desiderius, with his wife and daughter and the whole treasure of his palace besides. All the Lombards came from every city of Italy and submitted to the rule of the glorious Lord King Charles and of the Franks. Adalgis, the son of King Desiderius, fled, put to sea, and escaped to Constantinople.[1] After subduing Italy and setting it to rights, the glorious Lord King Charles left a Frankish garrison in the city of Pavia and by God's help returned triumphantly to Francia with his wife and the rest of the Franks.[2] When he arrived at Ingelheim, he sent four detachments to Saxony.[3] Three of them fought the Saxons and with God's help had the victory; the fourth did not see battle but returned home with much booty and no losses. The glorious king celebrated Christmas at the villa of Quierzy and Easter, too. And the date changed to

775

R While the king spent the winter at the villa of Quierzy, he decided to attack the treacherous and treaty-breaking tribe of the Saxons and to persist in this war until they were either defeated and forced to accept the Christian religion or entirely exterminated.

The pious and noble Lord King Charles held an assembly at the villa of Düren. From here he launched a campaign into Saxony and captured[1] the castle of Syburg,[2] restored the castle of Eresburg, and came as far as the Weser at Braunsberg.[3] There the Saxons prepared for battle since they wished to defend the bank of the Weser. With the help of God and by their own vigorous efforts, the Franks put the Saxons to flight; the Franks occupied both banks of the river, and many Saxons were slain there.

Then the Lord King Charles divided his army, and taking along as many as he wanted, he proceeded to the River Oker. There all the Saxon Austreleudi under Hassi came before him, gave as many hostages as he desired, and swore oaths of fealty to the Lord King Charles.[4] When the most gracious king returned from there, the Angrarii[5] came to the Bückegau[6] with Bruno and the rest of their magnates and gave hostages[7] as the Austrasians had done. On his return the king joined with another part of his army which by his order held the bank of the River Weser. The Saxons took them on at Lübbecke;[8] the Franks by the will of God had the victory and many Saxons of this group were slain.

R In the meantime the part of the army which he had sent to the Weser pitched camp at the place called Lübbecke. But the men acted carelessly, and were tricked by Saxon guile. When the Frankish foragers returned to the camp about the ninth hour of the day, Saxons mixed with them as if they belonged to them and thus entered the camp of the Franks. They attacked the sleeping or half-awake soldiers[9] and are said to have caused quite a slaughter among the multitude who were off guard. But they

NORSEMEN
SILENDI
Schleswig
OSTARSALT
WESTERN SEA
R. Eider
Esesfeld
R. Stor
Reric
HADELN
OBODRITES
WILZI
RÜSTRINGEN
WIHMUODI
FRISIA
Hollenstedt
LINONES
Bardowiek
Lune
Hohbuoki
BARDENGAU
Verden
ARENDSEE
R. Elbe
R. Aller
EASTPHALIANS
ANGRARII
BÜCKEGAU
Steinfurt
WESTPHALIANS
R. Ohre
Ohrum
R. Weser
Schöningen
R. Ems
WEISSGAU
R. Oker
Bocholt
Lippeham
DREINGAU
Sythen
R. Lippe
Seeburg
Syburg
R. Ruhr
THURINGIANS
R. Saale
R. Rhine
Inset refers to the map: "Sites of Saxon Campaigns"
R. Lahn
0
Miles
80

Saxony

were repulsed by the valor of those who were awake and resisted bravely. They left the Frankish camp after agreeing to the best terms they could get in their distress.[10]

Hearing this the Lord King Charles once more fell upon the Saxons with his army, inflicted on them an equally grave defeat, and carried away considerable booty from the Westphalians. They gave hostages as the other Saxons had done. When he had obtained the hostages, taken much booty, and three times caused much slaughter among the Saxons, the Lord King Charles with God's help returned home to Francia.

When he heard that the Lombard Hrodgaud was not keeping faith but breaking all oaths and planning to incite Italy to rebellion,[11] the Lord King Charles marched into Italy with a Frankish host.

He celebrated Christmas at the villa of Schlettstadt.[12] And the date changed to

776

The Lord King Charles entered Italy through Friuli. Hrodgaud was killed and the Lord King Charles celebrated Easter at the city of Treviso. He placed the cities he had captured under the command of Franks, that is, Cividale, Treviso, and the other places which had revolted, and returned again to Francia, successful and victorious.

Then a messenger came with the news that the Saxons had rebelled, deserted all their hostages, broken their oaths, and by tricks and false treaties prevailed on the Franks to give up the castle of Eresburg. With Eresburg thus deserted by the Franks, the Saxons demolished the buildings and walls. Passing on from Eresburg they wished to do the same thing to the castle of Syburg but made no headway since the Franks with the help of God put up a manly resistance. When they failed to talk the guards into surrender, as they had those in the other castle, they began to set up war machines to storm the castle. Since God willed it, the catapults which they had prepared did more damage to them than to those inside. When the Saxons saw that their constructions were useless to them, they prepared faggots to capture the fortress in one charge. But God's power, as is only just, overcame theirs. One day, while they prepared for battle against the Christians in the castle, God's glory was made manifest over the castle church in the sight of a great number outside as well as

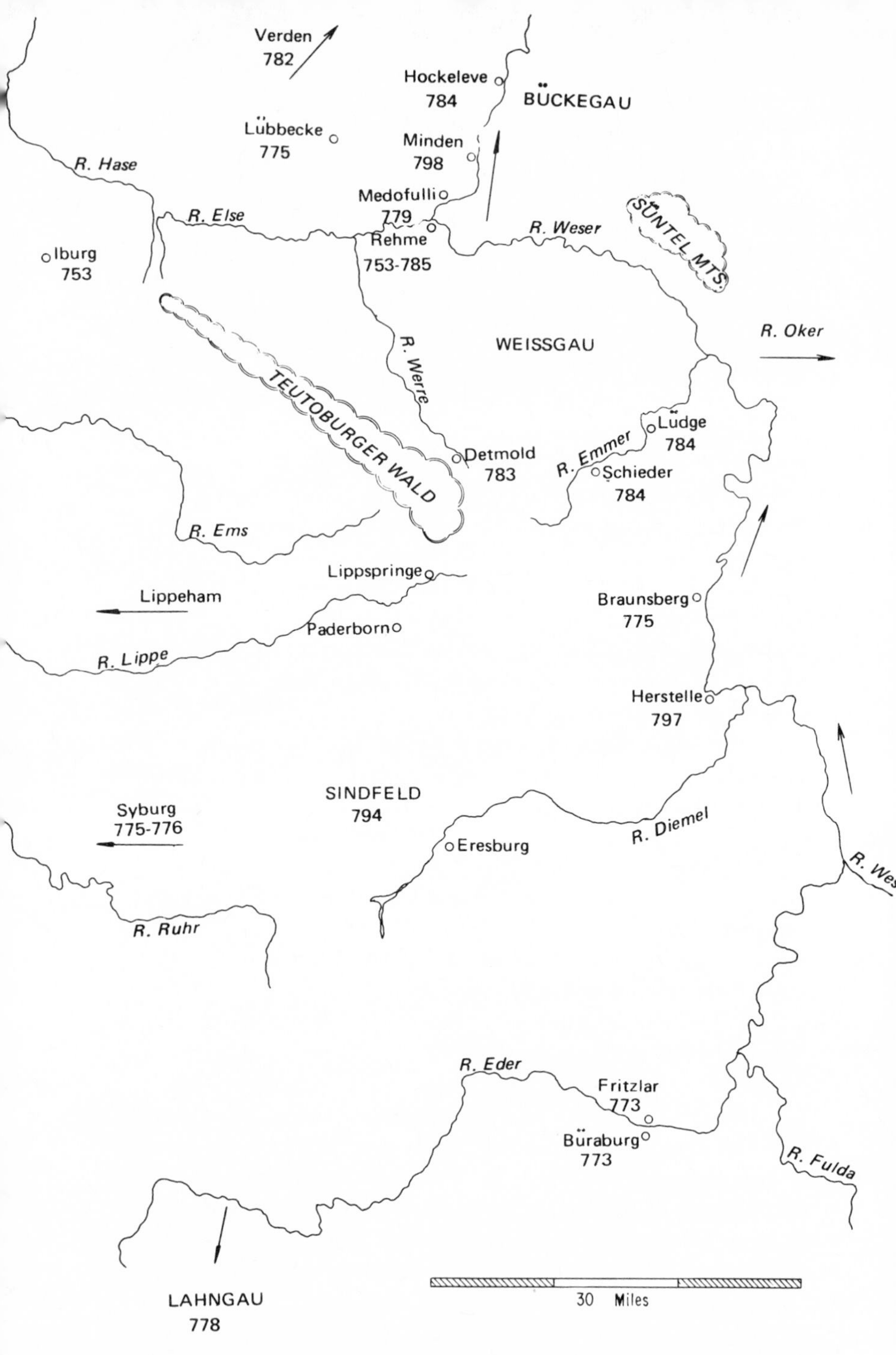

Sites of Saxon Campaigns

inside, many of whom are still with us. They reportedly saw the likeness of two shields red with flame wheeling over the church. When the heathens outside saw this miracle, they were at once thrown into confusion and started fleeing to their camp in terror. Since all of them were panic-stricken, one man stampeded the next and was killed in return, because those who looked back out of fear impaled themselves on the lances carried on the shoulders of those who fled before them. Some dealt each other aimless blows and thus suffered divine retribution. How much the power of God worked against them for the salvation of the Christians, nobody can tell. But the more the Saxons were stricken by fear, the more the Christians were comforted and praised the almighty God who deigned to reveal his power over his servants. When the Saxons took to flight, the Franks followed on their heels as far as the River Lippe slaughtering them. Once the castle was safe, the Franks returned home victorious.[1]

When the Lord King Charles came to Worms and heard what had happened he called an assembly there. He held his general assembly, and after deliberation suddenly broke through the fortifications of the Saxons with God's help. In great terror all the Saxons came to the source of the River Lippe; converging there from every point they surrendered their land to the Franks, put up security, promised to become Christians, and submitted to the rule of the Lord King Charles and the Franks.[2]

The Lord King Charles with the Franks rebuilt the castle of Eresburg and another castle on the River Lippe. The Saxons came there with wives and children, a countless number, and were baptized and gave as many hostages as the Lord King demanded. When the above castles had been completed and Frankish garrisons installed to guard them,[3] the Lord King Charles returned to Francia.

He celebrated Christmas at Herstal and Easter at the villa of Nijmegen. And the date changed to

777

The Lord King Charles for the first time held a general assembly at Paderborn. All the Franks gathered there and from every part of Saxony came the Saxons,[1] with the exception of Widukind, who was in revolt along with a few others. He fled with his companions into Nordmannia.[2] Saracens from Spain also came to this assembly, ibn al-Arabi and his son Deiuzefi—in Latin, Joseph—as well as his son-in-law.[3] Many Saxons were baptized and according to their custom pledged to the king their whole freedom and property if they should change their minds again in that detestable manner of theirs and not keep the Christian faith and their fealty to the Lord King Charles, his sons, and the Franks.

He celebrated Christmas at the villa of Douzy and Easter at the villa of Chasseneuil in Aquitaine.[4] And the date changed to

778

The Lord King Charles marched to Spain by two different routes.[1] One was by Pamplona, which the great king himself took as far as Saragossa. To Saragossa came his men from Burgundy, Austrasia, Bavaria, as well as Provence and Septimania, and a part of the Lombards. Arriving from two sides the armies united at Saragossa. The king received hostages from ibn al-Arabi and Abu Taher and many Saracens, destroyed Pamplona, and subjugated the Spanish Basques and the people of Navarre. Then he returned to Francia.

R On the heights of the Pyrenees the Basques prepared an ambush, attacked the rearguard, and threw the whole army into confusion. Although the Franks were obviously their betters in arms and valor, they nevertheless suffered a defeat due to the unfavorable terrain and the unequal method of fighting.[2] In this engagement a great many officers of the palace, whom the king had given positions of command, were killed; the baggage was plundered, and the enemy was able to vanish in all directions because he knew the lay of the land. To have suffered this wound shadowed the king's view of his success in Spain.[3]

When the Saxons heard that the Lord King Charles and the Franks were so far away in Spain, they followed their detestable custom and again revolted, spurred on by Widukind and his companions. The Lord King Charles was informed of this revolt at the city of Auxerre. Then the Lord King sent a Frankish host rushing to the defense against the Saxons. But these rebels advanced as far as the Rhine at Deutz, plundered along the river, and committed many atrocities, such as burning the churches of God in the monasteries and other acts too loathsome to enumerate.[4] When they suddenly heard of the return of the Lord King Charles and of the troops he had sent against them,

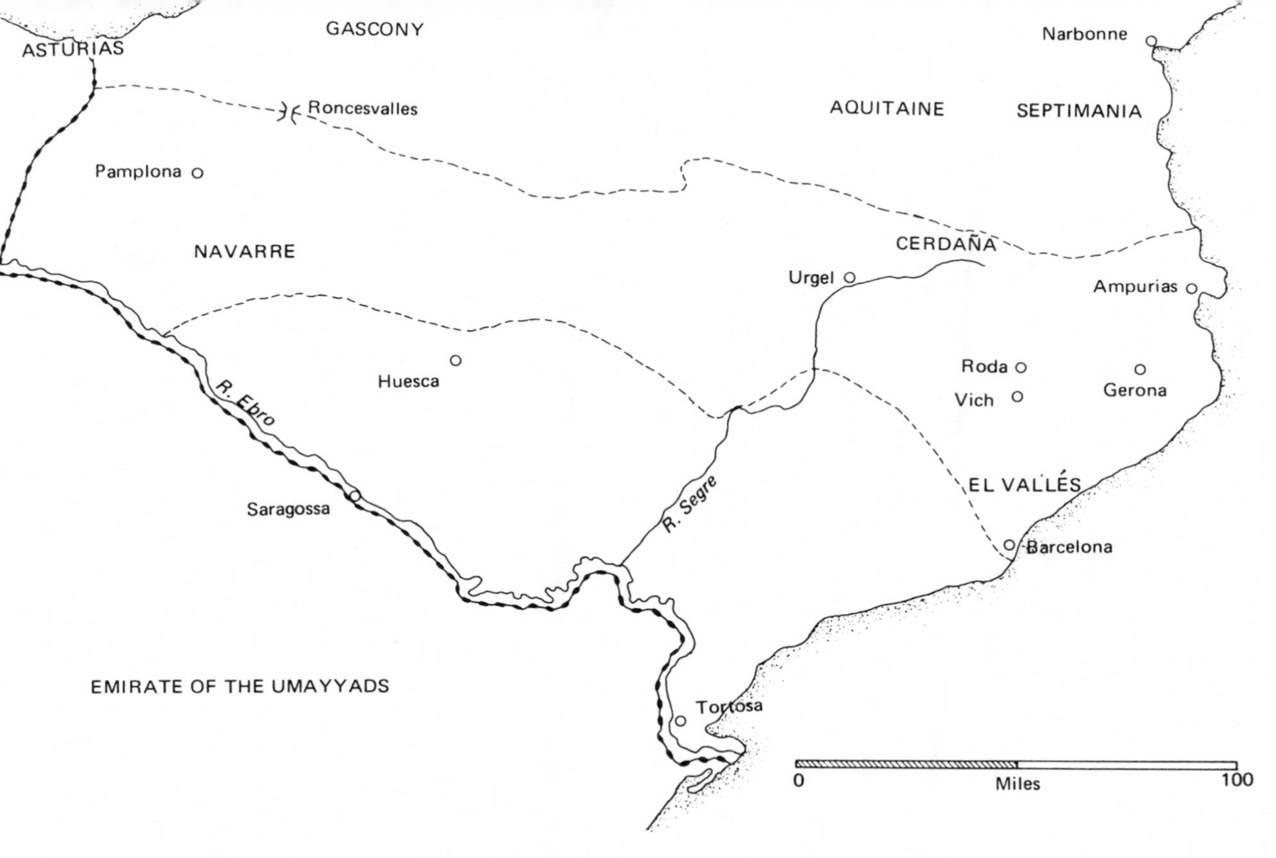

The Spanish March

the Saxons forsook the Rhine and returned to Saxony by way of the Lahngau. The Frankish detachments did not encounter them but found their trail and followed them as far as the River Eder near Leisa. There a battle started and was successfully completed. With the help of God the Franks had the victory. A great number of Saxons were slain, and those who escaped returned to Saxony in utter disgrace.

The most gracious king celebrated Christmas at the villa of Herstal and Easter, too. And the date changed to

779

The Lord King Charles marched into Neustria and arrived at the villa of Compiègne. On the king's return to Austrasia, Duke Hildebrand of Spoleto[1] put in an appearance with many presents before the great king at the villa of Verzenay.[2]

The assembly took place at the villa of Düren and a campaign was launched into Saxony. The Rhine was crossed at Lippeham,[3] and the Saxons wanted to put up resistance at Bocholt.[4] With the help of God they did not prevail but fled, abandoning every one of their bulwarks. The way was open for the Franks, and they marched into the land of the Westphalians and conquered them all. The rest who lived on the other side of the River Weser gave hostages and swore oaths when the Lord King Charles came upon them at Medofulli.[5] The glorious king then returned to Francia. He celebrated Christmas at Worms and Easter, too. And the date changed to

780

The Lord King Charles, on his way to straighten out the affairs of Saxony, advanced as far as the castle of Eresburg, and from Eresburg to the source of the River Lippe, where he held the assembly. From there he continued to the Elbe, and on this campaign all the people in the Bardengau and many of the Nordliudi were baptized at Ohrum[1] on the other side of the River Oker.[2] He reached the place where the Ohre flows into the Elbe. There the noble king settled all matters pertaining to Saxons and Slavs and then returned to Francia.

He then decided to go to Rome with his wife, the Lady Queen Hildegard,[3] in order to pray there. He celebrated Christmas in the city of Pavia, and the date changed to

781

After resuming this journey he celebrated Easter at Rome. There the Lord Pepin,[1] the son of the great Lord King Charles, was baptized by Pope Hadrian, who was also his sponsor. Two sons of the Lord King Charles were anointed kings by the same pontiff: the Lords Pepin and Louis,[2] the Lord Pepin to be king of Italy and the Lord Louis to be king of Aquitaine. On his return journey the Lord King Charles came to the city of Milan, and there his daughter, the Lady Gisela,[3] was baptized by Archbishop Thomas, who was also her sponsor. From Milan he returned to Francia. About this time Pope Hadrian sent two emissaries, Bishops Formosus and Damasus, to Duke Tassilo, along with Riculf, a deacon, and Eberhard, the master of the cupbearers, the emissaries of the Lord King Charles.[4] They were to warn and to beseech Tassilo to remember his former oaths and not to go back on his long-standing pledge to the Lord King Pepin, the great Lord King Charles, and the Franks. Then Tassilo, duke of the Bavarians, agreed to give hostages to the Lord King Charles and to appear before him. The Lord King agreed to this. The duke put in his appearance before the most pious king at the city of Worms. There he renewed his oaths and gave twelve selected hostages as pledge that he would do all that he had sworn to the Lord King Pepin regarding the Lord King Charles and his vassals. These hostages were received from the hand of Bishop Sinbert at the villa of Quierzy.[5] But Duke Tassilo did not long keep the promises he had made.

The glorious Lord King celebrated Christmas as well as Easter at the villa of Quierzy. And the date changed to

782

The Lord King Charles[1] embarked on a campaign and crossed the Rhine at Cologne. He held an assembly at the source of the River Lippe. All the Saxons came there except the rebel Widukind. Norse emissaries of King Sigifrid, Halptani with his companions, also appeared at this assembly, and so did Avars sent by the khagan and jugur.[2] When the assembly was over, the Lord King Charles returned to Francia.

As soon as he returned, the Saxons, persuaded by Widukind, promptly rebelled as usual. Before the Lord King Charles knew about this, he sent his emissaries Adalgis, Gailo, and Worad to lead an army of Franks and Saxons against a few defiant Slavs.[3] When the emissaries heard en route that the Saxons had revolted, they hurled themselves on the Saxon host as soon as they caught up with it, and from then on did not carry out their commission from the Lord King Charles. They made war on the Saxons and fought valiantly. The Franks slew many of the Saxons and had the victory. But two of the emissaries, Adalgis and Gailo, died in battle in the Süntel Mountains.

R Forsaking the campaign against the Slavs, they rushed with the East Frankish host to the place where they had heard the Saxons were assembling. In Saxony proper they were met by Count Theodoric, the king's kinsman, who had with him as many troops as he could hastily gather in Ripuaria[4] after he had heard of the Saxon revolt. He advised them through special messengers first to find out by patrols as fast as possible where the Saxons were[5] and what they were doing, and then, if the terrain permitted it, to attack them at the same time. This counsel was found laudable, and they advanced with the count as far as the Süntel Mountains, on whose north side the Saxon camp had been set up.[6] After Theodoric had pitched camp in this locality, the East Franks, as they had planned with the count, crossed the river, so as to be able to pass more easily around the mountains, and pitched camp on the river bank. When they discussed matters among themselves, they feared that the honor of victory might be Theodoric's alone if they should fight at his side. Therefore, they decided to engage the Saxons without him. They took up their arms and, as if he were chasing runaways and going after booty instead of facing an enemy lined up for battle, everybody dashed as fast as his horse would carry him for the place outside of the Saxon camp, where the Saxons were standing in battle array. The battle was as bad as the approach. As soon as the fighting began, they were surrounded by the Saxons and slain almost to a man. Those who were able to get away did not flee to their own camp but to Theodoric's on the other side of the mountain. The losses of the Franks were greater than the number might reveal since two of the envoys, Adalgis and Gailo, four counts, and up to twenty other distinguished nobles had been killed,[7] not counting those who had followed them, preferring to perish at their side rather than survive them.

When he heard of this,[8] the Lord King Charles rushed to the place with all the Franks that he could gather on short notice and advanced to where the Aller flows into the Weser. Then all the Saxons came together again, submitted to the authority of the Lord King, and surrendered the evildoers who were chiefly responsible for this revolt to be put to death—four thousand five hundred of them. This sentence was carried out.[9] Widukind was not among them since he had fled into Nordmannia.[10] When he had finished this business, the Lord King returned to Francia.

He celebrated Christmas at the villa of Thionville and Easter, too. And the date changed to

783

The worthy Lady Queen Hildegard died on April 30, which fell that year on the eve of the Ascension of the Lord. Since the Saxons had revolted again, the Lord King Charles conducted a campaign into Saxony and with only a few Franks advanced to Detmold. There the Saxons prepared for battle in a plain, but the Lord King Charles and the Franks assailed them vigorously as usual and the Saxons fled. With the help of God the Franks had the victory. An immense number of Saxons were slain at this place so that only a few escaped by flight. From Detmold the glorious king arrived in triumph at Paderborn and there assembled his army. He advanced as far as the River Hase,[1] where the Saxons had gathered again. There another battle was fought, and the number of Saxons killed was no less than before. With the help of God the Franks had the victory. Continuing his campaign the king crossed the Weser and went as far as the Elbe. From the Elbe he returned to Francia.

In the same year the Lady Queen Bertrada of good memory died on July 12. When the Lord King Charles came to Worms, he took the Lady Queen Fastrada as his wife.[2] He celebrated Christmas at the villa of Herstal and also Easter. And the date changed to

784

The Saxons rebelled again as usual and some Frisians along with them. Then the Lord King Charles set out on a campaign and crossed the Rhine at Lippeham. He entered Saxony and went here and there devastating the countryside until he reached Hockeleve.[1] Because of severe floods he decided to enter the land of the Eastphalians from the east by way of Thuringia and to send his son, the Lord Charles,[2] with a detachment against the Westphalians. This maneuver was carried out. The Lord King Charles marched through Thuringia as far as the Elbe and from there to Steinfurt and on to Schöningen.[3] After Charles and his son met there, the glorious king returned to Francia.

But the Westphalians wanted to gather at the River Lippe. When the Lord King Charles's son heard this, he marched against them with the host that had been sent with him, and they began the war in the Dreingau. With the help of God, the Lord Charles, son of the great King Charles, and the Franks had the victory, and many Saxons were killed. Since God willed it, he returned unharmed to his father at Worms. There it was decided with the Franks that the Lord King should march once more during wintertime into Saxony, which he did. He celebrated Christmas near Schieder in the Weissgau on the River Emmer at the villa of Lügde.[4] And the date changed to

785

The Lord King Charles continued the march into Saxony as far as Rehme on the Weser at the mouth of the River Werre. And because of the severe flood he returned from Rehme to the castle of Eresburg and had his wife, the Lady Queen Fastrada, and his sons and his daughters come to join him. There he remained for the whole winter and there the most excellent king celebrated Easter. While he was staying at Eresburg, he sent out many detachments and also went campaigning himself. He routed the Saxons who had rebelled, captured their castles, broke through their fortifications, and held the roads open until the right hour struck. Then he held a general assembly at Paderborn and from there he marched through all of Saxony wherever he wished, on open roads and with nobody putting up any resistance. He came into the Bardengau[1] and there he sent for Widukind and Abbi and had both brought before him.[2] He warned them that they could not escape unless they came to him in Francia. They asked for assurances that they would remain unharmed and these were given. Then the Lord King Charles returned to Francia and sent hostages to Widukind and Abbi by his emissary Amalwin. After receiving the hostages, the emissaries took Widukind and Abbi along and joined the Lord King Charles at the villa of Attigny. There

Widukind and Abbi were baptized with their companions. The whole of Saxony was then subjugated. In the same villa the often-mentioned glorious king celebrated Christmas and also Easter.

R The stubborn treachery of the Saxons quieted down for a few years, mainly because they could not find convenient opportunities for revolt. In the same year an ambitious conspiracy against the king arose across the Rhine among the East Franks, whose ringleader, as is certain, was Count Hardrad. But its discovery was quickly reported to the king, and by his effort this great conspiracy folded up quickly before it became a serious threat. Its authors were punished in part by being deprived of their eyes and in part by being sent into exile.[3]

And the date changed to

786

The Lord King Charles sent his army into Brittany under his emissary Audulf, the seneschal.

R After the island of Britain had been invaded by Angles and Saxons, a large part of its inhabitants crossed the sea and occupied the areas of Vannes and Corseult at the extreme end of Gaul. This people had been subjugated by the kings of the Franks and made tributary and it used to pay the imposed tax, although unwillingly. But since it refused to obey at this time, the king's seneschal Audulf was sent there. He broke down the arrogance of this treacherous tribe with marvelous speed.

There they conquered many Bretons with their castles and fortifications in swamps and in forests. As was said before, the Franks proved they could overcome many fortifications of the Bretons. By God's will they returned home victorious and presented the leaders of the Bretons to the Lord King at the assembly in Worms. Then the Lord King Charles, seeing that by the gift of God he enjoyed peace everywhere, decided to go to Italy in order to pray at the threshold of the blessed apostles, to settle the affairs of Italy, and to confer with the emperor's emissaries about a settlement, all of which he did.

R He considered it proper that he should take over the rest of the kingdom since he already had control of its ruler, the captive King Desiderius, and all of Lombardy. He did not delay long but promptly gathered the troops of the Franks and entered Italy in the cold of the winter season.

Then the Lord King celebrated Christmas at the city of Florence.[1] And the date changed to

787

On his expedition into Italy the Lord King Charles arrived in Rome and was received with great honors by the Lord Pope Hadrian. He spent some days with the Lord Pope. Arighis, duke of Benevento, because of the king's coming, sent his son Romuald with rich presents to demand of the Lord King that he should stay out of Benevento, and to let him know that he wished to do whatever the king said.[1] But neither the pope nor the Frankish magnates believed a word of this and decided with the Lord King Charles to enter Benevento to settle matters one way or the other, which they did. When they came to Capua, Duke Arighis forsook the city of Benevento and blockaded himself in Salerno. He was afraid and did not dare to see the Lord King Charles face to face. Instead, he sent emissaries and offered his two sons as hostages, that is, Romuald, whom the Lord King Charles had with him, and Grimoald, who was still with Arighis. He offered many presents as well, and more hostages to further his petition. Then the glorious Lord King Charles decided with the priests and the other magnates not to destroy this land and ruin its bishoprics and monasteries. He selected twelve hostages and as the thirteenth hostage he chose the son of the duke called Grimoald. After receiving presents all the Beneventans took oaths, including the duke and Romuald.

R Upon this the king conversed with the ambassadors of Emperor Constantine, who had been sent to him to ask for the hand of his daughter.[2]

The oft-named most pious king returned and celebrated Easter with the Lord Pope in Rome.

Emissaries of Duke Tassilo, that is, Bishop Arno and Abbot Hunric,[3] came to Rome and asked the pope to make peace between the Lord King Charles and Duke Tassilo. The Lord Pope, therefore, stepped in firmly and pleaded with the Lord King. The Lord King answered the pope that he had wished for peace and sought it for a long time but had not been able to obtain it by any means. He proposed to make peace at once. The Lord King wanted to settle with these emissaries in the presence of the Lord Pope, but the emissaries refused since they were afraid to make any commitments on their own. Recognizing their inconstancy and deceit the pope at once threatened to excommunicate the duke and his supporters unless they fulfilled the oaths which they had sworn to the Lord King Pepin and also to the Lord King Charles. The pope besought these emissaries to make sure Tassilo realized that he would carry out his threat unless the duke obeyed in everything the Lord King Charles, his sons, and the Frankish people, so that no bloodshed or violation of his territory should occur. If the duke in his stubbornness intended to disobey the words of the pope entirely, then the Lord King Charles and his army would be absolved from any peril of sin, and the guilt of whatever burning, murder, and other atrocities might occur in his country should then fall upon Tassilo and his supporters, and the Lord King Charles and the Franks would remain innocent.[4] When all this had been said, Tassilo's emissaries were dismissed. Then the Lord Pope and the glorious Lord King Charles took leave of one another. After receiving the papal blessings and completing his prayer the oft-mentioned excellent king returned to Francia.

The same most gracious king reached his wife, the Lady Fastrada, in the city of Worms. There they rejoiced over each other and were happy together and praised God's mercy. The Lord King convoked an assembly in the same city and reported to the clergy and the rest of his magnates on the upshot of his journey. After he had explained the affair with Tassilo, the king decided to send emissaries and ordered Tassilo to do everything according to the pope's instruction and the demands of justice, since he had promised under oath to be obedient and loyal in everything to the Lord King Charles, his sons, and the Franks, and to appear before him. But Tassilo rejected this and refused to come. Then the Lord King Charles with the Franks took steps to protect his rights, set out on a campaign into Bavaria with his army, and came in person to the Lechfeld above the city of Augsburg. He ordered another army to be raised consisting of East Franks, Thuringians, and Saxons, which was to assemble on the Danube at Pförring.[5] He ordered a third army to be raised in Italy. He also commanded King Pepin to advance with this army as far as Trent, to remain there himself, and to send his army ahead in full strength as far as Bolzano. Then Tassilo realized that he was surrounded on three sides and that all Bavarians, acknowledging the right of the Lord King and preferring to concede it to him rather than oppose him, were more loyal to the Lord King Charles than to him. Hedged in on every side, the duke came in person and putting his hands into the hands of the Lord King Charles he commended himself into vassalage. He returned the duchy which had been committed to him by the Lord King Pepin and admitted that he had sinned and acted unlawfully in every way. Then he renewed again his oaths and gave twelve selected hostages, adding as a thirteenth his son Theodo. After receiving hostages and oaths the glorious king returned to Francia.[6]

He celebrated Christmas at the villa of Ingelheim and also Easter. And the date changed to

788

The Lord King Charles convoked an assembly at the villa of Ingelheim. Tassilo came there as well as his other vassals on the order of the Lord King. Loyal Bavarians began to say that Tassilo, egged on by his wife,[1] was breaking his fealty and showing himself as downright treacherous, after he had surrendered his son with the other hostages and taken oaths. Tassilo could not deny it, but confessed later that he had made overtures to the Avars, had ordered the vassals of the Lord King to come to him, and had made an attempt on their lives. When his people took oaths, he told them to make mental reservations and swear falsely. What is worse, he confessed to having said that even if he had ten sons, he would rather have them all perish than keep the agreements and stand by what he had sworn. He also said that he would rather be dead than live like this. After all this had been proved against him, Franks, Bavarians, Lombards, and Saxons, and whoever else had come from every province to this assembly, condemned him to death, since they remembered his previous evil deeds and his desertion of the Lord King Pepin on a campaign, which is called *harisliz* in German. While all called out with one voice that he should impose the death sentence, the most pious Lord King Charles was moved by mercy. For the love of God and since the duke was his kinsman he prevailed upon these men, who were faithful to God and to him, that Tassilo should not die. Tassilo was asked by the most gracious Lord King what he wished to do. The duke requested permission to take the tonsure, enter a monastery, and do penance for so many sins in order to save his soul. His son Theodo was judged similarly, was tonsured, and sent to a monastery; a few Bavarians who chose to persist in their hostility against the Lord King Charles were sent into exile.[2]

In the same year a war was fought between Greeks and Lombards, that is, by Duke Hildebrand of Spoleto and Duke Grimoald, whom the Lord King Charles had made duke of the Beneventans. Winigis was sent there with a few Franks to oversee what they were doing.[3] With the help of God a victory was won by the Franks and the Lombards. A battle also took place at . . . between the Avars and the Franks who were stationed in Italy. With the help of the Lord the Franks won; the Avars fled and returned home disgraced and defeated.[4] A third battle was fought between Bavarians and Avars on the Ybbsfeld, and the emissaries of the Lord King Charles, Grahamannus and Otgar, were present with a number of Franks. With God's help victory went to Franks and Bavarians. All this Duke Tassilo and his rancorous wife, Liutberga, a woman hateful to God, had treacherously counseled. A fourth battle was started by the Avars, who wished to take revenge on the Bavarians. In this battle the emissaries of the Lord King Charles also took part, and since they were protected by the Lord the Christians won the victory. The Avars took to flight and in a great carnage many were struck down; others lost their lives by drowning in the Danube.[5]

R The Huns, as they had promised Tassilo, prepared two armies and attacked the March of Friuli with one and Bavaria with the other; but it was in vain. In both places they were defeated and put to flight and withdrew to their homes with great injury after losing many of their men. Planning to avenge this defeat, they again came to Bavaria with larger forces but were repulsed by the Bavarians in the first engagement, and an uncountable number of them were slain. In addition, many who attempted to flee and wanted to swim across the Danube were sucked down by the whirlpools of the river.[6]

In the meantime Emperor Constantine, enraged because he had been denied the king's daughter, instructed the patrician Theodore, governor of Sicily, with his other commanders to lay waste the territory of the Beneventans. When they carried out their orders, Grimoald and Hildebrand met them in Calabria with the troops they had been able to assemble. The king had installed Grimoald that year, after his father's death, as duke over the Beneventans; Hildebrand was duke of the people of Spoleto. With Grimoald and Hildebrand was the king's envoy Winigis, who afterwards succeeded Hildebrand in the duchy of Spoleto. In the ensuing battle they killed an immense number of the enemy; they won a victory without cost in equipment and men and brought back to their camp numerous prisoners and plenty of booty.

After all this the Lord King Charles came himself to Regensburg and arranged the borders and marches of the Bavarians so that with the protection of the Lord they could be held against the Avars. Then he returned and celebrated Christmas and Easter, too, at the palace of Aachen. And the date changed to

789

From Aachen a campaign was launched with the help of God into the land of the Slavs who are called Wilzi.[1]

R The Wilzi have always been hostile to the Franks and used to hate and harass their neighbors who were either subject to the Franks or allied with them and provoke them into war. Thinking he should not bear their arrogance any longer, the king decided to make war on them.

On the advice of Franks and Saxons he crossed the Rhine at Cologne, advanced through Saxony, reached the River Elbe, and had two bridges constructed, on one of which he built fortifications of wood and earth at both ends. From there he advanced further and by the gift of God subjected the Slavs to his authority. Both Franks and Saxons were with him in this army. In addition, the Frisians joined him by ship, on the River Havel, along with some Franks. He also had with him the Slavs called Sorbs and the Obodrites, whose chieftain was Witzan.[2]

R Entering the country of the Wilzi he ordered everything to be laid waste with fire and sword. But that tribe, although warlike and confident in its numbers, was not able to withstand the attack of the royal army for very long.[3] Therefore, as soon as he came to the city of Dragawit, who stands above the other kinglets of the Wilzi in age and lineage, Dragawit at once with all his people came forth from the city, gave the hostages he was ordered to provide, and promised by oath to keep faith with the king and the Franks. The other magnates and chieftains of the Slavs followed suit and submitted to the authority of the king.

After receiving hostages and numerous oaths he returned, guided by the Lord, to Francia. He celebrated Christmas and Easter, too, at Worms. And the date changed to

790

In the following year he did not undertake a campaign but again celebrated Christmas and also Easter in the city of Worms.

R He rested at Worms, received the envoys of the Huns, and on his part sent envoys to their princes. The point at issue between them was where the borders of their kingdoms should be. This festering dispute was the seedbed which nursed the subsequent war against the Huns. So it would not seem that he had grown idle and soft with leisure,[1] the king sailed up the River Main to his palace of Salz, which he had constructed on the River Saale in Germany.[2] From Salz he returned again downstream on the same river to Worms. While he was spending the winter there, the palace in which he lived was accidentally burned at night.[3]

And the date changed to

791

From Worms he set out for Bavaria and came to Regensburg where he assembled his army. After deliberating with Franks, Saxons, and Frisians they decided on a campaign because of the excessive and intolerable outrage committed by the Avars against the Holy Church and the Christian people, for which satisfaction could not be obtained through emissaries. With the help of the Lord they entered the land of the Avars. Heading for the River Enns[1] they decided there to hold processions and celebrate masses for three days. They implored God's help for the welfare of the army, for the assistance of our Lord Jesus Christ, and for victory over the Avars and revenge on them. The king marched on the south bank of the Danube, the Saxons with some Franks and most of the Frisians[2] on the north bank, until they came to an area where the Avars had prepared fortifications: on the south bank of the Danube by Cumeoberg,[3] on the north bank at a place called Kamp after the river which flows into the Danube here. When the Avars saw the army approach on both sides and the ships in the middle of the river, the Lord struck them with fear. They deserted their fortified positions, abandoning the elaborate defenses they had built, and took to flight. Christ guided his people and led both armies without harm into the Avar strongholds. Continuing its march the army advanced as far as the River Raab, and from there both armies returned along the two banks of the river to their own land, praising God for such a victory.[4]

R This campaign was accomplished without any misfortune, except that in the army under the king's command such a pestilence broke out among the horses that of so many thousands of them hardly the tenth part is said to have survived.

The Lord King Charles celebrated Christmas at Regensburg and also Easter. And the date changed to

792

Christmas and Easter at Regensburg again. The heresy of Felix was condemned there for the first time. Angilbert took him before Pope Hadrian, and having made a confession, Felix for the second time recanted his heresy. No military campaign was undertaken this year.

R Urgel is a city located on the heights of the Pyrenees. Its bishop, a Spaniard named Felix, was asked in a letter from Elipand, bishop of Toledo, what one should believe about the human nature of the Savior God, our Lord Jesus Christ, that is, whether in regard to His manhood He should be believed and proclaimed the real or the adopted Son of God.[1] Reckless and rash and contrary to the ancient doctrine of the Catholic Church he had not only pronounced Christ the adopted son but made stubborn efforts in books addressed to the above bishop to defend his perverse belief. He was taken to the king's palace in this matter —for the king rested at that time in the Bavarian city of Regensburg where he had spent the winter—was heard by the bishops assembled in council, and convicted of error. Sent to Rome before Hadrian, the Roman pontiff, he denounced and foreswore his heresy in the basilica of the blessed apostle Peter. When this had been done, he returned to his city.

While the king was spending the summer at Regensburg, a

conspiracy was made against him by his oldest son Pepin and some Franks,[2] who claimed that they were unable to bear the cruelty of Queen Fastrada and therefore conspired against the king's life.[3] When the conspiracy was revealed by the Lombard Fardulf, he was presented with the monastery of St.-Denis as a reward, because he had kept faith. Of the authors of the conspiracy some were executed by the sword for high treason and the others hanged on gallows, being punished with such deaths because of the crime they had planned.

A bridge of pontoons was built, connected by anchors and ropes so that it could be put together and taken apart. At Regensburg the king celebrated Christmas and Easter. And the date changed to

793

In the fall the king came by ship from Regensburg to the great trench between Altmühl and Rednitz, and there emissaries of the pope appeared with large presents. At that point a messenger brought the news that the Saxons had again broken faith.

R While the king wished to finish the war which he had begun and decided to march again into Pannonia, he was informed that the troops which Count Theodoric was leading through Frisia had been intercepted and destroyed by the Saxons in the county of Rüstringen on the Weser. When he received this information, he discontinued the march into Pannonia but concealed the magnitude of the loss.

The king was persuaded by self-styled experts that one could travel most conveniently from the Danube into the Rhine if a navigable canal was built between the Rivers Rednitz and Altmühl, since one of these rivers flows into the Danube and the other into the Main. So he went at once with his entire following to the place, gathered a large number of people, and spent the whole fall on this project. A ditch was dug between these two rivers, two thousand paces long and three hundred feet wide. But it was in vain; for due to continuous rain and because the swampy ground as such contained too much water, the work that was done did not hold. Whatever the diggers dug out during the day would sink back into its former place during the night.[1]

While he was occupied with this project, two very unpleas-

Campaigns in and beyond Pannonia

ant reports were brought to him from different parts of the country. One was about the general revolt of the Saxons; the other was that the Saracens had entered Septimania, fought a battle against the guards and counts of this border, and had returned home victorious after slaying many Franks.[2]

From there the king went by ship on the River Rednitz into the River Main and celebrated Christmas at St. Kilian's in Würzburg. And the date changed to

794

Easter was celebrated at Frankfurt,[1] and there a great council of Gallic, German, and Italian bishops met before the king and the emissaries of the Lord Pope Hadrian, two bishops named Theophylact and Stephen. There the heresy of Felix was condemned for the third time. This condemnation by the authority of the holy fathers was written into a book, and all priests signed this book with their own hands.[2] Queen Fastrada died there and was buried with honors at St. Alban's.[3] The Greeks held a spurious council, which they falsely called the Seventh, concerning the worship of images. It was rejected by the popes.

R The synod which had been held a few years earlier in Constantinople under Irene and her son Constantine and which they called not only the Seventh but a general council was found and declared to be neither the Seventh nor universal and rejected as entirely invalid by all.[4]

From Frankfurt the army set out in two detachments for Saxony. The most glorious Lord King Charles was with one; he sent his most noble son, the Lord Charles, to the other, by way of Cologne. The Saxons gathered in the plain called Sindfeld[5] and prepared for battle. But when they heard that they were surrounded on both sides, God frustrated their intentions, and they promised, with no such thing in mind, to become Christians and be loyal to the Lord King. The king returned to his palace of Aachen and there celebrated Christmas and Easter.[6] And the date changed to

795

R The Saxons gave hostages in the preceding summer and swore oaths, as they were ordered to, but the king did not forget their treachery.

In this year the king came to Kostheim, a suburb of the city of Mainz, and there he held his assembly. When he heard that the Saxons had, as usual, broken their promise to accept Christianity and keep faith with the king, he entered Saxony with an army and reached the Elbe at Lüne.[1] At that time, Witzin, the king of the Obodrites, was slain there by the Saxons.[2]

R This event further persuaded the king to beat down the Saxons promptly and made him hate the treacherous people even more.

To Saxony also came emissaries of the tudun, who possessed much power among the people and in the kingdom of the Avars. They declared that this tudun wished, with his land and people, to submit to the king and on his instruction accept the Christian faith. Once the Saxons had been soundly beaten, their country laid waste, and their hostages received, the king returned to Gaul and celebrated Christmas and Easter at the palace of Aachen.[3] And the date changed to

796

Pope Hadrian died, and as soon as Leo had succeeded to his place he sent envoys with presents to the king. He also delivered to him the keys to the tomb of St. Peter and the banner of the city of Rome.[1]

R Leo asked the king to send one of his magnates to Rome who would receive the submission of the Roman people and their oath of fealty.

Duke Eric of Friuli dispatched his men under the command of the Slav Wonimir into Pannonia and had them plunder the ring of the Avars, which had not been entered for ages. At that time the princes of the Avars were exhausted by internecine conflict; the khagan and the jugur had fought each other in a civil war and had been killed by their own people. The duke sent the treasure of the ancient kings, which had been piled up over many centuries, to the Lord King Charles at the palace of Aachen.[2] After receiving it and thanking God, the Giver of all good things, this most wise and generous man, the Lord's steward, sent Angilbert, his beloved abbot, with a large part of it to Rome, to the threshold of the apostles. The rest he distributed among his magnates, ecclesiastic as well as lay, and his other vassals.

In the same year the tudun in accordance with his promise came to the king with most of the Avars and submitted to him, with his people and land. He and his people were baptized and after receiving honorable gifts returned home.

R But the tudun was not willing to keep long the fealty he had pledged and not much later received the penalty of his treachery. Having mustered his armies the king entered Saxony while sending his son Pepin, the king of Italy, with an army into Pannonia. Pepin's embassies reached the king in Saxony. They first informed him that the khagan, whom the Avars themselves had appointed after the murder of his predecessors, had come with the rest of his magnates and met Pepin. The second told the king that Pepin was occupying the ring with his army. The Lord King marched through Saxony with his entire host and then returned to Gaul. In the palace at Aachen he was happy to see his son Pepin return from Pannonia bringing along the rest of the treasure. There he celebrated Christmas and Easter. And the date changed to

797

The city of Barcelona in Spain which had previously revolted against us was returned to us by its governor Zatun. He came to the palace in person and submitted with his city to the Lord King.[1] A campaign was launched into Saxony[2] and pursued beyond swamps and pathless places as far as the ocean. After the return from Hadeln—this is the name of the place where Saxony borders on the sea—the king accepted the submission of the whole Saxon people by receiving hostages and returned across the Rhine to Gaul.

In the palace at Aachen he received the Saracen Abdallah, the son of Emir ibn Muawijah. He had been deposed by his brother, was living in exile in Mauretania, and commended himself now to the Lord King.[3] Also an envoy of Nicetas, governor of Sicily, by the name of Theoctistos arrived with a letter from the emperor. The king received him with ceremony and dismissed him after a few days.

About the middle of November he entered Saxony with his army to take up winter quarters and having pitched camp at the River Weser ordered the site of the camp to be called Herstelle.[4] To this place envoys of the Avars came with rich presents.[5] From Herstelle he allowed the Saracen Abdallah to return to Spain with the king's son Louis; his son Pepin the king sent into Italy. In order to settle the affairs of Saxony he spent the whole winter in that country and celebrated Christmas and Easter there. And the date changed to

798

An envoy of King Alfonso of Galicia and Asturias by the name of Froia came to the king in Saxony and presented a most beautiful tent. But at the very time of Easter the Nordliudi who live beyond the Elbe rose in rebellion and took prisoner the royal envoys who had gone to obtain satisfaction from them. They executed some of the Franks on the spot and held the others for ransom. Some of these escaped; the rest were ransomed.

R They spared only a few in order to obtain ransom for them.[1] With the others they also put to death Godescal, the king's envoy, whom the king a few days before had sent to Sigifrid, king of the Danes. On his return about this time, he was intercepted by the instigators of this revolt and executed. When this was reported, the king was savagely aroused.

The king summoned an army and marched from Herstelle to Minden. After taking counsel he took up arms against the rebels, traversed the land, and laid waste the whole of Saxony between the Elbe and the Weser.

R But the Saxons from the far side of the Elbe were carried away with their own insolence because they had been able to kill the king's envoys with impunity. They took up arms and set out against the Obodrites. The Obodrites have always aided the Franks, ever since the Franks accepted them as their allies.

The Nordliudi were defeated in battle when they engaged Thrasco,[2] duke of the Obodrites, and our envoy Eburis.[3] Four thousand of them were slain on the battlefield; the rest fled, escaped, and entered into peace negotiations; but many of them also perished. The king received hostages, including those whom the Saxon nobles singled out as the most treacherous, and then returned to Francia.

When he arrived at the palace of Aachen, he received an embassy of the Greeks sent to him from Constantinople. The envoys were Michael, formerly governor of Phrygia, and the priest Theophilus. They carried a letter from Empress Irene, since her son, Emperor Constantine, had been arrested and blinded by his people the year before.[4] But this embassy was only concerned with peace. When he sent them back, he permitted Sisinnius, brother of Bishop Tarasius of Constantinople, to go along with them. Sisinnius had long before been taken as a prisoner of war in Italy.[5]

In this year the star called Mars could not be seen anywhere in the entire sky from July of the preceding year to July of this year. The Balearic Islands were plundered by Moors and Saracens. During the winter King Alfonso of Galicia and Asturias, after plundering Lisbon, the remotest city of Spain, as tokens of his victory, sent coats of mail, mules, and captive Moors to the Lord King by his envoys Froia and Basiliscus. In this palace the Lord King celebrated Christmas and Easter. And the date changed to

799

The Romans captured the pope at the Major Litanies, blinded him, and tore his tongue out. After being cast into prison, he escaped over the wall at night, went to the envoys of the Lord King, that is, Abbot Wirund and Duke Winigis of Spoleto, who were then at St. Peter's basilica, and was taken to Spoleto.

R When Pope Leo in Rome was riding on horseback from the Lateran to the church of the blessed Lawrence, which is called At the Roast, to participate in the litany, he fell into an ambush set up by the Romans near this church. He was thrown from his horse, his eyes, as it appeared to some observers, gouged out, and his tongue cut off; they left him lying in the street naked and half-dead. On the order of those responsible for this act he was then taken to the monastery of the holy martyr Erasmus, seemingly to recover there. But through the efforts of Albinus, his chamberlain, he was lowered over the wall at night, received by Duke Winigis of Spoleto, who on the news of this crime had rushed to Rome, and escorted to Spoleto.[1]

When the king received news of this event, he ordered the pope, as the vicar of St. Peter and Roman pontiff, to be led to him with highest honors. But still he did not give up the campaign which he had planned to carry into Saxony.

The Lord King set out for Saxony, crossed the Rhine at Lippeham, and stopped at Paderborn where he pitched camp. After splitting up his army he sent his son Charles with one part into the Bardengau to negotiate with the Slavs and to receive the Saxons coming from the Nordliudi. The other part remained with him. In the same place he received Pope Leo with highest honors and while waiting there for the return of his son Charles he dismissed Pope Leo with the same honors as he had bestowed on receiving him.[2] The pope at once proceeded to Rome and the king returned to his palace at Aachen.

On the same campaign an envoy of Michael, governor of Sicily, by the name of Daniel came to the Lord King and was dismissed again from there with great honors.

In the same year the tribe of the Avars broke the faith which it had promised, and Eric, duke of Friuli, after many successes, fell a victim to an ambush of its inhabitants near the city of Tarsatika in Liburnia.[3] Count Gerold, commander of Bavaria, perished in a battle against the Avars. The Balearic Islands, which had been plundered the year before by Moors and Saracens and had sought and received aid from us, submitted to us and with God's help and ours were defended against the raids of the pirates. Military insignia of the Moors were carried away in battle and presented to the Lord King.

Count Wido, commander of the Breton March, with his fellow counts, entered Brittany, traversed the whole land and conquered it. On the king's return from Saxony Wido presented to him the weapons of the leaders who had surrendered with their names inscribed on them. Each of these delivered his land, his people, and himself to the Franks and the whole province of Brittany was subjugated by the Franks, something which had never happened before.

In the same year a monk arrived from Jerusalem and brought blessings and relics of the Lord's Sepulcher, which the patriarch of Jerusalem sent to the Lord King. Hassan, governor of the city of Huesca, by his envoy sent the keys of the city with presents.[4] Christmas was celebrated in the same palace. And the date changed to

800

The king dismissed the monk from Jerusalem and sent back with him Zacharias, a priest of his palace, to deliver his presents for the Holy Places. He himself left the palace of Aachen in the middle of March and traversed the shore of the Gallic sea. He built a fleet on this sea, which was then infested with pirates, set guards in different places, and celebrated Easter at St.-Riquier in Centulum. From

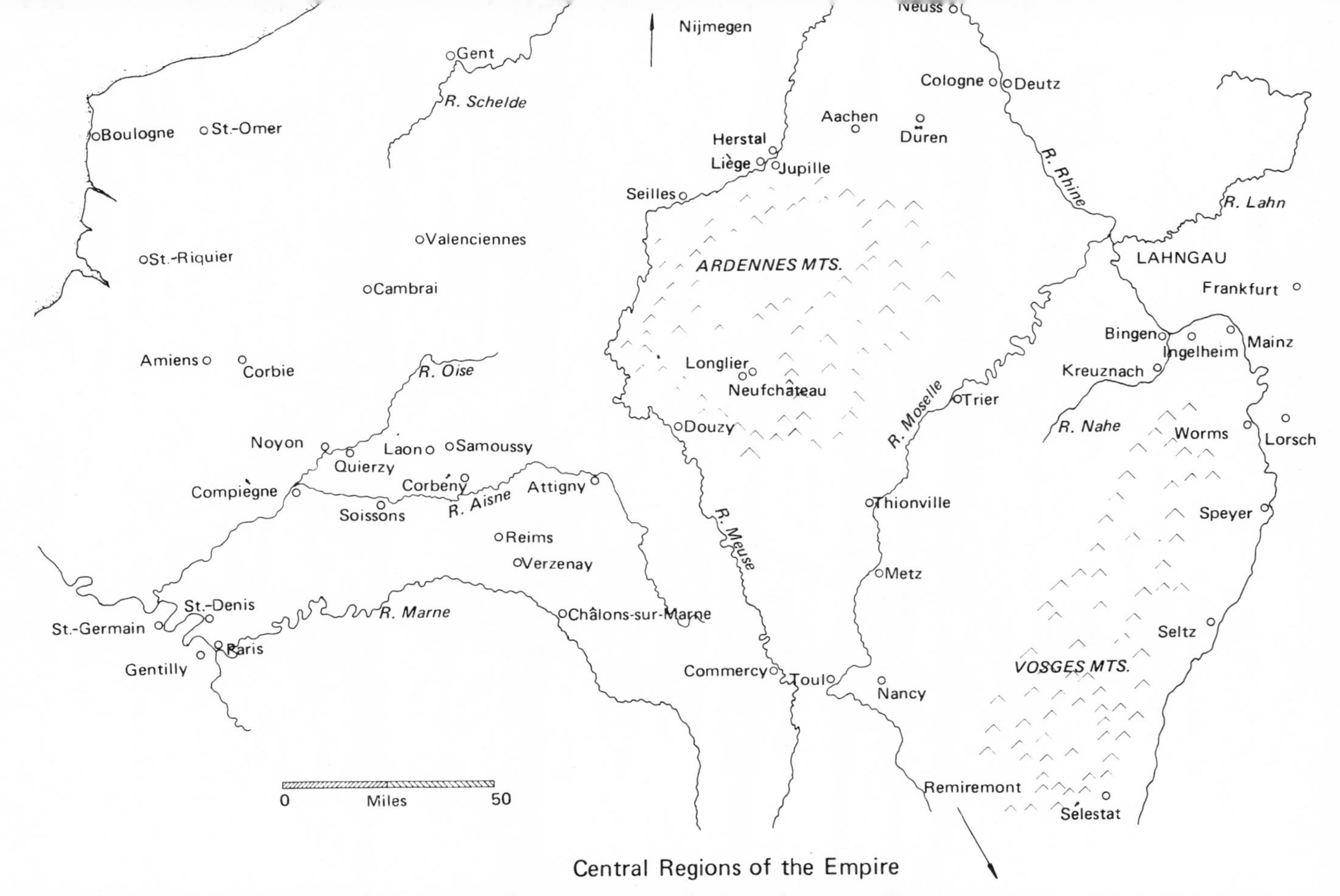

Central Regions of the Empire

Centulum he marched again along the shore of the ocean to Rouen, crossed the River Seine at this point, and arrived at Tours in order to pray at St. Martin's. There he stayed for a few days because of the bad health of his wife, the Lady Liutgarda; and there she died on June 4 and was buried.

From here he returned to Aachen by way of Paris and Orléans. On June 6 and likewise on June 9 there was a severe frost which did not, however, harm the harvest.

At the beginning of August he came to Mainz. Announcing an expedition into Italy, he left Mainz and went with his army to Ravenna. There he arranged a campaign against the Beneventans and after a delay of seven days headed for Rome and ordered the army under his son Pepin to go into the territory of the Beneventans and plunder it. When he approached Rome, Pope Leo came to meet him with the Romans at Mentana, twelve miles from the city, and welcomed him with the greatest humility and respect. After dining with the king in Mentana the pope immediately returned ahead of him to the city. On the next day he sent the banners of the city of Rome to meet him and ordered crowds of townspeople and pilgrims to line the streets and acclaim the king on his arrival. Standing with his clergy and bishops on the steps of the basilica of the blessed apostle Peter, he welcomed the king when he dismounted from his horse and ascended the stairs. A prayer was offered and while all were chanting the psalms the pope led the king into the basilica of the blessed apostle Peter. This took place on November 24.

Seven days later the king convoked an assembly, made known to everybody why he had come to Rome, and from that time on devoted himself daily to carrying out the tasks for which he had come. The most important and most difficult among these and the one he tackled first was the examination of the crimes with which the pope had been charged. Since nobody was willing to prove these charges, the pope mounted the pulpit of the basilica of the blessed apostle Peter, in the presence of the whole populace. With the Gospel in his hand, he invoked the name of the Holy Trinity and purged himself by oath from the charges.[1]

On the same day Zacharias returned from the East to Rome with two monks, one from Mount Olivet and the other from St. Saba's. These monks the patriarch of Jerusalem sent to the king with Zacharias. As a sign of his good will they brought along the keys of the Lord's Sepulcher and of Calvary, also the keys of the city and of Mount Zion along with a flag.[2] The king received them graciously, entertained them for a few days, and permitted them to return with rich rewards in the month of April. He celebrated Christmas at Rome. And the date changed to

801

On the most holy day of Christmas, when the king rose from prayer in front of the shrine of the blessed apostle Peter, to take part in the Mass, Pope Leo placed a crown on his head, and he was hailed by the whole Roman people: To the august Charles, crowned by God, the great and peaceful emperor of the Romans, life and victory! After the acclamations the pope addressed him in the manner of the old emperors. The name of Patricius was now abandoned and he was called Emperor and Augustus.[1]

A few days later he ordered those to be tried who had deposed the pope in the previous year. After the trial they were condemned to death according to the Roman law of lèse majesté.[2] But the pope, in Christian charity, pleaded for them with the emperor, who granted them life and freedom from mutilation, but because of the magnitude of their crime they were sent into exile. The leaders of this conspiracy were the nomenclator[3] Paschal, the treasurer Campulus, and many other high-ranking men of the city of Rome; they all received the same sentence at the same time. After settling public as well as ecclesiastic and private matters of the city of Rome, the pope, and all Italy (for the emperor did nothing but this all winter) he again sent an expedition under his son Pepin against the Beneventans. He left Rome after Easter, on April 25, and proceeded to Spoleto. While he was staying there, on April 30, in the second hour of the night, a tremendous earthquake occurred which severely shook the whole of Italy. Because of this tremor a large part of the roof of the basilica of the blessed apostle Paul with its wooden framework collapsed, and in some places mountains tumbled on top of cities. In the same year also some places along the Rhine, in Gaul, and in Germany were hit by earth tremors. Since the weather was mild a pestilence broke out.

From Spoleto the emperor came to Ravenna and after staying there for a few days continued to Pavia. There he received the news that envoys of Harun Emir al Mumenin, the king of the Persians, had arrived at the port of Pisa. He sent messengers to meet them and had them presented at court between Vercelli and Ivrea. One of them—for there were two—was a Persian from the East and the envoy of the Persian king, the other was a Saracen from Africa and the envoy of Emir Abraham, who ruled on the border of Africa in Fustât.[4] They reported that Isaac the Jew, whom the emperor four years earlier had dispatched with Lantfrid and Sigimund to the king of the Persians, was returning with large presents, but that Lantfrid and Sigimund had both died. Then the king sent Ercanbald, the notary, to Liguria to prepare a fleet on which the elephant and whatever else he brought along might be transported. After celebrating the feast of St. John the Baptist at Ivrea,[5] Charles crossed the Alps and returned to Gaul.

In the same summer the city of Barcelona in Spain was captured after a two-year siege. Its governor Zatun and many other Saracens were taken prisoner. In Italy the city of Chieti was also captured and burned, and its governor Roselmus taken prisoner; the castles belonging to this city surrendered. Zatun and Roselmus were brought before the emperor on the same day and condemned to exile.[6]

In the month of October of the same year Isaac the Jew returned from Africa with the elephant and arrived at Porto-Venere. Since he could not cross the Alps because of the snow, he spent the winter at Vercelli.

The emperor celebrated Christmas in his palace at Aachen. And the date changed to

802

Empress Irene sent the spatarius Leo as envoy from Constantinople to ratify a peace between Franks and Greeks.[1] When the envoy returned, the emperor on his part sent along to Constantinople Bishop Jesse of Amiens and Count Helmgaud to make peace with Irene.[2] Easter was celebrated in the palace of Aachen.[3]

On July 20 of this same year Isaac arrived with the elephant and the other presents sent by the Persian king, and he delivered them to the emperor at Aachen. The name of the elephant was Abul Abaz.

The city of Ortona in Italy surrendered.[4] Also Lucera, worn out by prolonged siege, was forced to surrender, and a garrison of our people was installed.[5]

The emperor was occupied with the chase in the Ardennes during the summer. He dispatched an army of Saxons to lay waste the lands of the Saxons on the far side of the Elbe.

Duke Grimoald of the Beneventans besieged Count Winigis of Spoleto in Lucera, where Winigis was in command. Worn out by ill-health Winigis was made to surrender, but was held in honorable captivity.[6]

The emperor celebrated Christmas at Aachen. And the date changed to

803

In this winter there was an earthquake around the palace and in neighboring areas and a large death toll was the result.

Winigis was released from captivity by Grimoald, and the emperor's emissaries returned from Constantinople. Along with them came envoys of Emperor Nicephorus, who ruled the commonwealth at that time, for they had deposed Irene after the arrival of the Frankish embassy. The names of the envoys were Bishop Michael, Abbot Peter, and the candidate Calistus. They met the emperor at Salz on the River Saale and received a written proposal for peace. They were dismissed with a letter from the emperor and returned by way of Rome to Constantinople.[1]

But the emperor marched into Bavaria and, after settling the affairs of Pannonia, returned to Aachen in the month of December and celebrated Christmas there. And the date changed to

804

The emperor spent the winter at Aachen. But in the summer he led an army into Saxony and deported all Saxons living beyond the Elbe and in Wihmuodi[1] with wives and children into Francia and gave the districts beyond the Elbe to the Obodrites.[2]

At the same time Godofrid, king of the Danes, came with his fleet and the entire cavalry of his kingdom to Schleswig on the border of his kingdom and Saxony. He promised to show up for a conference with the emperor, but was made wary by the counsel of his men and did not venture any closer. Instead, he communicated through envoys whatever he wanted to say. The emperor stayed at Hollenstedt on the River Elbe and sent an embassy to Godofrid to discuss the return of fugitives. About the middle of September he returned to Cologne. After dismissing the army he went first to Aachen and then into the Ardennes. He devoted himself to the chase and then returned to Aachen.

In the middle of November he was informed that Pope Leo wished to celebrate Christmas with him at whatever place that could be arranged. The king at once sent his son Charles to St.-Maurice and ordered him to receive the pope honorably. He himself came to meet him in the city of Reims. After welcoming him there he took the pope first to the villa of Quierzy, where he celebrated Christmas, and then to Aachen. Charles gave him many presents and since the pope wished to return by way of Bavaria had him escorted as far as Ravenna. The cause of his coming was this: in the past summer the emperor had been informed that in the city of Mantua the blood of Christ had been found. He sent to the pope and asked him to inquire into the truthfulness of this rumor. The pope made use of this opportunity to leave, traveled first to Lombardy to investigate the rumor, and after a rapid journey from there suddenly reached the emperor. He stayed with him for eight days and then, as was said, made his way back to Rome.[3] And the date changed to

805

Not long afterward the capcan, a prince of the Huns, approached the emperor because of the predicament of his people and asked him to give them a place to settle between Szombathely and Petronell. The Huns could not stay in their previous dwelling places on account of the attacks of the Slavs. The emperor received him graciously—for the capcan was a Christian by the name of Theodore—agreed to his request, and permitted him to return home with presents.

The capcan died a short while after returning to his people. And the khagan sent one of his magnates asking for the ancient dignity which the khagan used to have among the Huns. The emperor agreed to his request and ordered that the khagan, according to the ancient custom of the Huns, was to be lord over the whole kingdom.[1]

In the same year he sent the army under his son Charles into the country of the Slavs who are called Bohemians. Charles ravaged their native land from one end to the other and killed their chief

Lecho. Upon his return he went to see the emperor in the Vosges at Champ.[2] The emperor had left Aachen in July and headed by Thionville and Metz for the Vosges Mountains, where he went hunting. Once the army had returned, he moved on to the castle of Remiremont, where he remained for a while, and then he settled down for the winter in his palace of Thionville. Here his two sons Pepin and Louis came to him; here he celebrated Christmas. And the date changed to

806

Shortly after Christmas Willeri and Beatus, dukes of Venice, Paul, duke of Zara, and Donatus, bishop of the same city, came before the emperor with large gifts, as ambassadors of the Dalmatians. The emperor settled the affairs of the dukes and people of Venice as well as the affairs of Dalmatia.[1]

When they had been dismissed, the emperor held an assembly with the nobles and magnates of the Franks to confirm and preserve peace among his sons and to discuss the division of the empire into three parts, so that each son would know which part to protect and to rule if he should survive his father. A testament was drawn up ratifying this decision, and it was confirmed by the oaths of the Frankish magnates. Stipulations were laid down for the sake of preserving peace. All this was committed to writing and carried by Einhard to Pope Leo so that he would sign it.[2] After reading it the pontiff gave his consent and signed it with his own hand.

When he had dispatched both his sons, that is, Pepin and Louis, into their kingdoms, the emperor went by ship from the palace of Thionville down the Moselle and the Rhine to Nijmegen, where he celebrated the holy forty-days' fast and the most sacred feast of Easter.[3] After a few days he came from Nijmegen to Aachen and sent his son Charles with an army into the country of the Slavs who are called Sorbs and live on the River Elbe. On this campaign Miliduoch, duke of the Slavs, was killed. The army constructed two castles, one on the bank of the River Saale, the other one on the Elbe. When the Slavs had been pacified, Charles returned with the army and came to the emperor at Seilles on the Meuse.

A body of troops from Bavaria, Alamannia, and Burgundy was

also sent into the country of Bohemia, as in the previous year. After laying waste much of the land the army returned without serious losses.

In the same year a fleet was dispatched by Pepin from Italy to Corsica against the Moors who had pillaged the island. Without awaiting its arrival the Moors made away. But one of our men, Hadumar, count of the city of Genoa, was killed when he carelessly got into a fight with them. In Spain the people of Navarre and Pamplona, who had defected to the Saracens during the last years, were again placed under our authority.[4]

Emperor Nicephorus[5] dispatched a fleet under the command of the patrician Nicetas to reconquer Dalmatia. And the envoys, who about four years earlier had been sent to the king of the Persians, sailed through the very anchoring places of the Greek ships and returned to Treviso, into the shelter of the port, without being noticed by one of the enemies.

The emperor celebrated Christmas at Aachen. And the date changed to

807

During the previous year there was an eclipse of the moon on September 2. At that time the sun stood in the sixteenth degree of Virgo, and the moon in the sixteenth degree of Pisces. In this year, however, it was on January 31, on the seventeenth of the lunar month, when Jupiter was seen to pass through the moon. On February 11 at noon there was an eclipse of the sun, during which both stars stood in the twenty-fifth degree of Aquarius. There was again an eclipse of the moon on February 26 and in the same night enormous battle lines appeared in the sky. The sun stood in the eleventh degree of Pisces and the moon in the eleventh degree of Virgo. On March 17 the star Mercury was seen as a small dark spot a little above the center of the sun, and it was seen by us for eight days. When it first entered and left the sun, we could not observe it well because of clouds. Again on August 22 at the third hour of the night there was a lunar eclipse, while the sun stood in the fifth degree of Virgo and the moon in the fifth degree of Pisces. Thus, from September of last year to September of the present year the moon was eclipsed three times and the sun once.

Radbert, the emperor's emissary, died on his way back from the East. The envoy of the king of Persia by the name of Abdallah came to the emperor with monks from Jerusalem, who formed an embassy from the patriarch Thomas. Their names were George and Felix. This George is abbot of Mount Olivet, a native German and called, by his real name, Egilbald. They came to the emperor and delivered presents which the king of Persia sent to him, that is, a tent and curtains for the canopy of different colors and of unbelievable size and beauty. They were all made of the best linen, the curtains as well as the strings, and dyed in different colors. The presents of the Persian king consisted besides of many precious silken robes, of perfumes, ointments, and balsam; also of a brass clock, a marvelous mechanical contraption, in which the course of the twelve hours moved according to a water clock, with as many brazen little balls, which fall down on the hour and through their fall made a cymbal ring underneath. On this clock there were also twelve horsemen who at the end of each hour stepped out of twelve windows, closing the previously open windows by their movements. There were many other things on this clock which are too numerous to describe now.[1] Besides these presents there were two brass candlesticks of amazing size and height. All this was taken to the emperor in the palace at Aachen. The emperor kept the ambassador and the monks with him for a while and then sent them to Italy and told them to wait there till it was time to set sail.

In the same year he sent his marshal Burchard with a fleet to Corsica to defend the island against the Moors, who in past years used to come there and pillage. The Moors embarked, as usual, from Spain and went ashore first in Sardinia, where they waged a battle with the Sardinians and lost many men—three thousand are said to have died there. Then they came by a direct route to Corsica. Here they again engaged in battle with the fleet under Burchard's command, in a harbor of this island. They were defeated and put to flight with thirteen ships lost and most of their men killed. The Moors in this year were plagued by so much misfortune everywhere that they themselves admitted that this had happened because the year before they had unjustly carried away sixty monks from Pantelleria and sold them in Spain.[2] But some of these monks returned home again through the largesse of the emperor.

The patrician Nicetas who was staying in Venice with the fleet of Constantinople made peace with King Pepin. After concluding an armistice until the month of August, he weighed anchor and returned to Constantinople.[3]

In this year the emperor celebrated Easter and also Christmas at Aachen. And the date changed to

808

The winter was extremely mild and unhealthy at that time. When spring came, the emperor went to Nijmegen. After spending Lent and celebrating Holy Easter there, he returned again to Aachen.

Since he was informed that Godofrid, the king of the Danes, with his army had crossed over into the land of the Obodrites, he sent his son Charles with a strong host of Franks and Saxons to the Elbe, with orders to resist the mad king if he should attempt to attack the borders of Saxony.[1] Godofrid set up quarters on the shore for some days[2] and attacked and took a number of Slavic castles in hand-to-hand combat. Then he withdrew, suffering severe casualties. He expelled Thrasco, duke of the Obodrites, who did not trust the loyalty of his countrymen,[3] hanged on the gallows Godelaib, another duke, whom he had caught by treachery, and made two-thirds of the Obodrites tributary. But he lost the best and most battle-tested of his soldiers. With them he lost Reginold, his brother's son, who was killed at the siege of a town along with a great number of Danish nobles. But Charles, the son of the emperor, built a bridge across the Elbe,[4] and moved the army under his command as fast as he could across the river against the Linones and Smeldingi. These tribes had also defected to Godofrid. Charles laid waste their fields far and wide and after crossing the river again returned to Saxony with his army unimpaired.

On this expedition Godofrid had as his allies the Slavs called Wilzi,[5] who joined his forces voluntarily because of their ancient conflicts with the Obodrites. When Godofrid returned home, they also went home with the booty which they had been able to capture from the Obodrites. But Godofrid before his return destroyed a trading place on the seashore, in Danish called Reric, which, because of the taxes it paid, was of great advantage to his kingdom.[6] Transferring the merchants from Reric he weighed anchor and came with his whole army to the harbor of Schleswig. There he remained for a few days and decided to fortify the border of his kingdom against Saxony with a rampart, so that a protective bulwark would stretch from the eastern bay, called Ostarsalt, as far as the western sea, along the entire north bank of the River Eider and broken by a single gate through which wagons and horsemen would be able to leave and enter. After dividing the work among the leaders of his troops he returned home.

In the meantime Eardwulf, the king of the Northumbrians from the island of Britain, had been driven from his throne and country. He came to the emperor while the latter was still at Nijmegen and, after saying why he had come, continued to Rome. On his return from Rome he was taken back to his kingdom by the envoys of the Roman pontiff and the Lord Emperor. At that time Leo III ruled the Roman Church. As his envoy the deacon Aldulf, a Saxon from Britain, was sent to Britain. Two abbots were dispatched with him by the emperor, the notary Hruotfrid and Nanthar of St.-Omer.[7]

After having two castles built on the River Elbe by his envoys and placing troops in them for the defense against the attacks of the Slavs, the emperor spent the winter at Aachen and celebrated Christmas and Holy Easter in the same place.[8] And the date changed to

809

A fleet dispatched from Constantinople put ashore first in Dalmatia and then in Venice. While staying there for the winter, part of it anchored off the island of Comacchio and skirmished with the garrison stationed there. The fleet was defeated, put to flight, and returned to Venice. Paul, commander of the fleet, was apparently under orders in his desire to negotiate with the Lord Pepin, king of Italy, about the terms of a peace between Franks and Greeks. But he was prevented in all his attempts by Willeri and Beatus, dukes of Venice, who even prepared an ambush against him, and departed when he recognized their treachery.[1]

In the west the Lord King Louis entered Spain with his army and besieged the city of Tortosa on the River Ebro. When he had devoted some time to the siege and had seen that he could not take the city quickly, he gave up and returned to Aquitaine with his army unimpaired.

When Eardwulf, king of the Northumbrians, had been taken back to his kingdom and the envoys of emperor and pontiff were returning, all crossed without mishap except one of them, the deacon Aldulf, who was captured by pirates and taken to Britain. But he was ransomed by one of King Cenwulf's men and returned to Rome.[2]

In Tuscany the Greeks named Orobiotae[3] ravaged the port city of Piombino. Also the Moors came to Corsica from Spain and plundered a city on the very Sunday of Holy Easter, leaving behind nothing but the bishop and a few of the old and infirm.

In the meantime Godofrid, king of the Danes, sent word by some merchants that he had heard of the emperor's wrath against him because he had led an army against the Obodrites the year before and revenged himself for injuries done to him. Godofrid added that he would like to purge himself of the charges made against him and that the Obodrites had broken the peace first. He also requested that a meeting between his counts and the emperor's should take place beyond the Elbe near the borders of his kingdom. There they could establish what both parties had done and determine what redresses were to be made. This the emperor did not refuse. A conference was held with Danish nobles beyond the Elbe at Badenfliot.[4] Both sides brought up and elaborated on a number of matters and then departed, leaving the entire question unsettled. But Thrasco, duke of the Obodrites, first surrendered his son as a hostage to Godofrid as Godofrid demanded, and then gathered an army of his people. Supported by the Saxons, he attacked the neighboring Wilzi and laid waste their fields with fire and sword. Returning home with immense booty and with even more help from the Saxons, he conquered the largest city of the Smeldingi.[5] By these successes he forced all who had defected from him to join him again.

When these things had come to pass, the emperor returned from the Ardennes to Aachen and in November held a council about the procession of the Holy Spirit, a question which John, a monk of Jerusalem, had first raised.[6] To reach a decision on this matter Bernhar, bishop of Worms, and Adalhard, abbot of the monastery of Corbie, were sent to Rome to Pope Leo.[7] At this same council they also examined the condition of the churches and the lives of those who were to serve God in them. But they decided nothing, apparently because of the magnitude of the problems.

Since he had heard much about the arrogance and pride of the Danish king, the emperor decided to build a castle on the other side of the Elbe and to garrison it with a Frankish force. For this purpose he gathered men in Gaul and Germany equipped with arms and all other necessities, and ordered them to be taken by way of Frisia to their destination. In the meantime Thrasco, duke of the Obodrites, was treacherously killed by Godofrid's men at the trading place of Reric. When the location for the founding of a castle had been explored, the emperor appointed Count Egbert to be responsible for this matter, ordering him to cross the Elbe and to occupy the site. This place is located on the River Stör and is called Esesfelth. Egbert and the Saxon counts occupied it and began to fortify it about March 15.[8]

Count Aureolus died. He had been stationed on the border of Spain and Gaul, on the other side of the Pyrenees over against Huesca and Saragossa. Amorez, the governor of Saragossa and Huesca, assumed the count's position, placed garrisons in his castles, and sent an embassy to the emperor, promising that he was willing to submit to him with everything he had.[9]

An eclipse of the moon occurred on December 26.

810

When the imperial envoys came to Amorez, governor of Saragossa, he requested a conference with the guards of the Spanish border, promising that at this conference he would submit with all his people to the emperor. Although the emperor gave his consent, complications arose which prevented this formal submission from taking place.[1] The Moors with a fleet of immense size, which had been gathered by the whole of Spain, landed first in Sardinia, then in Corsica. Since they found no garrison there, they conquered almost the entire island.

In the meantime King Pepin, aroused by the treachery of the Venetian dukes, ordered Venice to be attacked by land and by sea. After the capture of Venice and the submission of the dukes he sent the same fleet to ravage the shores of Dalmatia. But when Paul, governor of Cephalonia, came to the aid of the Dalmatians with the eastern fleet, the royal fleet returned home.[2]

Hruodtrude, the emperor's eldest daughter, died on June 6.[3]

While the emperor was still at Aachen, considering an expedition against King Godofrid, he received the news that a fleet of two hundred ships from Denmark had landed in Frisia, that all the islands off the coast of Frisia had been ravaged, that the army had already landed and fought three battles against the Frisians, that the victorious Danes had imposed a tribute on the vanquished, that already one hundred pounds of silver had been paid as tribute by the Frisians, and that King Godofrid was at home. That, in fact, is how things stood. This information aroused the emperor so much that he sent out messengers everywhere to gather an army. Leaving the palace without delay, he decided first to go and meet the fleet, then to cross the Rhine at Lippeham and wait for the troops which had not yet arrived. While he stayed there for a few days, the elephant which Harun, the king of the Saracens, had sent him, suddenly died. When the troops had finally assembled, the emperor hastened to the Aller at the greatest possible speed, set up camp where it flows into the Weser, and then waited for what would come of King Godofrid's threats. Inflated by the vain hope of victory, this king boasted that he wished to fight the emperor in open battle.[4]

But while the emperor had his quarters in the place mentioned, news of various matters was brought to him. It was reported that the fleet which ravaged Frisia had returned home and King Godofrid had been murdered by one of his retainers; that the castle of Hohbuoki on the Elbe,[5] with Odo, the emperor's envoy, and a garrison of East Saxons, had been captured by the Wilzi; that his son Pepin, the king of Italy, had died on July 8; and that two embassies to make peace had arrived from different countries, one from Constantinople, the other from Cordova. When the emperor had received all these reports, he settled the affairs of Saxony as far as circumstances at that time permitted and returned home. On this campaign an epidemic broke out among the cattle which was so severe that almost no animals remained to feed such a large army. All perished to the last head. Not only there but in all provinces subject to the emperor the mortality of this kind of animal ran very high.[6]

Arriving at Aachen in the month of October, the emperor received the embassies mentioned and made peace with Emperor Nicephorus and with Abul Aas, king of Spain. He gave back Venice to Nicephorus and received Count Haimric, who at one time had been taken prisoner by the Saracens and whom Abul Aas now sent back.[7]

In this year both sun and moon were eclipsed twice; the sun on June 7 and November 30, the moon on June 21 and December 15. The island of Corsica was again ravaged by the Moors.

Amorez was expelled from Saragossa by Abd ar-Rahman, the son of Abul Aas, and forced to enter Huesca.

After the death of Godofrid, king of the Danes, Hemming, the son of his brother, succeeded to his throne and made peace with the emperor.[8]

811

The emperor settled with the spatarius Arsafius, who was envoy of Emperor Nicephorus, dismissed him, and to ratify this peace[1] sent his own envoys, Bishop Haido of Basle,[2] Count Hugo of Tours, and the Lombard Aio of Friuli, to Constantinople. With them were the spatarius Leo, a Sicilian by birth, and Willeri, duke of Venice. The former of these two had fled ten years earlier from Sicily to the emperor in Rome and now was sent back, since he wanted to return to his homeland; Willeri had been deprived of his office because of treachery and was ordered to be returned to his lord in Constantinople.

The peace announced between the emperor and Hemming, the king of the Danes, was only sworn on arms because of the severity of the winter, which closed the road for traveling between the parties. Only with the return of spring and the opening of the roads, which had been closed because of harsh frost, did twelve magnates of each party and people, that is, of Franks and Danes, meet on the River Eider at Heiligen and confirm the peace by an exchange of oaths according to their customs. The nobles on the Frankish side were Count Walach, son of Bernard, Count Burchard, Count Unroch,[3] Count Odo, Count Meginhard, Count Bernard, Count Egbert, Count Theothari, Count Abo, Count Osdag, and Count Wigman. On the Danish side there were Hankwin and Angandeo, Hemming's brothers, and, in addition, other men distinguished among this people: Osfrid nicknamed Turdimulo, Warstein, Suomi, Urm, another Osfrid, son of Heiligen, and Osfrid of Schonen, and Hebbi and Aowin.

After peace had been made with Hemming and the general assembly held at Aachen according to custom, the emperor sent into three parts of his kingdom an equal number of armies. One went beyond the Elbe against the Linones, which ravaged their territory and restored the castle of Hohbuoki on the Elbe destroyed by the Wilzi in the preceding year. The second went into Pannonia to end the disputes among Huns and Slavs. The third was dispatched against the Bretons to punish their treachery. They all returned home unharmed after carrying out their orders successfully.

In the meantime, the emperor himself went to the port city of Boulogne in order to inspect the fleet whose construction he had ordered the year before. There the ships in question had assembled. At Boulogne he restored the lighthouse constructed a long time ago to guide the course of sailors and had a fire lit on its top at night. From Boulogne he came to the River Scheldt at Ghent and inspected the ships built for the same fleet. About the middle of November he came to Aachen. The envoys of King Hemming, Aowin and Hebbi, came to meet him and brought presents and assurances of peace. Envoys had also arrived at Aachen from Pannonia and waited for him, namely the canizauci,[4] prince of the Avars, and the tudun and other nobles and leaders of the Slavs who live along the Danube. They had been ordered to come before the prince by the commanders of the troops dispatched into Pannonia.

Meanwhile, Charles, the eldest son of the Lord Emperor, died on December 4.[5] The emperor spent the winter at Aachen.

812

Not much later the news arrived that Hemming, king of the Danes, had died. Sigifrid, the nephew of King Godofrid, and Anulo, the nephew of Heriold and of the former king, both wished to succeed him. Being unable to agree on who should be king, they raised troops, fought a battle, and were both killed. The party of Anulo won, however, and made his brothers Heriold and Reginfrid their kings. The defeated party out of necessity had to go along with Anulo's party and did not reject the brothers as their kings. They say that ten thousand nine hundred and forty men died in that battle.

Emperor Nicephorus after many remarkable victories died in the province of Moesia in a battle against the Bulgars.[1] His son-in-law Michael became emperor and received and dismissed in Constantinople the envoys of the Lord Emperor Charles, who had been sent to Nicephorus. With these men he sent his own envoys, Bishop Michael and the protospatarii Arsafius and Theognostus, through whom he ratified the peace proposed by Nicephorus. At Aachen, where they came before the emperor, they received from him in church the document of the treaty, acclaimed him according to their custom, that is, in Greek, and called him "Emperor" and "Basileus." When they came to Rome on their journey home, they received the same charter of an agreement or an alliance a second time from Pope Leo in the basilica of the holy apostle Peter.[2]

When the envoys had been dismissed and the general assembly held in the usual manner at Aachen, the emperor sent his grandson Bernard, son of Pepin, to Italy.[3] A fleet was said to be coming from Africa as well as Spain to lay waste Italy. Because of this rumor the emperor ordered Wala, son of his father's brother Bernard, to stay with him until the outcome of the matter would assure the safety of our people.[4] Part of this fleet went to Corsica and part to Sardinia. The part which came to Sardinia was almost totally destroyed.

Also a fleet of the Norsemen landed in Ireland, the island of the Scots, and in a battle with the Scots many of the Norsemen were killed, and the fleet returned home after shameful flight.

Peace was made with Abul Aas, king of the Saracens;[5] also with Grimoald, duke of the Beneventans, and twenty-five thousand gold solidi were paid as tribute by the Beneventans.[6]

A campaign was carried out against the Wilzi, and hostages were received from them.

Heriold and Reginfrid, kings of the Danes, sent an embassy to the emperor, asking for peace and requesting that their brother Hemming be released.

In this year there was an eclipse of the sun on May 15 after midday.[7]

813

The emperor spent the winter at Aachen, and when the mild season of spring set in, he sent Bishop Amalhar of Trier and Abbot Peter of the monastery of Nonantola to Constantinople in order to ratify the peace with Emperor Michael.[1]

He invited his son Louis, king of Aquitaine, to a general assembly at Aachen, placed the crown on his head, and shared the title of emperor with him. His grandson Bernard, son of his son Pepin, he placed in charge of Italy and ordered to be called king.[2] Also on his order councils were held by the bishops in all of Gaul to improve the condition of the churches, one at Mainz, another at Reims, a third at Tours, a fourth at Chalon, a fifth at Arles. Of the canons issued in the individual councils a collection was made before the emperor at that assembly. Anyone who wants to know them can find them in the above-named five cities, although copies are also available in the archives of the palace.[3]

From this assembly several Frankish and Saxon nobles were sent beyond the Elbe to the borders of the Norsemen. They came to make peace, at the request of the Danish kings, whose brother they intended to return. When an equal number—they were sixteen—of Danish magnates met them at the stipulated place, peace was sworn by mutual oaths and the brother of the kings was returned. The kings themselves at this time were not at home but had marched with an army toward Westarfolda,[4] an area in the extreme northwest of their kingdom across the northern tip of Britain, whose princes and people refused to submit to them. When they returned after conquering the Britons and received their brother, who had been sent from the emperor, the sons of King Godofrid gathered troops from everywhere and made war upon the kings. The sons of King Godofrid were assisted by not a few of the Danish nobles who for some time after leaving their homeland had been in exile with the Swedes. Since hosts of their countrymen joined the sons of Godofrid from all over the land of the Danes, they easily drove the kings from the kingdom after a battle.

Count Irmingar of Ampurias prepared an ambush near Majorca against the Moors who were returning with much booty from Corsica to Spain. Irmingar captured eight Moorish ships, on which he found more than five hundred Corsican prisoners. The Moors wanted revenge and ravaged Civitavecchia in Tuscany and Nice in the province of Narbonne. They also attacked Sardinia, but were repelled and defeated in battle by the Sardinians and turned back after losing many of their men.

Emperor Michael achieved little success when he made war on the Bulgars. On his return home he laid down the imperial headband and became a monk. In his place Leo, son of the patrician Bardas, was made emperor.[5] Krum, king of the Bulgars, who two years before had killed Emperor Nicephorus and driven Michael out of Moesia, was elated by his luck and advanced with his army to the very confines of Constantinople, pitching his camp before the gate of the city. But as he rode his horse around the walls Emperor Leo ordered a sally and intercepted the reckless king. Krum was gravely wounded and forced to save himself by flight and to return to his homeland in disgrace.

814

While spending the winter at Aachen, the Lord Emperor Charles departed this life on January 28, in about his seventy-first year, in the forty-seventh year of his reign, in the forty-third since the conquest of Italy, and in the fourteenth since he had been named Emperor and Augustus.[1]

A large number of messengers informed Louis of this event at the royal villa of Doué[2] in Aquitaine, where he was then spending the winter. Thirty days later he arrived at Aachen and succeeded his father with the full consent and support of all Franks. Turning his mind to the administration of the kingdom which he had assumed, he first heard and dismissed the foreign envoys who had come to his father. He then received the other envoys who had been sent to his father but had come to him instead.

The most important among the latter was the mission sent from Constantinople. When Emperor Leo, Michael's successor, dismissed Bishop Amalhar and Abbot Peter, who had been sent to Michael but had come to him, he dispatched his own envoys along with them to the Lord Charles. These were the spatarius Christopher and the deacon Gregory. Through them Emperor Leo delivered the ratified text of a treaty of alliance. When they had been received and dismissed, the Lord Louis directed his envoys, Bishop Nordbert of Reggio and Count Richoin of Padua, to Emperor Leo to renew friendship with him and to ratify the aforementioned pact.[3]

After holding a general assembly of his people at Aachen he sent envoys into all parts of his kingdom to render justice and relieve the oppression of the people. He sent for Bernard, king of Italy, his nephew, presented him with gifts, and dismissed him again. With Duke Grimoald of the Beneventans he made a solemn treaty similar to that of his father, namely that the Beneventans should pay an annual tribute of seven thousand solidi. Then he sent Lothair, one of his two sons, to Bavaria and the other son, Pepin, to Aquitaine.

Heriold and Reginfrid, kings of the Danes, had been defeated and expelled from their kingdom the year before by the sons of

The Carolingian Empire at the Death of Charlemagne in 814
DENMARK
OBODRITES
FRISIA
SAXONY
WILZI
MERCIA
WESSEX
THURINGIA
HESSE
SORBS
R. Elbe
FLANDERS
R. Rhine
BOHEMIANS
FRANCIA
R. Meuse
R. Seine
MORAVIANS
BRITTANY
Corseult
Rennes
BRETON MARCH
Vannes
ALAMANNIA
BAVARIA
R. Danube
AVARS
R. Loire
CARINTHIA
PANNONIA
BURGUNDY
FRIULI
AQUITAINE
Lyons
KINGDOM OF ITALY
LIBURNIA
R. Rhone
DALMATIA
PATRIMONY OF ST. PETER
PROVENCE
Nice
ASTURIAS
GASCONY
SERBS
SEPTIMANIA
Marseille
DUCHY OF SPOLETO
SPANISH MARCH
Added in 812
EMIRATE OF THE UMAYYADS
CORSICA
Rome
DUCHY OF BENEVENTO

Godofrid, against whom they regrouped their forces and again made war. In this conflict Reginfrid and the oldest son of Godofrid were killed. When this had come to pass, Heriold despaired of his cause,[4] came to the emperor, and put himself under his protection. The emperor received him and told him to go to Saxony and to wait for the proper time when he would be able to give him the help which Heriold had requested.

815

The emperor commanded that Saxons and Obodrites should prepare for this campaign, and twice in that winter the attempt was made to cross the Elbe. But since the weather suddenly turned warm and made the ice on the river melt, the campaign was held up. Finally, when the winter was over, about the middle of May, the proper time to begin the march arrived. Then all Saxon counts and all troops of the Obodrites, under orders to bring help to Heriold, marched with the imperial emissary Baldrich across the River Eider into the land of the Norsemen called Silendi.[1] From Silendi they went on and, finally, on the seventh day, pitched camp on the coast at . . . . There they halted for three days. But the sons of Godofrid, who had raised against them a large army and a fleet of two hundred ships, remained on an island[2] three miles off the shore and did not dare engage them.[3] Therefore, after everywhere laying waste the neighboring districts and receiving hostages from the people, they returned to the emperor in Saxony, who at that time was holding the general assembly of his people at Paderborn.[4] There all nobles and envoys of the East Slavs came to him.

But before he arrived, while he was still at home, the emperor was informed that some Roman nobles had conspired to murder Pope Leo in the very city of Rome. Since the pontiff had been informed in advance, all the ringleaders were butchered on his order. The emperor was annoyed with these events. He settled the affairs of the Slavs and of Heriold, and, leaving Heriold behind in Saxony, returned to his palace in Frankfurt. Then he dispatched his nephew Bernard, king of Italy, who had been with him in Saxony, to Rome in order to get to the bottom of the report he had heard. When Bernard came to Rome, he fell ill, but whatever he could find out he passed on to the emperor[5] through Count Gerold,[6] who had been assigned to him as an envoy for this purpose. The pope's envoys, Bishop John of Silvacandida, the nomenclator Theodore, and Duke Sergius, followed Gerold and satisfied the emperor with regard to all charges leveled against their lord.

Envoys of the Sardinians from the city of Cagliari arrived with presents.

The peace made with Abul Aas, king of the Saracens, and kept for three years, was broken because it gained no advantage for the Franks, and war was resumed against him.

Bishop Nordbert and Count Richoin returned from Constantinople bringing back the charter of the treaty which Emperor Leo had given them.[7] They reported among other things that an extremely severe earthquake had occurred there for five continuous days in the month of August. Owing to this earthquake, they declared, many buildings of this city collapsed, and in other cities people were buried in ruins.[8] In Gaul, too, the city of Saintes in Aquitaine reportedly suffered an earthquake in September. The Rhine, swollen by rain[9] in the Alps, caused an unusual flood.

When the Romans saw that Pope Leo was lying on his sickbed, they raised a body of troops and first plundered the manors which the pope had lately built on the land of each city, and then set them on fire. Subsequently, they decided to go to Rome and to carry away by force what, as they complained, had been stolen from them. When King Bernard heard of this, he dispatched a body of troops under Duke Winigis of Spoleto, put down the revolt, and made these people stop what they had started. He informed the emperor through his envoys of what had happened.

816

When the winter was over Saxons and East Franks were ordered to campaign against the Slavonic Sorbs who refused obedience. They carried out their orders energetically and without much effort suppressed the insolence of the rebels. As soon as a city had been captured, rebellious elements of the population promised submission and calmed down.

The Basques, who live beyond the Garonne and in the Pyrenees, moved by their usual recklessness, conspired and started a general revolt. This was set off by the emperor's removal of Sigiwin their duke, because of his boundless arrogance and wicked ways. But in two campaigns they were beaten so thoroughly that surrender and petition for peace could not be carried out fast enough for them.

In the meantime Pope Leo died on May 25 in the twenty-first year of his pontificate, and in his place the deacon Stephen was elected and took office. Not two months had passed since his consecration when he set out in great haste to see the emperor, sending ahead two envoys to report his consecration to the emperor. When the emperor heard of this, he decided to meet the pope at Reims. He sent emissaries ahead to guide him there, but was first to arrive and received the pope with great honors. The pope at once let the emperor know the purpose of his coming and after the customary solemn Masses had been celebrated, he crowned the emperor by placing a diadem on his head. They then exchanged many gifts, celebrated splendid banquets, and established a firm friendship between them. After making other arrangements advantageous to the Holy Church of God, as much as time permitted, the pontiff set out for Rome, the emperor for his palace at Compiègne.[1]

While staying there he received the envoys of the Obodrites and the envoys from Spain of Abd ar-Rahman, son of King Abul Aas, who had been sent to him. After remaining at Compiègne for more than twenty days he proceeded to Aachen to spend the winter there.

817

Envoys of Abd ar-Rahman, son of Abul Aas, king of the Saracens, were dispatched from Saragossa and came to ask for peace. They were received by the emperor at Compiègne and then told to travel ahead of him to Aachen. When the emperor arrived in Aachen, he received an envoy of Emperor Leo by the name of Nicephorus who had been sent from Constantinople because of the Dalmatian question. Since Cadolah, who was in charge of that frontier, was not present but was believed to be arriving shortly, Nicephorus was ordered to wait for him. After Cadolah's arrival, negotiations took place between him and the emperor's envoy about the complaints which Nicephorus submitted. Since this matter concerned a great number of Romans as well as Slavs and apparently could not be settled if all parties were not present, a decision was postponed until then. For this purpose Albgar, nephew of Unroch, was sent to Dalmatia with Cadolah and the imperial envoy. The envoys of Abd ar-Rahman were also sent back. They had been kept waiting for three months and were beginning to think they would never get home.[1]

Because of Heriold's persistent aggression,[2] the sons of Godofrid, king of the Danes, also sent an embassy to the emperor, asked for peace, and promised to preserve it. This sounded more like hypocrisy than truth, so it was dismissed as empty talk and aid was given to Heriold against them.

On February 5 in the second hour of the night there was an eclipse of the moon and a comet appeared in the constellation Sagittarius.

Meanwhile, Pope Stephen died on January 25, not three months after his return to Rome.[3] Paschal was elected as his successor. As soon as he had been solemnly consecrated, he sent gifts and an apologetic letter to the emperor. In the letter he claimed that the papal dignity had been forced on him not only against his will but even against his most violent resistance. But he sent another embassy, asking that the covenant made with his predecessors should also be solemnly concluded with him. The nomenclator Theodore brought this message and was granted his request.[4]

When the emperor left church on Maundy Thursday after the holy office was over, the wooden arcade through which he was walking collapsed on top of him and knocked him to the ground, with more than twenty of his companions. This happened because the arcade was made of shoddy material. The worn-out and rotten crossbeams could no longer hold up the weight of the framework and wainscoting above them. While this accident gravely injured most of those who fell down with him, the emperor's injuries were minor: the handle of the sword he was wearing bruised the lower part of his chest on the left side, the back of his right ear was injured, and his right thigh near the groin was hit by a heavy piece of wood. Through the diligence of the physicians who took care of him he evidently made a rapid recovery, since twenty days after it happened he went hunting at Nijmegen.

On his return from Nijmegen he held the general assembly of the people as usual at Aachen. On this occasion he crowned his first-born son Lothair and shared with him the name of emperor. His other sons he appointed kings, placing one over Aquitaine and one over

Bavaria.[5] When the assembly was over and he was heading for the Vosges to go hunting, he was met by the envoys of Emperor Leo. He received them in the palace of Ingelheim near the city of Mainz. Finding that their message was no different from the one which Nicephorus, envoy of the same emperor, had recently brought, he speedily dismissed them and continued toward his destination.

When the news of the revolt of the Obodrites and of Sclaomir arrived, he ordered through his envoy that counts be stationed for the defense on the River Elbe to protect the borders assigned to them. The cause of the revolt was that Sclaomir was to share with Ceadrag, son of Thrasco, the royal power over the Obodrites which Sclaomir had held alone after the death of Thrasco. This matter exasperated Sclaomir so much that he solemnly declared he would never again cross the Elbe and come to the palace. He at once sent an embassy across the sea, made friends[6] with the sons of Godofrid, and coaxed them to send an army into Saxony beyond the Elbe. Their fleet came up the Elbe as far as the castle of Esesfeld and ravaged the entire bank of the River Stör. Gluomi, commander of the Norse border, led his foot soldiers overland with the Obodrites to the same castle. But since our people offered them violent resistance, they gave up the siege of the castle and departed.

In the meantime, the emperor returned to Aachen from his hunting trip in the Vosges. He was informed that his nephew Bernard, king of Italy, on the counsel of some depraved men, was planning to set up an unlawful regime and that he had already occupied all entrances to Italy, that is the Cluses, and received homage from all the cities of Italy.[7] This report was partly true and partly false. The emperor hastily prepared to enter Italy with a host gathered from all over Gaul and Germany in order to nip these movements in the bud. At hearing this, Bernard despaired of his cause, mainly because every day he saw that he was being deserted by his people. He laid down his arms and surrendered to the emperor at Chalon.[8] The others followed suit. They not only laid down their arms and surrendered but voluntarily, the minute they were asked, revealed everything as it had happened.[9] The leaders of this conspiracy were Eggideo, the first among the king's friends, his chamberlain Reginhard, and Reginhar, son of Count Meginhar, whose maternal grandfather Hardrad once conspired in Germany with many noblemen of the province against

Emperor Charles.[10] Apart from these men many other distinguished nobles were caught at the same crime, among them also some bishops: Anshelm of Milan, Wolfold of Cremona, and Theodulf of Orléans.[11]

818

After the treachery had come to light, the conspiracy had been uncovered,[1] and all conspirators were at his mercy, the emperor returned to Aachen. When the forty-day fast was over, a few days after Holy Easter, the ringleaders of the plot who have been named above, and the king with them, were condemned to death by the sentence of the Franks. But the emperor ordered them only to be blinded and the bishops to be deposed by the decree of a council and to be put into monasteries. The rest, according to the degree of their guilt or innocence, were to be exiled or tonsured and to live in monasteries.[2]

When the conspiracy had been settled in this manner, the emperor went with an immense army to Brittany and held a general assembly at Vannes. From Vannes he marched into the province mentioned, captured the rebels' fortifications, and without much effort, quickly brought the whole province into line. Morman, who had usurped royal authority in this province against the established custom of the Bretons, was killed by the emperor's army, and after that no Breton was found to offer resistance or dare refuse either obedience or the hostages demanded by the emperor.

After the completion of this campaign and the dismissal of the army the emperor returned to Angers. Queen Irmengardis, his wife, whom he had left behind sick, died of her ailments two days after his return on October 3.

On July 8 there was an eclipse of the sun.[3]

The emperor returned to Aachen by way of Rouen, Amiens, and Cambrai to spend the winter there. When he came to Herstal, he met envoys of Duke Sigo of the Beneventans, who brought gifts and justified the duke with regard to the murder of Duke Grimoald, his predecessor. The envoys of other peoples were also there, that is, of the Obodrites, of Borna, duke of the Guduscani,[4] and of the Timociani,[5] who had recently revolted against the Bulgars and come over to our side; also of Ljudovit, duke of Lower Pannonia, a schemer and agitator, who tried to accuse Count Cadolah, commander of the March of Friuli, of brutality and arrogance.[6] When these had been heard and dismissed, the emperor went to Aachen to spend the winter there.

819

Sclaomir, king of the Obodrites, was taken to Aachen by the commanders of the Saxon border and the emperor's envoys in command of the army of Saxons and East Franks. This army had been sent beyond the Elbe in the same year to take revenge for Sclaomir's treachery. The nobles of his people, who had been told to appear at the same time, charged him with many crimes. When Sclaomir was unable to refute the charges by a reasonable defense, he was condemned to exile and his kingdom given to Ceadrag, son of Thrasco. Similarly also, Lupus Centulli the Basque was sent into exile for life.[1] He had clashed in battle that year with Counts Berengar of Toulouse and Warin of Auvergne. In this battle he lost his brother Garsand, a man of exceptional folly, and came close to being killed himself, but saved his life by flight. He came before the emperor and was unable to purge himself of the treachery of which the two counts vehemently accused him.

An assembly was held at Aachen after Christmas at which many matters regarding the condition of the churches and monasteries were brought up and settled. Some greatly needed chapters, as yet still lacking, were drawn up and added to the laws. When this was done, the emperor married Judith, daughter of Count Welf, after looking over many daughters of the nobility.[2]

Another assembly was held at the palace of Ingelheim in July, and because of Ljudovit's revolt, an army was sent from Italy into Pannonia. This army got nowhere and returned with nothing to show for its efforts. Carried away by his own insolence, Ljudovit sent envoys to the emperor, acting as if he wanted peace. He proposed several conditions to be met before he would do as he was told. When the emperor did not accept these conditions and proposed others through his envoys, Ljudovit decided to continue in his treacherous course and sent envoys around to the neighboring tribes, trying to incite them to war. The Timociani had broken with the Bulgars and wished to come over to the emperor's side, submitting to his authority. But Ljudovit blocked this move and with specious reasoning led them on to drop their plan and join his perfidious revolt.

When the army returned from Pannonia, Cadolah, duke of Friuli, died of fever in this march. Baldrich succeeded him. When he entered Carinthia, which was under his command, he came upon Ljudovit's host. With a handful of men, he attacked it on the march along the River Drave, destroyed a good many of the enemy, routed his host, and drove it out of that province.

With a large body of men, Borna, the duke of Dalmatia, came upon Ljudovit, who had been advancing against him, on the River Kulpa. At the first encounter the Guduscani deserted Borna, but he escaped under the cover of his bodyguard. In this battle Ljudovit's father-in-law, Dragomosus, perished. He had deserted his son-in-law and joined Borna when his rebellion began. After the Guduscani returned home, they were again conquered by Borna. But Ljudovit seized the opportunity and with a strong force invaded Dalmatia in December, ravaging the whole land with fire and sword. When Borna saw that he was no match for Ljudovit, he stored all he could in his castles, and attacked Ljudovit's army with crack troops. Hampering him now in the rear and now on the flank, he wore him down day and night and would not let him stay unpunished in his province. In the end he forced Ljudovit to retreat from his territory after suffering heavy losses. Three thousand men of Ljudovit's army were killed, more than three hundred horses captured, and baggage and all sorts of spoils seized. Borna took care to inform the emperor through his envoys how this was done.

In the west Pepin, son of the emperor, on his father's order entered Gascony with an army, carried away the agitators, and so pacified the whole province[3] that no rebellious or disobedient man could be found.

On the emperor's order Heriold was taken to his ships by the Obodrites and sailed back to his homeland to take over the kingdom. Two of the sons of Godofrid are said to have made an alliance with him to share the throne; two others were driven out of the country. But this is believed to have been done by trickery.[4]

After dismissing the assembly the emperor first went to Kreuznach, then came to Bingen and traveled down the Rhine to Koblenz; from there he passed on to the Ardennes for the chase. Having gone hunting as usual, he returned to Aachen to spend the winter there.

820

In January an assembly was held in Aachen. The matter of Ljudovit's rebellion came up and the decision was made to dispatch three armies from three directions at once in order to lay waste

Ljudovit's territory and curb his pretensions. Through envoys and then in person, Borna offered his opinion on what should be done.[1]

At this assembly Count Bera of Barcelona, who for a long time had been accused by his neighbors of bad faith and treason, tried to contend with his accuser in combat on horseback but was defeated. He was first condemned to death for lèse majesté but then pardoned by the mercy of the emperor and taken away into exile to Rouen.

When the winter was over and the grass could provide fodder for the horses,[2] the three armies were sent against Ljudovit. One of them came from Italy by way of the Noric Alps; the second through the province of Carinthia; the third by Bavaria and Upper Pannonia. The two which moved on the right and left went slowly, since one was hindered in the Alps by enemy forces, while the other was slowed down by the length of the route and by the River Drave, which had to be crossed. But the one in the center, which entered by way of Carinthia, although meeting resistance in three places, luckily overcame it each time, crossed the Drave, and arrived at its destination more rapidly. Ljudovit undertook nothing against this force but lay low with his men behind the bulwark of a castle that he had built on a steep mountain. He reportedly said nothing about war or peace, either in person or through his envoys. But when the armies had united, they ravaged almost the whole land with fire and sword and then returned home without suffering any serious losses. But the army which marched through Upper Pannonia suffered a misfortune when crossing the Drave. From the unhealthy land and water, it was severely stricken with dysentery, to which a considerable part of it succumbed. These three armies had been recruited in Saxony, East Francia, and Alamannia, as well as Bavaria and Italy. After their return home the people of Carniola, who live along the River Save and border almost on Friuli, surrendered to Baldrich, and so did those of the Carinthians who had defected from us to Ljudovit.

The treaty made between us and Abul Aas, king of Spain, which did not satisfy either party, was purposely broken, and war against him was resumed.[3]

In the Italian sea pirates captured and sank eight merchant ships on their return from Sardinia to Italy.[4] From the land of the Norsemen, on the other hand, thirteen pirate vessels set out and tried to plunder on the shore of Flanders, but were repelled by guards. But because of the carelessness of the defenders, some wretched huts were burned down and a small number of cattle taken away. When the Norsemen made similar attempts on the mouth of the River Seine, the coast guards fought back, and the pirates retreated empty-handed after losing five men. Finally, on the coast of Aquitaine they met with success, thoroughly plundered a village by the name of Bouin[5] and then returned home with immense booty.

In this year great disasters occurred on account of continued rain and the excessive humidity. A pestilence affecting both men and cattle raged far and wide so that hardly any part of all the Frankish kingdom could be found immune from this plague or untouched by it. Grain and vegetables were rotting away in the persistent rains or could not be gathered or, when gathered, were spoilt. Little wine was produced this year, and what little there was turned out tart and sour since there was not enough warm weather. In some places water from the flooded rivers did not run off from low-lying areas,[6] and this flooding prevented seeding in the fall, so that almost no grain was sown before the warm spring season. There was an eclipse of the moon on January 28 in the second hour of the night.

After the assembly at Quierzy was over and the emperor had finished his usual autumn hunt, he returned to Aachen.

821

In February an assembly was held at Aachen and war against Ljudovit was planned. Provisions were made for three armies to take turns during the next summer and ravage the fields of the traitors. A similar decision was made about the Spanish March and the commanders of this border were ordered to carry it out. They agreed to hold another assembly at Nijmegen in May and the counts who were to appear there were given their orders.

On account of this the Lord Emperor, after celebrating Easter,[1] went by ship down the Meuse. There he reviewed the division of the kingdom among his sons which had been worked out and put into writing during the preceding years. He had the division ratified by the oaths of those magnates who could be present at that time.[2] At the same place he received the envoys of Paschal, the Roman pontiff, Bishop Peter of Civitavecchia and the nomenclator Leo, and dismissed them quickly. He also appointed the counts who were present for the

Pannonian campaign, and after a short stay returned to Aachen. A few days later he traveled across the Ardennes to Trier and Metz. From there he headed for the castle of Remiremont, where he spent the rest of the summer and half the fall hunting in the remote stretches of the Vosges Mountains.

In the meantime, Borna, duke of Dalmatia and Liburnia, died, and his nephew Ladislas was appointed his successor on the bidding of the people and with the emperor's approval. News also arrived of the death of Leo, emperor of Constantinople, who had been assassinated in his palace by several noble conspirators, notably Michael, the commander of the guards.[3] Michael reportedly received the imperial headband by the vote of the people and the effort of the praetorian guards.

Fortunatus, patriarch of Grado, was accused before the emperor by the priest Tiberius of encouraging Ljudovit to persist in his treacherous revolt and of helping him construct castles by supplying craftsmen and builders. On this account Fortunatus was ordered to appear at the palace. At first he set out for Istria, as if he intended to comply with the order. From there he secretly returned to the city of Grado and then, while no one but his fellow conspirators suspected anything, seized the opportunity to sail secretly away. Arriving at the city of Zara in Dalmatia, he told the commander of this province why he had fled. The latter immediately placed him on board a ship and sent him to Constantinople.

In the middle of October a general assembly was held at the villa of Thionville with many Franks present. At this assembly in solemn ceremony the Lord Lothair, first-born son of Lord Emperor Louis, married Irmengarda, daughter of Count Hugo.[4] Envoys of the Holy Roman Church also came there, the chief of the notaries Theodore and the sacristan Florus, and delivered rich gifts. The counts who had already returned from Pannonia were also present at this assembly. They had laid waste the entire territory of the renegades clinging to Ljudovit and then returned home since nobody met them with troops in battle. At this assembly the most pious emperor revealed his most singular mercy to those who had conspired with his nephew Bernard in Italy against his life and throne. He made them appear before him and granted them not only life and limb but in his great generosity also gave back to them the possessions which according to law they had forfeited to the treasury. He also called back Adalhard from Aquitaine, where he lived in exile, and again set him up as abbot and head of the monastery of Corbie, where he had been before.[5] He returned Adalhard's brother Bernhar to the same monastery after he had been pardoned. The emperor returned to Aachen after finishing whatever he had begun for the good of the kingdom and once the oath which part of the nobility had sworn at Nijmegen had been taken by all. After the solemn celebration of the wedding of his son Lothair, he sent him to Worms to spend the winter there.

Everything was quiet on the Danish front in this year, and Heriold was received as partner in the rule[6] by the sons of Godofrid. This is believed to have caused the peaceful relations among them at this time. But since Ceadrag, prince of the Obodrites, was charged with treachery and with having entered into an alliance with the sons of Godofrid, his rival Sclaomir was sent back to his homeland. When Sclaomir came to Saxony, he fell ill and died after receiving the sacrament of baptism.

Sowing was prevented in the fall in several areas because of continuous rain. This fall was followed by a winter so long and cold that not only brooks and rivers of medium size were covered with thick ice but even the biggest and most important streams, such as the Rhine, the Danube, the Elbe, the Seine, as well as the other rivers of Gaul and Germany that flow into the ocean. For more than thirty days heavy wagons crossed over the rivers as if they were bridges. When this ice melted, it did grave damage to the villages along the Rhine.

822

In the land of the Thuringians, in the neighborhood of a river, a block of earth fifty feet long, fourteen feet wide, and a foot and a half thick, was cut out, mysteriously lifted, and shifted twenty-five feet from its original location. Likewise, in eastern Saxony toward the Sorbian border in the wilderness near Arendsee, the ground was raised into a dam. Within a single night, without any human effort, it formed a rampart-like embankment one Gallic mile in length.[1]

Duke Winigis of Spoleto in his declining years put off secular garb and entered the monastic life. But not much later he was stricken by disease and died. Suppo, count of Brescia, replaced him.

After talking it over with his bishops and magnates, the Lord Emperor was reconciled to his brothers whom he had ordered to be tonsured against their will. He made a public confession and did penance for this as well as for what he had done to Bernard, son of his brother Pepin, and to Abbot Adalhard, and Adalhard's brother Wala. He did this at the assembly which he held in the presence of the whole people at Attigny in August of the same year. At this assembly he also tried with great humility to make up for any similar acts committed by him or his father.[2]

An army was sent from Italy into Pannonia to finish the war against Ljudovit. On its arrival Ljudovit withdrew from the city of Sisak and fled to the Serbs, a people that is said to hold a large part of Dalmatia. After treacherously murdering the only one of their dukes who had received him, he took over his city. Yet he still sent his envoys to the emperor, promising that he was willing to appear before him.[3]

In the meantime the Saxons, on the emperor's order, built a castle at Delbende[4] on the other side of the Elbe, drove out the Slavs who had previously held the place, and put a garrison of Saxons in the castle for the defense against the invasions of the Slavs.

The counts of the Spanish March crossed the River Segre into Spain, laid waste the fields, burned down a number of villages, and returned with considerable booty. After the fall equinox, the counts of the Breton March invaded the land of a rebellious Breton named Wihomarc. The whole territory was ravaged by fire and sword.

When the assembly at Attigny was over, the emperor went hunting in the Ardennes. He sent his son Lothair into Italy with the monk Wala, his relative and the brother of Abbot Adalhard, and Gering,[5] master of the doorkeepers, on whose counsel he was to rely in matters public and private.[6] He ordered Pepin to go to Aquitaine, but first had him take as his wife the daughter of Count Theotbert of Madrie and then made him depart to the west after the celebration of his wedding. When the chase in the fall was over, the emperor crossed the Rhine and went to Frankfurt to spend the winter there.

At Frankfurt he convoked a general assembly, and with the magnates whom he had ordered to appear there he took care, as usual, of all that pertained to the welfare of the eastern parts of his kingdom. At this assembly he received embassies and presents from all the East

Slavs, that is, Obodrites, Sorbs, Wilzi, Bohemians, Moravians, and Praedenecenti,[7] and from the Avars living in Pannonia. Embassies from Nordmannia were also at this assembly, from Heriold as well as from the sons of Godofrid. After he had heard and dismissed all of these, he spent the winter at the same place. For this purpose new buildings had been constructed according to his orders.

823

An assembly was held at the same place in May, at which not only all the nobles of Francia were ordered to appear but those from East Francia, Saxony, Bavaria, Alamannia and neighboring Burgundy, and from the Rhineland. Two brothers, kings of the Wilzi, named Milegast and Cealadrag, who quarreled with each other over their kingdom, appeared before the emperor at this assembly, among the other embassies of barbarians which had either been ordered to come or had come of their own accord. The two were sons of Liub, king of the Wilzi, who had shared the kingdom with his brothers, but as the eldest had held supremacy over the whole kingdom. When he died in battle against the eastern Obodrites, the people of the Wilzi made his son Milegast their king, since he was the eldest. Milegast was an unworthy ruler of the kingdom which had been committed to him according to popular custom. He was deposed and the kingship was conferred on his younger brother. Because of this matter both appeared before the emperor. When the emperor had heard them and realized that the will of the people was more in favor of the younger brother's holding the office, he decided that Cealadrag should keep the office conferred on him by the people. He nevertheless gave gifts to both of them and sent them back to their homeland after they had taken oaths to keep the agreement.

During the assembly at Frankfurt, Ceadrag, prince of the Obodrites, was accused in the emperor's presence of infidelity to the Franks and of having failed to appear before the emperor for a long time. Envoys were sent to him on that account. With these envoys Ceadrag sent back some nobles of his people to the emperor. Through them he promised to appear before the emperor next winter. Lothair followed the instructions of his father and dispensed justice in Italy. When he was about to return, he went to Rome at Pope Paschal's request, was honorably received, and on the holy day of Easter received the crown of the kingdom and the title of Emperor and Augustus. From Rome he returned to Pavia in June and met his father. Lothair reported the laws he had made or initiated in Italy to the emperor. Adalhard, count of the palace, was then sent to Italy and instructed to take along Mauring, count of Brescia, and to complete the laws which Lothair had begun.[1]

He made his brother Drogo, who was leading the life of a monk, head of the church of Metz upon the consent and election of the clergy of that city and believed that he should be made bishop.[2]

At the same assembly it was agreed that the next assembly should be held in November at the palace of Compiègne. After the meeting, when the nobles had been dismissed and the emperor was on the point of leaving, he was informed that Ljudovit had perished. When Ljudovit, after leaving the Serbs, went to Liudemuhsl, uncle of Duke Borna, and stayed with him for a while, he was murdered by Liudemuhsl's treachery.

It was also reported that Theodore, chief of the notaries of the Holy Roman Church, and his son-in-law, the nomenclator Leo, had been first blinded and then decapitated in the Lateran, and that this fate had befallen them because they had always acted loyally toward the young emperor Lothair. There were also some who said that this had been done on either the order or the advice of Pope Paschal. Adalung, abbot of the monastery of St. Vaast,[3] and Hunfrid, count of Chur, were dispatched with orders to get to the bottom of this matter. But before they departed, envoys of Pope Paschal arrived, Bishop John of Silvacandida and Benedict, archdeacon of the Holy Apostolic See, pleading with the emperor to exonerate the pope from the infamous rumor that he had consented to the murder of the men in question.

When the emperor had given a reasonable answer and dismissed them, he ordered his envoys to go to Rome, as previously decided, and to find out the truth. The emperor himself spent the rest of the summer in the county of Worms and then in the Ardennes. When the fall hunting season was over, he came, as he had planned, to Compiègne on November 1.

The envoys who went to Rome could not determine exactly what had happened. Pope Paschal, with a large number of bishops, purged himself by oath from any complicity in this deed. On the other hand, he defended with great vigor the murderers of the above-mentioned men because they belonged to the family of St. Peter, condemned the dead as guilty of lèse majesté, and proclaimed that they had been justly slain. He, therefore, sent to the emperor Bishop John of Silvacandida and the librarian Sergius, as well as the subdeacon Quirinus and the master of horse Leo along with the aforementioned envoys who had been dispatched to him. When the emperor heard from these men as well as from his own envoys of the pontiff's oath and the vindication of the defendants, he believed that there was nothing else for him to do in this matter and sent Bishop John and his companions back to the pope with a suitable answer.

Ceadrag, prince of the Obodrites, lived up to his promises and came to Compiègne with several nobles of his people. He gave an acceptable explanation for his failure over so many years to present himself to the emperor. Although he appeared culpable in several respects, he not only remained scot-free because of the merits of his ancestors but was permitted to return to his kingdom after being presented with gifts.

Also Heriold came from Nordmannia, asking for help against the sons of Godofrid, who threatened to drive him out of his country. To explore this matter more thoroughly Counts Theothari and Hruodmund were sent to the sons of Godofrid. Traveling ahead of Heriold they carefully studied the dispute with the sons of Godofrid as well as the condition of the whole kingdom of the Norsemen and informed the emperor of all they could find out in these lands. They returned with Archbishop Ebbo of Reims,[4] who had gone to preach in the land of the Danes on the counsel of the emperor and with the approval of the Roman pontiff and had baptized many converts to the faith during the previous summer.

In this same year several prodigies are said to have occurred. The most significant among these were an earthquake in the palace of Aachen and a girl of about twelve years who abstained from all food for ten months in the village of Commercy in the area of Toul. In the Saxon county of Firihsazi twenty-three villages were burned by fire from heaven, and lightning struck out of a clear sky at daytime. Near the Italian city of Como, in the village of Gravedona, there was a picture painted in the apse of the church of St. John the Baptist of Holy Mary holding the infant Jesus in her lap and of the Magi offering presents that was dimmed and almost wiped out with age. This picture shone for two days with such clarity it seemed to viewers that its ancient beauty almost surpassed the splendor of a new picture. But the same clarity did not brighten the images of the Magi except for the presents which they offered. In many areas the produce of the fields was destroyed by a raging hailstorm, and in a few places real stones of tremendous weight were seen to fall with the hail. Houses are also said to have been struck by lightning, and everywhere men and animals were killed with unusual frequency by strokes of lightning. There followed a great pestilence and mortality which raged furiously throughout Francia, carrying away by violence countless people of both sexes and of all ages.

824

N., king of the Bulgars, sent envoys with peace overtures to the emperor. When the emperor had received them and had read the letters they brought, he was moved by the novelty of this matter to explore more thoroughly the cause of this unprecedented legation which never before had come to Francia. He sent Machelm, a Bavarian, with these envoys to the king of the Bulgars.[1]

The winter was cold and very long. The extreme cold killed not only animals but some people, too. There was an eclipse of the moon on March 5 in the second hour of the night. Suppo, duke of Spoleto, was reported to have died.

In the meantime the envoys of the Roman pontiff returned to Rome and found the pope in bad health and already near death. In fact he died within a few days after their arrival. Two men were elected to take his place due to a conflict of the people. The party of the nobility prevailed, and Eugenius, titular archpriest of St. Sabina, was ordained as successor. The subdeacon Quirinus, one of those who had served on the former embassy, brought the news of this event to the emperor.[2]

At the assembly announced for June 24 and held at Compiègne the emperor resolved to make an expedition into Brittany. He also planned to send his son and co-emperor Lothair to Rome, so that Lothair would in his stead make binding decisions with the new pontiff and the Roman people on whatever the occasion seemed to demand. Lothair embarked for Italy after the middle of August to carry out his father's order. But because the famine was still very severe, the emperor postponed the campaign he had planned against Brittany until the beginning of autumn. Only then did he gather his troops from every corner and advance to the city of Rennes on the Breton border. There he divided his host into three parts, of which he put two under the command of his sons Pepin and Louis. Retaining command of the third, he entered Brittany and laid waste the whole land with fire and sword. When he had spent more than forty days on this campaign and had received the hostages he had demanded from the faithless Bretons, he returned to the city of Rouen on November 17, where his wife was expecting him.

He also ordered the envoys being sent by the Emperor Michael to meet him at Rouen. Fortunatus, patriarch of Venice, had returned and appeared before him with these envoys. They brought letters and presents from the emperor and declared that they had been sent to ratify peace. They said nothing good about Fortunatus. Among other things they raised the question of image worship, on account of which they said they were to go to Rome and consult the head of the Apostolic See.[3] When the emperor had heard their message, given an answer, and dismissed them, he ordered them to be taken to Rome, where they said they wanted to go. He also questioned Fortunatus about the reason for his flight and sent him for an investigation to the Roman pontiff. The emperor himself went to Aachen, where he had decided to spend the winter.

After arriving at Aachen and celebrating Christmas there, he was informed that the envoys of the king of the Bulgars were in Bavaria. He contacted them and made them wait there until the right moment. The emperor also received the envoys of the Obodrites who are commonly called Praedenecenti and live in Dacia on the Danube as neighbors of the Bulgars, of whose arrival he had been informed. When they complained about vicious aggression by the Bulgars and asked for help against them, he told them to go home and to return when the envoys of the Bulgars were to be received.

Since Suppo had died at Spoleto, as was mentioned, Adalhard the Younger, count of the palace, received the duchy. He died of fever after holding the office for barely five months. Mauring, count of Brescia, was elected his successor. At the time he received the news of his appointment he was sick and he died within a few days.

Counts Aeblus and Asinarius had been sent to Pamplona with Basque forces. When they had completed their assignment and were on their march back, they were lured into an ambush by the treachery of the mountain people, surrounded, and taken prisoner. The troops which they had with them were destroyed almost to a man. Aeblus was sent to Cordova, but Asinarius, being a relative of his captors, was mercifully permitted to return home.

Lothair went to Rome, according to the instruction of his father, and was honorably received by Pope Eugenius. After informing the pope of his mandate and gaining his consent, Lothair ordered the affairs of the Roman people, which for a long time had been confused due to the wickedness of several popes. As a result of Lothair's intervention all who had been injured by the loss of their fortune were marvelously consoled by the return of their possessions. This was brought about, with the help of God, by Lothair's appearance on the scene.

A few days before the summer equinox of this year, when a sudden change in the air whipped up a storm, an enormous chunk of ice is said to have fallen with the hail in the country around Autun. It is said to have been fifteen feet long, seven feet wide, and two feet thick.

825

The emperor celebrated the holy feast of Easter as usual at Aachen, and when the gentle season of spring smiled he went to Nijmegen for the chase. He ordered the envoys of the Bulgars to come to Aachen about the middle of May, since he decided to return to Aachen in order to hold an assembly. This gathering had been announced to his magnates when he came back from Brittany.

On his return to Aachen after the hunting season was over, he received the Bulgar embassy. The question at issue was the determination of the borders between Franks and Bulgars. Almost all the nobles of Brittany were present at this assembly. Among them was Wihomarc, who by his treachery had thrown the whole of Brittany into confusion and by his senseless obstinacy had provoked the emperor to the above-mentioned campaign. He was finally following saner counsel,[1] and, as he said himself, did not hesitate to place himself under the protection of the emperor. The emperor forgave him and after presenting him with gifts permitted him to return home with the other nobles of his people. But with the treachery peculiar to his nation, as he had before, he broke the faith which he had promised. He did not cease to molest his neighbors with all his energy, burning and plundering until he was cornered and slain in his own house by the men of Count Lambert.[2] After receiving the embassy of the Bulgars, the emperor sent suitable letters to their king by the same envoys.

When he had dismissed the assembly, the emperor set out for Remiremont in the Vosges Mountains to go hunting, and there he received his son Lothair, who was on the way back from Italy. After the chase he returned to Aachen, where he held the customary general assembly of his people in August. Among various embassies at this assembly the emperor listened to the envoys of the sons of Godofrid from Nordmannia. He ordered the peace for which they asked to be made with them in the Danish March in October. When all business to be considered at this assembly had been completed, he departed from Nijmegen with his elder son, sending his younger son Louis to Bavaria.[3] After the fall hunting season the emperor returned to Aachen at the beginning of winter.

In the vicinity of Toul by the village of Commercy a twelve-year-old girl named N., after receiving Holy Communion from the hand of the priest at Easter, reportedly abstained first from bread and then from all other food and drink. She fasted to such an extreme that she took absolutely no bodily nourishment and lived for full three years without any desire for eating. She began to fast in the year of the Lord's Incarnation 823, as noted above in the report on that year, and in the present year, 825, at the beginning of November, she ceased to fast and began to take food and to live by eating like the rest of mortals.

826

When the envoys of the Bulgars reported to their king what they had accomplished, he sent his first ambassador again with letters to the emperor and requested that the borders be determined without further delay, or, if this was not acceptable to the emperor, that each should guard his frontiers without a peace treaty. The emperor delayed his answer because of the rumor that the king of the Bulgars had either been driven out or murdered by one of his nobles. He ordered the ambassador to wait and dispatched Bertrich, count of the palace, to Counts Baldrich and Gerold, the guards of the Avar border, in the province of Carinthia, in order to sift out the truth of the rumor. When Bertrich came back and reported nothing certain one way or the other the emperor received the envoy but made him return without a letter.

In the meantime about February 1 King Pepin, the emperor's son, came with his magnates and the guards of the Spanish border to Aachen as ordered, for the emperor had spent the winter there. After consulting with them the emperor made his decision on the protection of the western frontier against the Saracens. Then Pepin returned to Aquitaine and spent the summer in the place assigned to him.

But the emperor left Aachen in the middle of May and arrived at Ingelheim about June 1. He held an assembly there that was heavily attended, receiving and dismissing many embassies from various countries. The most important and distinguished among these was the embassy of the Holy Apostolic See, which consisted of Bishop Leo of Civitavecchia, the nomenclator Theophylact, and Dominic, abbot of Mount Olivet,[1] from the land beyond the sea. The envoys of the sons of Godofrid, king of the Danes, had also been sent there to make peace and clinch an alliance, and from the lands of the Slavs were some nobles of the Obodrites who spoke against their duke, Ceadrag. Besides all these, Tunglo, one of the magnates of the Sorbs, was accused of having refused obedience. These two were informed that the emperor would punish them in accordance with their treachery if they failed to come to his assembly in the middle of October. Some nobles of the Bretons also appeared whom the guards of that border wished to present.

At the same time Heriold came with his wife and a great number of Danes and was baptized with his companions at St. Alban's in Mainz. The emperor presented him with many gifts before he returned home through Frisia, the route by which he had come. In this province one county was given to him, the county of Rüstringen, so that he would be able to find refuge there with his possessions if he were ever in danger.[2]

Counts Baldrich and Gerold, commanders of the Pannonian border, were at this assembly and testified that up to this moment they had not been able to detect a movement of the Bulgars against us. With Baldrich came a priest from Venice by the name of George, who claimed that he could build an organ.[3] The emperor sent him to Aachen with the treasurer Thancolf and ordered him to be provided with everything needed for the building of the instrument.

A general assembly was planned for the middle of October and all other business settled as usual. The emperor then traveled with his retinue across the Rhine to the royal villa of Salz. There envoys of the people of Naples came to him, and when they had received an answer they returned home again.[4] At Salz Aizo's flight and treachery were brought to his attention: how he artfully entered Vich, was received by the people of Roda whom he cunningly deceived and whose city he destroyed, fortified the stronger castles of this country, sent his brother to Abd ar-Rahman,[5] king of the Saracens, and requested and accepted this king's aid against us. Although the news of this matter infuriated the emperor, he believed that nothing should be done on the spur of the moment and decided to wait for the arrival of his counselors. When the fall hunting was over, about October 1, he traveled down the Main to Frankfurt.

From there he came to Ingelheim in the middle of October and held the general assembly of his people as had been planned. At this assembly he also received Ceadrag, duke of the Obodrites, and Tunglo, who had both been charged with treachery. He permitted Tunglo to return home after securing Tunglo's son as a hostage. But Ceadrag he kept with him, although he sent the rest of the Obodrites away. He dispatched envoys to the Obodrites and told them to inquire whether the people wanted Ceadrag to be their ruler. The emperor himself went to Aachen, where he had decided to spend the winter. The envoys sent to the Obodrites returned and informed him that the opinion of this people about their king blew hot and cold but that the better and nobler people agreed he should come back. The emperor, therefore, had him restored to his kingdom, after receiving the hostages he had demanded.

While this was going on, Hilduin, abbot of the monastery of the holy martyr Dionysius,[6] petitioned Rome for the relics of the holy martyr Sebastian. Eugenius, who was then head of the Holy Apostolic See, granted his request. Hilduin interred the relics in the basilica of St.-Médard in the city of Soissons. As long as they were lying unburied next to the tomb of St. Médard an incredible and inexpressible number of marvels occurred, manifesting miraculous power[7] in all kinds of healings, through divine grace in the name of this most blessed martyr. Some of these miracles are said to have been so amazing as to exceed the faith of man's limited mind.[8] Of course it cannot be doubted that our Lord Jesus Christ, for whom this most blessed martyr is known to have suffered, can do everything He wishes by His divine omnipotence, in which every creature in heaven and on earth is subject to Him.

827

The emperor sent the priest and abbot Helisachar[1] and with him Counts Hildebrand and Donatus to stamp out the revolt in the Spanish March. Before their arrival Aizo, trusting in the assistance of the Saracens, had inflicted much damage on the guards of this border. By constant invasions he had worn them out so thoroughly that some of them deserted the castles which they were to defend and retreated. Willemund, son of Bera, defected to him as did some others equally anxious for change, which is just what might be expected of this fickle people. They joined the Saracens and Moors and molested Cerdaña and Vallés with daily robbing and burning. Abbot Helisachar, dispatched with others by the emperor to calm down the Goths and Spaniards living in this territory, made many prudent arrangements due to his personal concern over the problem and to the counsel of his companions. Bernard, count of Barcelona, stubbornly resisted the ambushes of Aizo and the cunning and treacherous machinations of those who had defected to him and frustrated their daring attempts. An army sent to Aizo's aid by Abd ar-Rahman, king of the Saracens, was reported to have arrived at Saragossa. Abumarvan, a relative of the king, had been made its commander, and he promised, on the assurance of Aizo, that victory was not in doubt. Against Abumarvan the emperor sent his son Pepin, king of Aquitaine, with innumerable Frankish troops and ordered him to defend the borders of his kingdom. This would have been done if the army had not arrived in the march too late, due to the negligence of the leaders he had put in command.[2] This delay was so disastrous that Abumarvan laid waste the fields and burned the villages around Barcelona and Gerona, pillaged everything he found outside the cities, and retreated to Saragossa with his army intact before our men ever caught sight of him. People were sure they saw battle lines and shifting lights in the sky at night and that these marvels foreboded the Frankish defeat.

The emperor held two assemblies. One was at Nijmegen because Hohrich, son of Godofrid, the king of the Danes, had falsely promised to appear before the emperor. The other was at Compiègne, where he accepted the annual gifts and gave instructions to those who had to be sent to the Spanish March on how they were to proceed. He himself stayed at Compiègne, Quierzy, or other neighboring palaces until the beginning of winter.

In the meantime the kings of the Danes, that is, the sons of Godofrid, deprived Heriold of his share in the kingship and forced him to leave Nordmannia.

The Bulgars sent an army on ships up the Drave and harassed the Slavs living in Pannonia with fire and sword. They expelled the Slavic chieftains and appointed Bulgar governors instead.[3]

Pope Eugenius died in August. The deacon Valentine was elected by the Romans in his place and ordained, but held the pontificate for barely one month. On his death Gregory, titular priest of St. Mark's, was elected, but was not ordained until the emperor's envoy had come to Rome and investigated the popular election.[4]

Envoys of Emperor Michael were sent from Constantinople to the emperor to ratify their treaty. They arrived at Compiègne in September. The emperor received them graciously and heard and dismissed them.

In October the bodies of the most blessed martyrs of Christ, Marcellinus and Peter, were removed from Rome and translated to Francia. There they became famous through many signs and miracles.[5]

828

In February an assembly was held at Aachen at which the events in the Spanish March were given special consideration over other matters. The envoys who had commanded the army were found guilty and punished as they deserved by losing their offices.[1] Baldrich, duke of Friuli, was also deprived of the offices he held and the march which he had ruled alone was divided among four counts. Because of his cowardice the army of the Bulgars had ravaged with impunity the borderland of Upper Pannonia. Bishop Halitgar of Cambrai and Abbot

Ansfrid of the monastery of Nonantola were sent to Constantinople and, as they reported on their return, were received by Emperor Michael with great honor.[2]

In June the emperor came to his villa at Ingelheim and for several days held an assembly there. At this assembly he resolved to send his sons Lothair and Pepin with the army into the Spanish March and told them exactly what to do. He heard the message of the pope's emissaries, chief of the notaries Quirinus and the nomenclator Theophylact, who had come to him there, and dismissed them. Then he went to the villa of Frankfurt. He stayed there for a while, then turned to Worms and continued to Thionville. From Thionville he sent his son Lothair with a large body of Frankish troops into the Spanish March. When Lothair arrived at Lyons, he stopped to wait for news of the coming of the Saracens. While he waited, he had a conference with his brother Pepin. When they heard that the Saracens were either afraid to come to the march or unwilling to do so, Pepin returned to Aquitaine and Lothair to his father at Aachen.

Near the border of Nordmannia in the meantime negotiations were planned to ratify the peace between Norsemen and Franks and to discuss the affair of Heriold. For this business counts and margraves came from almost all of Saxony. But Heriold was too thirsty for action. He broke the peace that had been agreed upon and confirmed by hostages, and burned and pillaged some small villages of the Norsemen. Upon hearing this the sons of Godofrid immediately gathered troops. Our people were stationed on the bank of the River Eider, not expecting any trouble.[3] The sons of Godofrid advanced toward the march, crossed the river, and attacked the Franks, driving them out of their castle and putting them to flight. They took everything from them and retreated with all their forces to their camp. Then they deliberated how to ward off revenge for this action. They dispatched an embassy to the emperor and explained that need had compelled them against their will to do this, that they were ready to give satisfaction, and that it was entirely up to the emperor how amends should be made in order to preserve peace between the two parties.

Count Boniface, who at that time was entrusted with the defense[4] of the island of Corsica, sailed around Corsica and Sardinia with a small fleet. His brother and some of the other counts of Tuscany sailed with him. When he did not find a single pirate on the sea, he crossed over to Africa and landed between Utica and Carthage. He attacked a large number of the inhabitants who had suddenly gathered, fought a battle with them, and put them to flight after routing them at least five times. After slaying a great number of Africans and losing some of his own companions because of their daring, he retreated to his ships. This feat gave the Africans a healthy respect for them.

The setting moon was eclipsed on July 1 at dawn, and again on December 25, that is, on Christmas, at midnight.

The emperor came to Aachen about Martinmas[5] to spend the winter. When he had settled in, he devoted the entire winter to various assemblies convoked for current matters of state.[6]

829

When the winter was over an earthquake occurred at Aachen during the holy forty-day fast, a few days before Holy Easter. A violent storm broke loose. During its course, not only humbler houses were unroofed but even the basilica of the Holy Mother of God, called the Chapel, lost much of its roof of lead tiles.[1]

The emperor, delayed by various affairs, remained at Aachen until July 1. He finally decided to depart with his retinue for the general assembly to be held at Worms in August. But before he left he received the news that the Norsemen planned to invade Saxony on the far side of the Elbe and that their army was approaching our borders. On hearing this he sent into all parts of Francia, ordering the general levy of his people to follow him as fast as they could to Saxony. He announced at the same time that he planned to cross the Rhine at Neuss about the middle of July.

But when he found out that the rumor about the Norsemen was false, he came to Worms in the middle of August, as had been planned before. He held a general assembly there and as usual accepted the annual presents brought to him. He also received a great number of embassies which had come to him from Rome and Benevento as well as from other distant countries and dismissed them again. After the assembly he also sent his son Lothair to Italy. He appointed as chamberlain in his palace Bernard, count of Barcelona, who up to that time had been the commander of the Spanish March.[2] After properly settling the other affairs which seemed to be the business of this assembly and sending the people home, he went to the villa of Frankfurt for the fall hunting. When this was over he wintered at Aachen and there celebrated Martinmas, the feast of the blessed apostle Andrew, and Holy Christmas with much joy and exultation.

NITHARD'S

Histories

[Book I: 814—40]

When you had innocently suffered your brother's persecutions for almost two years, as you, my lord, know best, you ordered me, before we entered the city of Châlons, to write the history of your time.[1] This assignment, I confess, would have been pleasant and welcome if the press of events had allowed me time to do it justice. But if you find this work less ample or less polished than it should be, considering the importance of the events, you and your people owe me all the more forbearance since you know that as I wrote I was caught up in the same turmoil as you were.

I was inclined, it is true, to pass over events that occurred in the time of your pious father, but the real cause of your conflicts will become clearer to the reader if I begin by touching upon some matters known to have taken place in his time. Besides, it also seems highly inadvisable to omit altogether the venerable memory of your grandfather, and therefore my story shall begin with him.

[1]

When Emperor Charles of blessed memory, rightfully called
814 the Great by all nations, died at a ripe old age, about the third hour of the day, he left the whole of Europe flourishing. For in his time he was a man who so much excelled all others in wisdom and virtue that to everyone on earth he appeared both terrible and worthy of love

and admiration. Thus, he made his whole reign in every way glorious and salutary, as was apparent to everyone. But above all I believe he will be admired for the tempered severity with which he subdued the fierce and iron hearts of Franks and barbarians. Not even Roman might had been able to tame these people, but they dared do nothing in Charles's empire except what was in harmony with the public welfare. He ruled happily as king for thirty-two years and held the helm of the empire with no less success for fourteen years.

[2]

Louis was the heir of all this excellence. He was the youngest of Charles's legitimate sons and succeeded to the throne after the death of the others. As soon as he had certain news of his father's death, he came straightway from Aquitaine to Aachen. No one objected when he asserted his authority over the nobles arriving on the scene but reserved judgment on those whose loyalty seemed doubtful.[2] At the beginning of his rule as emperor he ordered the immense treasures left by his father to be divided into three parts; one part he spent on the funeral; the other two parts he divided between himself and those of his sisters who were born in lawful wedlock.[3] He also ordered his sisters to remove themselves instantly from the palace to their monasteries. His brothers Drogo, Hugo, and Theodoric, who were still very young, he made companions of his table and ordered to be brought up in his palace.[4] To his nephew Bernard, Pepin's son, he
817 granted the kingdom of Italy. Since Bernard defected from Louis a little later, he was taken prisoner and deprived of his sight as well as his life by Bertmund, governor of the province of Lyons.[5] From that time on Louis feared that his younger brothers might later stir up the people and behave like Bernard. He therefore had them appear before his general assembly, tonsured them, and put them under free custody into monasteries.

When this had been taken care of, he made his sons enter legal marriages and divided the whole empire among them so that Pepin was to have Aquitaine, Louis Bavaria, and Lothair, after his father's death, the whole empire.[6] He also permitted Lothair to hold the title of emperor with him. In the meantime Queen Irmengardis, their mother, died, and a short time later Emperor Louis married Judith,
823 who gave birth to Charles.[7]

[3]

After Charles's birth, Louis did not know what to do for him since he had already divided the whole empire among his other sons. When the distressed father begged their help on Charles's behalf, Lothair finally gave his assent and swore that his father should give to Charles whatever part of the kingdom he wished. He assured Louis by oath that in the future he would be Charles's protector and defender against all enemies. But after being incited by Hugo, whose daughter Lothair had married, Mathfrid, and others, he later regretted what he had done and tried to undo it.[8] This behavior did not in the least escape his father and Judith. So from then on Lothair secretly sought to destroy what his father had arranged. To help him counter Lothair's plot the father employed a man named Bernard, who was duke of Septimania. He appointed Bernard his chamberlain, entrusted Charles to him, and made him the second man in the empire. Bernard recklessly abused the imperial power which he was supposed to strengthen and undermined it entirely.[9]

Aug. At that time Alamannia was handed over to Charles by decree.[10]
829 Lothair, as if he had at last found a good reason to complain, called upon his brothers and the whole people to restore authority and order in the empire.[11] They all suddenly converged on Louis at Compiègne,
April made the queen take the veil, tonsured her brothers, Conrad and
830 Rudolf, and sent them to Aquitaine to be held by Pepin.[12] Bernard took to his heels and escaped to Septimania. His brother Herbert was captured, blinded, and imprisoned in Italy. When Lothair had taken over the government, he held his father and Charles in free custody. He ordered monks to keep Charles company; they were to get him used to the monastic life and urge him to take it up himself.[13]

But the state of the empire grew worse from day to day, since all were driven by greed and sought only their own advantage. On account of this the monks we have mentioned above, as well as other men who deplored what had happened, began to question Louis to see if he were willing to reconstruct the government and stand behind it if the kingdom were restored to him. Above all he was to promote religious worship, by which all order is protected and preserved. Since he readily accepted this, his restoration was quickly agreed upon. Louis chose Guntbald, a monk, and secretly sent him to his sons Pepin and Louis. Guntbald went ostensibly on religious business, but he promised

Sites of the Conflicts between Louis the Pious and His Sons

that Louis would increase the kingdom of both Pepin and Louis if
they would assist the men who wanted him back on the throne. The
megen promise of more land made them only too eager to comply. An
t. 830 assembly was convoked, the queen and her brothers were returned to
Louis, and the whole people submitted again to his rule. Then those
achen who had been on Lothair's side were taken before the general as-
Feb. sembly and either condemned to death or, if their lives were spared,
831 sent into exile by Lothair himself. Lothair also had to be content with
Italy alone and was permitted to go there only on the condition that
in the future he would not attempt anything in the kingdom against
his father's will.[14]

When matters rested at this and there seemed to be a moment's respite, the monk Guntbald, whom we mentioned above, immediately wanted to be second in the empire because he had done so much for Louis' restoration. But Bernard, who had formerly held this position, as I said before, tried eagerly to regain it. Also Pepin and Louis, although their kingdoms had been enlarged as promised, nevertheless both tried hard to be first in the empire after their father. But those who were in charge of the government at that time resisted their desires.

[4]

833 At the same time Aquitaine was taken from Pepin and given to Charles, and the nobility which was on King Louis' side did homage to Charles.[15] This event infuriated the malcontents whom I mentioned. They let it be known that the government was poorly run and incited the people to demand fair rule. They freed Wala, Helisachar, Mathfrid, and the others who had been sent into exile and urged Lothair to seize power.[16] Under the same pretext and by continual petitions, they also won over to their side Gregory, pontiff of the supreme Roman See, so that his authority would help them do what they planned.

The emperor with all his forces confronted the three kings, his
sons, with their immense army, and Pope Gregory with his entire
Roman entourage. They all gathered in Alsace and set up camps at
Mount Siegwald.[17] By promising various favors the sons prevailed
upon the people to defect from their father. After most of his men
June had fled Louis was eventually captured. His wife was taken from him

and sent into exile to Lombardy, and Charles was held with his father under close guard.[18]

Pope Gregory, filled with regret over his journey, returned to Rome later than he had planned. Lothair had seized the empire again, but what he had so unjustly and easily won, he justly lost again even more easily, the second time around. Pepin and Louis saw that Lothair intended to seize the whole empire and make them his inferiors, and they resented his schemes.[19] Hugo, Lambert, and Mathfrid also disagreed as to which of them should be second in the empire after Lothair. They began to quarrel, and, since each of them looked out for his own, they entirely neglected the government. When the people saw that, they were distressed. Shame and regret filled the sons for having twice deprived their father of his dignity, and the people
Feb. for having twice deserted the emperor. Therefore, they all now
834 agreed on his restoration and headed for St.-Denis, where Lothair was
then holding his father and Charles.

Seeing that this flare-up was more than he could deal with, Lothair took up arms before the others had assembled, released his father and Charles, and hurried by forced marches to Vienne.[20] When the emperor was returned to them, a large number of men present were ready to use force in support of the father against the son. They flocked with the bishops and the whole clergy into the basilica of St.-Denis, offered praise to God in all piety, placed crown and arms upon their king, and then assembled to deliberate on the remaining matters.[21]

Louis refrained from pursuing Lothair, but sent envoys after him who were to order him to leave promptly across the Alps.[22] When Pepin came to him, Louis received him graciously, thanked him for what he had done toward his restoration, and allowed him to return to Aquitaine as Pepin requested. There was a gathering of the emperor's vassals who used to run the government and had fled. With these men he marched quickly to Aachen to spend the winter there. Finally, his son Louis came to him. The emperor received him joyfully and told him to stay with him for his protection.

When in the meantime those who guarded Judith in Italy heard that Lothair had fled and Louis ruled the empire, they seized Judith and escaped. They arrived safely at Aachen and delivered her as a welcome present to the emperor. But she was not admitted to the royal bed until she had established her innocence of the offenses with which she had been charged. In the absence of an accuser she did so by an oath taken with her kinsmen before the people.[23]

[5]

834 At this time Mathfrid, Lambert, and the others of Lothair's party were in the Breton March. Wido and all the men between the Seine and Loire were dispatched to drive them out. They assembled in a large force. The small number of Lothair's men put them at a great disadvantage, but at least they moved as one man. Wido's large army made him and his men secure but quarrelsome and disorganized. No wonder they fled when it came to battle. Wido was slain as well as Odo, Vivian, Fulbert, and an uncounted number of the people.[24] The victors hastily informed Lothair of this, urging him to come to their assistance with an army as fast as he could. Lothair gladly complied and came with a large force to Chalon, laid siege to the city, and
June stormed it for three days. After he had finally captured the place, he
834 burned the city and its churches. He ordered Gerberga to be drowned in the Saône like a witch and Gozhelm and Senila to be beheaded. But he granted Warin his life, forcing him to swear he would support Lothair in the future with all his might.[25]

Lothair and his men were in high spirits because of their two successful battles and hoped for an easy conquest of the whole empire. They marched to the city of Orléans to deliberate on unsettled business. Upon hearing this the emperor assembled a strong army in Francia. With the aid of Louis and all his men on the far side of the Rhine, he set out to take revenge for the great crime committed by his son against the empire. Hoping that he might cause the Franks to defect as before, Lothair decided on a direct confrontation. So the two forces met and pitched camp by a river near the village of Chouzy.[26] But the Franks were sorry that they had deserted their emperor twice, and considered it shameful to commit the same act again. They spurned any attempt to make them defect. Lothair saw
Aug. that this was no time for either flight or fight and finally gave up the
834 struggle. First it was agreed that within a stipulated number of days he would cross the Alps and in the future not dare to enter the territory of Francia or make a move without his father's consent. Lothair and his men swore that they would keep these promises.

[6]

835/36 When these matters had been settled, the father ruled the empire with his former advisers.[27] He realized that as long as he lived the people would not desert him, as had been their habit before. He
837/38 convoked an assembly at Aachen in winter and gave Charles a part of the kingdom bounded in the following way: from the sea along the borders of Saxony as far as the borders of the Ripuarians, all of Frisia; in the lands of the Ripuarians the counties of Moilla, Haettra, Hammolant, and Maasgau; the whole land between the Meuse and Seine as far as Burgundy with the county of Verdun, and in Burgundy the counties of Toul, Ornois, Blois, Blasois, Perthois, the two counties of Bar; the counties of Brienne, Troyes, Auxerre, Sens, Gatinais, Melun, Étampes, Chatres, and Paris; and then along the Seine as far as the ocean and along the coast as far as Frisia all bishoprics, abbeys, counties, royal estates, and everything within the above boundaries and all that went with them, wherever it was located and was known to belong to the emperor.[28] He gave this to his son Charles with all divine and paternal authority and implored the mercy of Almighty God that it remain in his hands.

838 Hilduin, abbot of the church of St.-Denis, and Gerard, count of the city of Paris, and all others living within this territory came together and took an oath of fealty to Charles. When Lothair and Louis heard of this they were very much annoyed and arranged a conference. During their meeting they saw that there was no adequate excuse for being angry about anything that had happened. They shrewdly concealed that they intended to do anything against their father's will and broke up. This meeting raised a storm, but it subsided quickly.[29] The emperor then came to Quierzy about the middle of September and easily suppressed another revolt. He conferred arms and crown upon Charles as well as a part of the kingdom between Seine and Loire. He also reconciled Pepin and Charles, at least to all appearances; then he graciously permitted Pepin to return to Aquitaine and sent Charles into the part of the kingdom he had given him. On Charles's arrival all inhabitants of those lands came to commend themselves to him and swear fealty.

839 It was then announced that Louis had revolted against his father and intended to seize the entire part of the kingdom on the far side of the Rhine. When his father heard what he was doing, he came to

Grant to Charles in 837

Mainz, where he convoked an assembly, crossed the Rhine with his army, and forced Louis to flee into Bavaria.[30] Then he returned jubilantly to Aachen, since by God's will he had the victory wherever he turned.[31] Louis was getting old and his mind was beginning to falter because of his many troubles. Queen Judith and those nobles who were working for Charles, as Louis wished them to, feared that the hatred of the brothers would pursue them until death if the emperor died without settling his affairs. For this reason they thought it wise for Louis to secure the support of one of his sons and that at least this son and Charles could work together and resist the malcontents if the others were unwilling to preserve harmony after their father's death.

Since the matter was urgent, they discussed it day and night until they came to the unanimous decision that an alliance be made with Lothair if he proved trustworthy. For Lothair, as I said earlier,[32] had sworn at one time before father, mother, and Charles that the emperor should give Charles whichever part of the kingdom he wished. Lothair promised that he would agree to the decision and protect Charles against all enemies as long as he lived. This oath encouraged Charles's partisans to choose emissaries and send them to Lothair in Italy. They promised that all his crimes against Louis would be forgiven and the whole kingdom except Bavaria divided between himself and Charles, if he would enforce his father's will regarding Charles from now on. Since this arrangement seemed acceptable to Lothair and his men, both parties swore to their good intentions and pledged to carry them out.

[7]

Accordingly they all came to Worms where an assembly had
30 May been convoked.[33] At this assembly Lothair humbly fell at his father's
839 feet in the presence of all and said: "I know, Lord Father, that I have sinned before God and you.[34] I don't ask for your kingdom but for your forgiveness and that I may be worthy of your grace." Louis behaved like a pious and mild father. He forgave the petitioner for what he had done and granted him his grace, if he would never again injure Charles or the kingdom against his father's will. Louis kindly raised and kissed him and thanked God for the lost son with whom he had been reconciled. Then they went to dine together, postponing until the next day talks on the other matters which they had sworn

they would discuss. On the next day they began their conference. As he wished to carry out what his emissaries had sworn, the father said: "Look, my son, as I promised, the whole kingdom is lying before you; divide it as you please. If you divide it, Charles shall have the choice of the parts. But if we divide it, the choice will be yours."

For three days Lothair tried to divide the empire but was not at all able to do so. He then sent Joseph and Richard to his father asking that Louis and his men should divide the kingdom and he be granted the choice of the parts. They assured the king's party by the oath they had already sworn that the only reason Lothair would not divide the kingdom was his ignorance of the land. Therefore, the father with his men divided the whole kingdom, except Bavaria, as equally as possible. Lothair and his men chose the part east of the Meuse and received it immediately. He agreed that the western part should be conferred on Charles and announced with his father before the whole people that they wished things to be settled in this way. Then the father reconciled the brothers as best he could, fervently imploring them to love each other.[35] He also begged them with many exhortations to protect one another, professing that nothing in the world meant more to him.

July 839 When all this was settled, the father graciously and peaceably sent Lothair to Italy, enriched by the grace of his forbearance and the gift of the kingdom. He reminded Lothair how often he had broken the oaths he had so frequently sworn to his father, and how often Louis had forgiven him his offenses. He warned Lothair, entreating him fervently not to break those agreements which they had recently made and which he had confirmed as his will before all the people.

[8]

At the same time the father received the news that Pepin had died.[36] There were some who waited to see what Louis would order to be done about his grandsons' share in the kingdom. But others seized Pepin's eldest son, also named Pepin, and set up an unlawful regime. On this account the emperor settled his business with Lothair as reported and then went with Charles and his mother by way of Chalon[37] to Clermont. There he graciously received those who waited for him. Since he had once given Aquitaine to Charles, he advised and even commanded the Aquitanians to do homage to his son. They all did homage and swore fealty to him. After this the emperor sought for ways to curb the usurpers.

At this very time Louis, as usual, came out of Bavaria and invaded Alamannia, accompanied by a number of Thuringians and Saxons whom he had stirred up. This event called the emperor from Aquitaine, and he left Charles with his mother at Poitiers, celebrated holy Easter at Aachen, and then continued his march to Thuringia.[38] After his son Louis had been driven back the emperor forced him to buy his way through the land of the Slavs and to flee to Bavaria. When this conflict was settled the emperor convoked an assembly at the city of Worms, for July 1, to which he summoned his son Lothair from Italy to talk about Louis with himself and other trusted men.

20 June 840 When things had come to this pass, with Lothair in Italy, Louis on the far side of the Rhine, and Charles in Aquitaine, Emperor Louis, their father, died on an island near Mainz on June 20. His brother Drogo, bishop and archchaplain, buried him with due honors at St. Arnulf's in his city of Metz in the presence of bishops, abbots, and counts. Louis lived for sixty-four years, ruled Aquitaine for thirty-seven years, and held the imperial title for twenty-seven years and six months.[39]

[BOOK II: JUNE 840–JUNE 841]

I have laid bare the roots of your conflicts as far as time and talent permitted. Now every reader who wants to know why Lothair resolved to pursue you and your brother after your father's death may judge for himself, connect the threads, and see whether Lothair acted lawfully. I shall now try to show, as far as memory and talent serve me, how vigorously he carried out his plans. But I ask you to consider the difficulties which arose for my humble self from this trouble and entreat you to overlook any omissions in this work of mine.

[1]

June 840 **When** Lothair heard of his father's death, he immediately sent **emissaries** everywhere, especially all over Francia. They proclaimed that he was coming into the empire which had once been given to him. He promised that he wished to grant everyone the benefices which his father had given and that he would make them even bigger. He gave orders also that oaths of fealty should be exacted from those who were still uncommitted. In addition, he ordered that all should join him as fast as they could; those who were unwilling to appear he threatened with death. He himself advanced slowly since he wanted to find out how the wind was blowing before he crossed the Alps.

Presently, men from everywhere joined him, driven by either

greed or fear. When Lothair saw that, his prospects and power made him bold, and he began to scheme about how he might best seize the whole empire. He decided to send an army against Louis first, since this would not take him out of his way, and to devote himself with all his might to the destruction of Louis' forces. In the meantime he was shrewd enough to send emissaries to Charles in Aquitaine, informing Charles that he was friendly toward him, as their father had demanded and as was proper for one to feel toward a godchild. But he begged him to spare their nephew, Pepin's son, until he had spoken to him. Having settled this, he turned to the city of Worms.

At that time Louis had left part of his army as a garrison in Worms and had gone to meet the Saxons who were in revolt. But after a small skirmish Lothair put the defenders to flight and, crossing the Rhine with his entire army, headed for Frankfurt. Here they suddenly came upon each other, Lothair approaching from one side and Louis from the other.[1] After peace had been arranged for the night, they pitched their camps, not exactly in brotherly love, Lothair right at the place where they had met and Louis at the point where the Main flows into the Rhine. Since Louis' opposition was vigorous and his brother was not sure that he could make him give in without a fight, Lothair thought it might be easier to get the better of Charles first. He therefore put off battle with the understanding that he would meet Louis again at the same place on November 11. Unless an agreement could be negotiated beforehand, they would settle by force what each of them was going to get. And so, giving up his initial schemes, Lothair set out to subdue Charles.

[2]

July 840 At this time Charles had come to Bourges to the assembly which Pepin was going to attend, as his men had sworn. When Charles had learned what he could from everybody, he selected as ambassadors Nithard and Adalgar[2] and dispatched them as speedily as possible to Lothair, enjoining and entreating him to remember the oaths they had sworn each other and to preserve what their father had arranged between them. He also reminded him that he, Charles, was his brother and godson. Lothair should have what belonged to him; but should also permit Charles to have without a fight what his father had granted him with Lothair's consent. Charles pledged, if Lothair should do this, that he was willing to be loyal and subject to him, as it is proper to behave toward one's first-born brother. Besides, Charles promised that he would wholeheartedly forgive whatever Lothair had done to him up to that time. He implored him to stop stirring up his people and disturbing the kingdom committed to him by God, and sent word to Lothair that peace and harmony should rule everywhere. This peace he and his people considered most desirable and were willing to preserve. If Lothair did not believe this, Charles promised to give him whatever assurances he wanted.

Lothair pretended to receive this message kindly, but permitted the emissaries to return with greetings only and the reply that he would answer fully through his own envoys. Moreover, he deprived Charles's emissaries of the benefices which his father had given them because they did not want to break their fealty and join him. In this way he unwittingly betrayed his designs against his brother. Meanwhile, all men living between the Meuse and the Seine sent to Charles, asked him to get there before the land was taken over by Lothair, and promised to wait for his arrival. Charles quickly set out
Aug. with only a few men and marched from Aquitaine to Quierzy.[3] There
840 he received graciously those who had come from the Charbonnière and the land on this side of it.[4] Beyond the Charbonnière, however, Herefrid, Gislebert, Bovo, and the others duped by Odulf disregarded their sworn fealty and defected.[5]

[3]

At the same time a messenger coming from Aquitaine announced that Pepin and his partisans wanted to attack Charles's mother. Charles left the Franks at Quierzy by themselves, but ordered them to move his way if his brother should attempt to subdue them before his return. In addition, he dispatched Hugo, Adalhard, Gerard, and Hegilo to Lothair.[6] Repeating everything that he had said before, he entreated Lothair again for God's sake not to subvert Charles's men and further to whittle away at the kingdom which God and his father had given to Charles with Lothair's consent. After making this appeal to Lothair he rushed into Aquitaine, fell upon Pepin and his men, and put them to flight.

Meanwhile, Lothair was returning from the confrontation with
Oct. Louis and being joined by every man on this side of the Charbon-
840 nière. He thought it best to cross the Meuse and advance as far as the Seine.[7] On his way there Hilduin, abbot of St.-Denis, and Gerard,

count of the city of Paris, came and met him. They had broken their fealty and defected from Charles. When Pepin, son of Bernard, king of the Lombards, and others saw this treachery, like slaves they also chose to break their word and disregard their oaths rather than give up their holdings for a little while.[8] That is why these men broke faith, followed the example of those we mentioned already, and submitted to Lothair. Then Lothair became bold and crossed the Seine,[9] sending ahead, as he always did, to the inhabitants between the Seine and the Loire men who were to make them defect by threats and promises. He himself followed slowly, as usual, heading for the city of Chartres. When he learned that Theodoric and Eric were on the way with the rest who had decided to join him, he resolved to proceed as far as the Loire, putting his confidence in his great numbers. Charles returned from the pursuit in which he had dispersed Pepin and his followers, and since he had no place where he could safely leave his mother, they both hastily departed for Francia.

[4]

In the meantime Charles heard of all these defections and that Lothair was determined to hound him to the death with an immense army, while Pepin on one side and the Bretons on the other had raised arms against him. So he and his men sat down to think about all these troubles. They easily found a simple solution. Since they had nothing left but their lives and their bodies, they chose to die nobly rather than betray and abandon their king.

Nov. 840 They headed in Lothair's direction, and both sides thus approached the city of Orléans. They pitched camps at a distance of barely six Gallic miles from each other, and both parties dispatched emissaries. Charles only asked for peace and justice, but Lothair tried to think of a way he could deceive and get the better of Charles without a fight. This scheme came to nothing because of strong resistance on the other side. Then Lothair hoped that his own forces would continue to grow from day to day, and he thought he might be able to conquer his brother more easily when Charles's following had further dwindled.

But he was disappointed in the hope and refrained from battle. The condition of the truce was that Charles should be granted Aquitaine, Septimania, Provence, and ten counties between the Loire and the Seine, with the stipulation that he should be satisfied with them and remain there for the time being until they met again at Attigny on May 8.[10] Lothair promised that he was indeed willing to talk over and settle the interests of both parties by mutual consent. The leaders of Charles's party also realized that the problems at hand were more than they could handle. They feared, if it came to a battle, that they might be hard put to save the king in view of their small numbers, and all of them set great store by his talents. So they consented to the stipulations if only Lothair from now on would be as loyal a friend to Charles as a brother should be, permit him to hold peacefully the lands he had allotted to him, and in the meantime also refrain from hostilities against Louis. Otherwise they should be absolved from the oath they had sworn.

By this device they both rescued their king from danger and soon freed themselves from an oath. For those who had sworn this had not yet left the house when Lothair tried to seduce some of them from Charles and by the next day in fact he received a few defectors. He immediately sent into the lands which he had assigned to his brother, to stir up trouble so that they would not submit to Charles. Then he moved on in order to receive homage from those coming to him out of Provence and tried to think of ways to overcome Louis by force or deception.

[5]

In the meantime Charles came to the city of Orléans and gave a warm welcome to Theobald and Warin who had come to him from Burgundy with some other men. Then he turned toward Nevers to meet Bernard, whom he had ordered to come there.[11] But Bernard put off his appearance before Charles as usual, claiming he had sworn to Pepin and his men that neither of them should enter into an agreement with anybody without the other's consent. So he declared that he would go to Pepin. If he could prevail upon his men to come with him, he said this would suit him well; but if not, then he promised to take back his oath, to return to Charles within fifteen days, and to submit to his rule.

Jan. 841 For this reason Charles came again to Bourges to meet Bernard. When Bernard arrived and proved to have done nothing at all, Charles was greatly annoyed about the tricks this man had played first on his father and now on him. Fearful that he might not be able to catch him in any other way, Charles decided to make a surprise attack upon him. But Bernard saw it coming at the last minute, took to flight, and barely escaped. Charles managed to kill some of Bernard's people and left others behind wounded and half dead. Some who were not injured he captured and treated as prisoners of war. Their entire baggage he allowed to be plundered.

At this Bernard grew humble and a little later approached Charles as a contrite petitioner, declaring that he had always been true to him. He also said that recently he had wished to be loyal, had it been possible, and, in spite of the outrage done to him, was going to be unswervingly faithful in the future. And if anyone called him a liar, he promised to refute the charge by force of arms. Charles believed this and accepted Bernard as a friend, proving his good will by bestowing presents on him and his favor as well. He also told him to coax Pepin and his followers to submit to Charles as he had promised.

841 When this affair was settled, he turned to the city of Le Mans to win Lambert, Eric, and the others to his side.[12] He received them with great kindness and then at once sent to Nomenoi, duke of the Bretons, in order to find out whether or not he was willing to submit to his authority. The duke followed the advice of the majority, sent presents to Charles, and promised under oath to keep faith in the future.

When this business was out of the way and the time for the assembly to meet at Attigny[13] was approaching, Charles wondered what he and his men would have to do to act prudently and yet not violate their good faith. He therefore called together his confidential advisers, described how matters stood, which was already known to everybody, and then asked them how they believed he and his men could best extricate themselves from their predicament. He declared that he wished wholeheartedly to serve the public welfare and would not hesitate to die for it if that should be necessary.

At these words everybody's courage seemed to rise. They recalled the snares which in the days of his father Lothair had tried to set for the emperor and Charles and after their father's death, with the same relentlessness, against his brothers. Everyone remembered especially the oaths which Lothair had recently broken. They declared that they wished Charles could readily obtain full justice from Lothair, but had no reason to believe he could. Therefore, they all considered it advisable that Charles should not fail to come to the announced assembly if at all possible. Should Lothair be willing to put the public welfare ahead of his own, as he had promised, this would please everybody, and they would welcome him. But if not, then Charles should rely on the justice of his case and thus on the help of God and of his vassals and not fail to claim with all his might whatever part of the kingdom his father had given him with the consent of the vassals on both sides.

[6]

Thus, Charles ordered all his partisans in Aquitaine to follow him and his mother. Those from Burgundy and the land between the Loire and the Seine who wished to be under his authority were also *March 841* to come along. But he himself with all present set out on the aforementioned march, although it seemed difficult. Reaching the Seine, he found Guntbold, Warnar,[14] Arnulf, Gerard,[15] and all counts, abbots and bishops from the Charbonnière and this side of it. They had apparently been left there by Lothair to prevent Charles from crossing the river if he should do so without Lothair's permission. Besides, the river had flooded so that it could not be forded and those who guarded it had either smashed all the boats to bits or sunk them. Gerard had also destroyed every bridge he found. So crossing the river was not an easy matter and gave no end of trouble to those who wanted to get to the other side.

While their minds were busy with plans for dealing with all these difficulties, they learned that merchant ships had been driven from the mouth of the Seine by a violent tide and had drifted ashore near Rouen. When he arrived on the scene Charles filled twenty-eight *March 841* of the boats with armed men.[16] He got on board himself and sent messengers to announce that he was on his way and that he forgave everyone who wished to be forgiven for what he had done. To those who did not seek his pardon he announced that they should let him have the kingdom given to him by God and go live somewhere else. They would not agree to this, but when they saw the fleet approaching and recognized both Charles and the cross on which they had taken their oath, they immediately left the riverbank and took to flight.[17]

April 841 Charles was unable to pursue them because the horses delayed his crossing. He now headed for St. Denis to praise God and pray there. When he arrived, Charles found out that those whom he had put to flight had united with Arnulf, Gerard, and the rest and planned to surprise Theobald, Warin, Otbert, and the others who were on their way to Charles under orders from him.[18] So Charles continued to St.-Germain[19] to offer his prayers there. After traveling all night long, at dawn he safely met Warin with his companions where the Loing flows into the Seine.[20] He continued the march with them and reached the city of Sens.

From here he set out at night and made his way through the forest of Othe, hoping that his enemies were in this forest, as had been reported to him,[21] for he had decided to attack them wherever and however he could. And he would have done it, too, if those who were in fear of their lives had not learned that death was waiting at their doorstep. This news frightened them terribly and everyone fled wherever he could. Charles could not pursue them because his companions and horses were tired out, so he devoted Maundy Thursday to rest and on the next day proceeded to the city of Troyes.

14 April 841

[7]

While Charles was thus heavily engaged, Lothair, as I said before, bent his whole mind to subjugating Louis by deceit or force, or, preferably, destroying him altogether.[22] In this enterprise he included Bishop Otgar of Mainz and Count Adalbert of Metz, who were just the men for the job, since both of them had a mortal hatred of Louis.[23] Adalbert had by then recovered from the disease which had incapacitated him for almost a year, so he could now take part in the fratricide. His counsel was considered so valuable in those days that nobody wanted to dispute a word of it. At his suggestion Lothair assembled a countless multitude from every side and set off across the Rhine. As usual, he sent messengers ahead to try to seduce the fickle populace by threats and promises. Louis' followers feared that they might not be able to resist such an immense army. Some of them defected, going over to Lothair, and some fled, leaving Louis behind in very great difficulty. Since there was no help in sight anywhere, Louis departed with the few men he had and retreated to Bavaria.

April 841

After this defeat, Lothair believed Louis was finished. So he left Duke Adalbert, whom we mentioned earlier as count, behind to obtain the people's oath of fealty, and at all costs to prevent Louis from going to Charles. But Lothair himself prepared to march against Charles after finding out that he had crossed the Seine.[24] On his way to Aachen to celebrate Easter, Lothair quickly sent scouts ahead since he wanted to know exactly where Charles was and with whom.

April 841

[8]

Something really strange and remarkable happened to Charles on this holy eve of Easter. Neither he nor anyone else in his entourage had anything with him but their arms, horses, and the shirts on their backs. But when Charles stepped from his bath and was going to put on the same clothes he had taken off, suddenly messengers from Aquitaine were standing outside with his crown and all his royal and liturgical attire.

Who could fail to be amazed that a few men, strangers almost, had been able to carry so many talents of gold and a countless number of gems over so many stretches of land and remain unharmed while pillage threatened everywhere. What is most surprising, I believe, is that they were able to arrive at the proper place and on the proper day and hour, although not even Charles himself knew where he and his people were supposed to be. It even seemed that this could only have happened by divine favor and divine will. Charles's companions were filled with amazement and everybody was inspired with high hopes for salvation. Then Charles and his whole entourage jubilantly turned to the celebration of the feast.

When it was over he kindly received Lothair's envoys and made them dine with him. He ordered them to return the next day, promising to send his own emissaries to take care of the matter which his brother had submitted to him. Lothair's embassy wanted to know why Charles had crossed the boundaries which Lothair had set for him without permission.[25] But since the deed was done, he ordered Charles to remain there, at least for the time being, where Lothair's emissaries found him, until he was instructed whether he should come to the meeting place agreed on beforehand or to another which suited Lothair better.

Through his own emissaries Charles answered that he had gone beyond the stipulated boundaries because Lothair had gone back on all the good things which he had promised and sworn by oath. In violation of his sworn oath Lothair had stirred up several of Charles's men and put them under his own rule; he had deprived others of their lives, and, furthermore, as much as he could, he had stirred up the lands which he should have made subject to Charles. But worst of all, he had made war on his brother and forced him to seek the help of the pagans. Despite Lothair's breaches of faith, Charles declared he would come to the meeting which they had mutually arranged. If Lothair wished to look for ways to assure the common good as he had promised, this would please Charles. But if not, then Charles would wholeheartedly obey the counsels of his vassals and do the will of God for the kingdom which had been given to him by God and his father with the consent of his people.

After making all this clear to Lothair, Charles set out on his march and arrived at Attigny one day earlier than had been agreed
7 May on. But Lothair deliberately failed to appear. Instead, he sent one
841 messenger after another with various complaints and took precautions lest Charles should suddenly attack him.

[9]

May In the meantime envoys had come from Louis who announced
841 that he would help Charles if only he knew how.[26] Charles answered that help was just what he needed, thanked him for his good will, and immediately sent back the same emissaries so that they could get things moving right away. For four days and more he waited there for Lothair's arrival, but Lothair never came. Then Charles convoked an assembly and deliberated how he might act more prudently toward Lothair in the future.

Some said he should go and meet his mother since she was on her way with the Aquitanians. But the majority either advised him to march against Lothair or declared that he should at least decide on a place to wait for Lothair's arrival. They felt he should do this because if he changed his itinerary everyone would say he had run away. Such talk would only embolden Lothair and his followers. Besides, those men who had been afraid to join either party so far would pin their hopes on Lothair and flock to him everywhere. This is exactly what happened when, in spite of much objection, Charles was won over to the former view.

So he went to the city of Châlons.[27] When he had received his mother and the men of Aquitaine there, the report suddenly arrived

March 841 that Louis had fought a battle against Adalbert, duke of the Austrasians, and defeated him; that he had crossed the Rhine and was coming as fast as possible to help Charles.[28] This news spread rapidly through the whole camp, and Charles's overjoyed followers all thought they should set out to meet Louis.

When Lothair heard what was going on, he announced to his assembled men that Charles had taken flight and that he wished to pursue him as quickly as possible. By this stroke he both raised the spirits of his faithful followers and encouraged lukewarm ones to come over to his side, turning them into more solid supporters. Charles pitched camp in an inaccessible place surrounded by swamps and water, and only then learned he was being followed by Lothair. Immediately, he set out to meet him, so that there would be nothing in the way of an open battle if that was what Lothair had in mind. On hearing this Lothair set up camp and gave his worn-out horses two days of rest. Lothair and Charles kept jockeying their positions, frequently exchanging emissaries, but without being able to settle anything. All this time Louis and Charles were coming closer and closer to each other and finally they met.[29] At their meeting they discussed and deplored the unrestrained violence with which Lothair had treated them and their men, intending to deliberate the next day on what might best be done in the future.

They met at dawn and held a council at which they complained a great deal about their calamity. When both had finished the story of their sufferings at Lothair's hands, they decided unanimously to select noble, wise, and well-meaning men from the holy order of bishops and the laity. They would send Lothair word by these men of what their father had arranged between them and what they had suffered from him after their father's death. Moreover, they would implore Lothair to remember Almighty God and to grant peace to his brothers and to the entire church of God. He was to concede to each what rightly belonged to him according to the expressed will of father and brother. They also were to offer Lothair whatever they had in their entire army except horses and arms, so that he would yield to their rightful demands. If he would heed these warnings and requests, they would be pleased. But if not, Charles and Louis declared, they could most certainly hope for divine help, as long as they looked only for a fair settlement and made this offer to their brother in all humility. This plan seemed reasonable. Indeed it was so, and they immediately carried it out.

[10]

But Lothair considered the offer useless and rejected it.[30] He sent word by his own envoys that he wanted nothing but a battle, and he immediately set out to meet Pepin, who was on his way to Lothair from Aquitaine. Louis and his men quickly learned of this and were deeply worried, for they were very worn out by the length of their march as well as by battles, many troubles, and, above all, the lack of horses. Despite their condition they feared that they might leave an unworthy memory to their descendants if a brother failed to give aid to his brother. To avoid this disgrace they preferred to submit to every misery and even, if necessary, to death rather than lose their reputation for invincibility. This greatness of soul enabled them to overcome their sadness and to cheer each other up, and they joyfully set out in great haste to reach Lothair as soon as possible.

21 June 841 Near the city of Auxerre both armies met each other unexpectedly. Lothair immediately moved a short distance out of his camp, with his armed men, fearing that his brothers might plan to attack him at any minute. Since his brothers realized what he was up to, they left some men behind to make camp, and, taking along others who were armed, immediately marched against Lothair. They exchanged emissaries and arranged a truce for the night. The camps were at a distance of about three Gallic miles from each other. A small swamp and a forest lay between them, which made it hard to get back and forth.

22 June 841 At daybreak Louis and Charles sent word to Lothair that they were very unhappy with his rejection of peace and insistence on battle. But since he wanted it that way, that was the way it would be. If there had to be a battle, though, there should at least be no treachery. They first ought to invoke God with fasting and prayers. Then, they promised to give Lothair a place to cross the swamp if he wanted to face them on their side of it. They wanted nothing to prevent the confrontation of the armies and to fight without any deceitful tricks. They ordered their emissaries to swear their good faith if Lothair accepted the proposal, and if not, they asked him to permit them to cross over to his side and their emissaries would swear to that. As usual, Lothair promised to answer by his own envoys. But when the emissaries had returned, Lothair immediately set out, heading for Fontenoy to set up camp there.[31] The brothers rushed after Lothair on the same day, passed him, and set up their camp near the village *June 841* of Thury. On the next day the armies, ready for battle, moved out for some distance from their camps.

Louis and Charles sent word ahead to Lothair, telling him to remember that they were brothers, to leave the Church of God and the whole Christian people in peace, to concede to his brothers the lands given to them by their father with Lothair's consent, and to keep the lands his father had left him, not because he deserved them, but out of mercy alone. They offered him as a present whatever could be found in their whole army with the exception of arms and horses. If that did not please him, they would each grant him a portion of the kingdom, one as far as the Charbonnière, the other as far as the Rhine. If he were to reject this, they would divide all of Francia into equal parts, and whichever part he wished should be under his rule.

To this Lothair answered, as usual, that he would communicate by his own envoys whatever was acceptable to him. He promptly sent Drogo, Hugo, and Hegibert, informing Louis and Charles that they had never made such proposals to him before and that he wanted time to consider them.[32] The fact of the matter was that Lothair was manufacturing delays because Pepin had not yet arrived. But he had Ricuin, Hirmenald, and Frederic swear that he requested this armistice only because he wanted to seek the common good of both his brothers and the whole people, as justice among brothers and Christian people demanded.[33]

June 841 Louis and Charles believed this oath. When both sides had sworn peace, for this day and the next, and to the second hour[34] of the third, which fell on June 25, they returned to the camp to celebrate St. John's Mass on the next day. Lothair secured Pepin's support on that very day and then sent word to his brothers that they should consider how he might discharge the august office of emperor, since they knew that this title had been solemnly conferred on him; furthermore, that he was happy to look after the interests of them both. Lothair's emissaries were asked whether Lothair was willing to accept the proposals submitted by Louis and Charles or whether he had given them a definitive declaration of his own. But the emissaries answered they had not been told what to say about that.

24 June Any hope for justice and peace from Lothair seemed to have
841 vanished. So Charles and Louis told him, if he could think of nothing better, he should either accept one of their proposals or know that they would put the issue in the hands of God on the next day, June 25, as I said before, at the second hour, a course of action which Lothair had forced on them against their will. Lothair arrogantly rejected their proposal, as he always did, answering them that they
18 Oct. would see what he was going to do. While I was writing this at the
841 Loire[35] near St. Cloud, an eclipse of the sun occurred in Scorpio in the first hour[36] of October 18, a Tuesday. After breaking off these
25 June negotiations Louis and Charles rose at dawn, occupied the peak of a
841 mountain near Lothair's camp with about one-third of their army, and waited for Lothair's arrival and the striking of the second hour, as their men had sworn. When both had come, they fought a violent battle on the brook of the Burgundians.[37] Louis and Lothair were engaged in heavy fighting in a place called Brittas; there Lothair was overcome and fled. The troops which Charles confronted at the place commonly called Fagit immediately took flight. But the part of our army which attacked Adalhard and the others at Solemnat, and to which I gave vigorous assistance with God's help, fought bitterly.[38] There the fight was a draw, but in the end all of Lothair's party fled.[39]

With the end of the first battle that Lothair fought this book may end.

[BOOK III: JUNE 841–MARCH 842]

Although I am ashamed to hear of anything bad in my people, it especially pains me when I have to report it. Therefore, I was inclined, without deliberately ignoring my orders, to consider my work complete with the longed-for end of the second book. But I have agreed to add a third book of the events in which I myself took part, lest some misguided man dare to record them inaccurately.

[1]

After the battle had been vigorously fought to the end, as I said before, Louis and Charles deliberated on the battlefield what should be done about their scattered opponents. Some were filled with rage and advised pursuing the enemy, but some, especially the kings themselves, took mercy on their brother and the people. As always, Charles and Louis wished piously that their opponents would turn away from evil greed and with God's grace join them and be of one mind in true justice, now that they had been smitten with God's judgment in this defeat. They suggested things be left to the mercy of Almighty God. Since everyone agreed to this they ceased fighting and plundering and returned to camp about the middle of the day to talk over what they ought to do next.

The booty and the slaughter were immense and truly astonishing, but the mercy of the kings and of the entire people was equally re-

26 June 841 markable. For several reasons they decided to celebrate Sunday in the same place. After Mass on Sunday they buried friends and enemies alike, the faithful and the faithless, and with equal sincerity comforted as best they could those felled by blows and only half-alive. They also sent messengers after the foes who had fled the scene and offered them pardon of all offences if they wished to return in good faith.

After that the kings and their followers in their grief over their brother and the Christian people began to ask the bishops what they should do in this situation. So all the bishops, acting as one man, came together to hold council. A public assembly found that Louis and Charles had fought for justice and equity alone, as God's judgment had made clear. For this reason every one of them, he who commanded as well as he who obeyed, was to consider himself in this conflict an instrument of God, free from responsibility. But whoever knew that he had either counseled or committed anything on this campaign from wrath or hatred or vainglory or any passion, was to confess secretly his secret sin and be judged according to the measure of his guilt. To honor and praise God's display of justice, a three-day fast was arranged and celebrated gladly and solemnly. This was done for the remission of the sins of their deceased brothers (for they knew they were not faultless and had committed many sins, willingly and unwillingly), so that with God's help they might be freed from them; and, finally, so that the Lord, Who up to that moment had been their succor and protector[1] in a just cause, would forever remain so.

[2]

30 June 841 When this was taken care of, Louis decided to march to the Rhine. Charles, on the other hand, for various reasons, but mainly to attempt to overcome Pepin, thought it best to move into Aquitaine. Bernard, duke of Septimania, although no further from the place of the above battle than about three leagues, had not helped either party. But as soon as he learned that Charles had won a victory, he sent his son William to the king with orders to do homage to Charles if the latter were willing to give him the benefices which William held in Burgundy. Bernard also boasted that he was willing and able to make Pepin and his people submit to Charles by the most advantageous of treaties. Charles received this embassy kindly and did as Bernard asked, reminding him that he should make good his promise to win over Pepin and his people.

Since everywhere troubles seemed to have vanished and all had high hopes, Louis proceeded with his men to the Rhine. Charles and his mother headed for the Loire. But the public welfare was unduly neglected. Once separated, everyone carelessly wandered off wherever he felt like going. When Pepin heard of this, he put off the alliance with Charles in which he had been interested a moment earlier. Bernard, it is true, came to Charles, but did not agree to do homage. But some men deserted Pepin and the only advantage Charles got from the whole campaign was the homage of these defectors.[2]

In the meantime Adalhard and the others whom Charles had sent to the Franks to learn if they were willing to return to him, came to Quierzy, where the Franks had asked him to send envoys. They found only a few men there, however. These men said they would not hesitate to join Charles on the spot if he were present; since he was not, they claimed not to know if he were even alive. For Lothair's partisans had spread the rumor that Charles died in battle and that Louis was wounded and had fled. It was, therefore, not advisable, they said, in such uncertain circumstances, to make a treaty with anybody. But Guntbold and the rest who had joined forces made moves to attack Charles's emissaries and would actually have done so if they had dared. For this reason Adalhard and the others sent to Charles, asking him to try to come and help them as fast as he could and to see if he could find out whether the Franks were really willing to join him, as they maintained. The emissaries themselves, however, went to the city of Paris to wait for Charles's arrival.

Aug. 841 As soon as Charles received their news, he at once set out for this region. When he reached the Seine, he met Adalhard with the others at Épône.[3] Charles was worried about the impending conference which he had arranged with his brother at Langres for September 1. But he still thought it best to reach Langres by a fast march through Beauvais, Compiègne, Soissons, and further on, by Reims and Châlons. His aim was to keep the appointment with his brother and yet to give any Frank who wished to do so the chance to join his side. But the Franks looked with contempt at the small number of his followers, as the Aquitanians had done, and under various pretexts postponed submission to him for the time being.

Seeing their reaction, Charles quickened his march. When he reached the city of Soissons,[4] the monks of St.-Médard came out to meet him and begged him to translate the bodies of Sts. Médard,

Sebastian, Gregory, Tiburtius, Peter and Marcellinus, Maria, Martha, Audifax and Abacuc, Honesimus, Maresma, and Leocadia into the basilica where they now rest and which had then been partly constructed. He agreed to that, remained at Soissons, and, as they had requested, translated the bodies of the saints on his own shoulders with all due veneration. By a solemn charter he added the village of Berny to the estates of this church.[5]

After taking care of this, he proceeded to Reims.[6] When he got there he was informed that Louis was unable to come to the meeting they had arranged at Langres because Lothair threatened his kingdom with a hostile force. Also his uncle Hugo and Gislebert, count of the Maasgau, sent word that they would join Charles with other men if he should enter their territory.[7]

[3]

1 Sept. 841 So Charles marched toward St.-Quentin both to help his brother and to receive these men if they really wanted to join him. There he met Hugo, who had let Charles know he was coming. From St.-Quentin, Charles headed for the area of Maastricht. As soon as Lothair heard what Charles was up to, he broke off his pursuit of Louis, which he had only just decided on anyway. Lothair then set out from Worms to the assembly which had been convoked at Thionville, and thought about how he might attack Charles.

When Charles heard of this at Wasseiges, he sent Hugo and Adalhard to coax Gislebert and the others over to his side.[8] He also sent Rabano to Louis, letting him know that Charles had come to help him;[9] that Lothair, on hearing this, had stopped pursuing Louis and was going to attack Charles with all his troops. Charles begged and pleaded with Louis to do all he could to help him at once, as he had in the past. He also sent the venerable Bishop Emmon[10] to Lothair with the standard orders to beg Lothair in all humility to remember that Charles was his brother and godson; to remember what their father had arranged between them, which Lothair and his men had sworn to preserve, and also to remember that only recently divine judgment had made it clear which side God was on. If he would rather forget these things, he should at least not persecute the Holy Church of God any more, have mercy on the poor, the widows, and the orphans, and stop attacking the kingdom given to Charles by his father with Lothair's consent. Above all, Lothair should not compel Christian people to face each other again in a mutual slaughter. After making his position clear to Lothair, Charles went to the city of Paris to wait for the arrival of his brother Louis and his other vassals whom he had summoned.

When Lothair heard what Charles was doing, he headed for the same city, because he had with him a considerable force of Saxons, Austrasians, and Alamanni. With every confidence in their support he came to St.-Denis. He found there about twenty ships; in addition, as usual in September, the Seine was shallow and easy to ford. In view of this Lothair and his men boasted that it was a simple matter for them to come across and pretended that they were eager to do just that.

So Charles ordered some men to guard Paris and Meulan,[11] and others to take up positions wherever he knew there were fords or ferries. He himself pitched camp in a central position, across from St.-
Oct. Denis near St.-Cloud so he could if necessary prevent Lothair from
841 crossing or help his men if Lothair should plan to attack them anywhere.[12] To make it easy to learn where help was needed, he arranged signs and guards at critical points, as is usually done on the coast.[13] Besides, strange to tell, while the sky was clear and, as far as we knew, no rain had then fallen for two months, the Seine suddenly began to rise and of its own accord made all the fords impassable.

When this was the way things turned out, and Lothair saw that he was prevented from crossing anywhere, he sent word to Charles that he was ready to make peace with him if Charles would give up his sworn alliance with his brother Louis. Lothair said he would withdraw from the alliance with Pepin, which had also been confirmed by oaths. Charles should have the land west of the Seine except Aquitaine and Septimania and they should be united in eternal peace. The truth was that Lothair believed this ruse might make it easier for him to trick them both and seize the whole empire.

But Charles answered him that he was unwilling to break the treaty which he had made with his brother out of necessity. Furthermore, he added, it seemed not a bit fair to him that he should surrender to Lothair the kingdom from the Meuse to the Seine which his father had given him, especially, since so many of the nobility in these areas now supported him. It was quite improper that these nobles should be deceived about his loyalty to them. Since winter was not far off, Charles proposed that each, if he so desired, should keep the benefices which their father had given them. But in the spring, unless they had reached an agreement by old arrangements or new ones, they all should meet, either with a few men or their entire following, and decide by force of arms what each could rightfully claim. Lothair rejected this proposal as usual and turned from St.-Denis to Sens to meet Pepin, who was coming to him from Aquitaine. Charles, on the other hand, looked for ways to unite with Louis to gain support.

[4]

Oct. 841 In the meantime Charles was informed that his sister Hildegard[14] had taken one of his men, Adalgar, prisoner and was holding him in captivity with her in the city of Laon.[15] This inspired Charles to select men who were right for the task and, though it was late in the day,[16] to rush at once to Laon. The city was about thirty leagues away. He rode all night, in spite of the severe cold, and about the third hour of the day his sister and the inhabitants of Laon suddenly learned that Charles was there with a tremendous force and the entire city about to be surrounded by armed men.[17] Terrified by this news and realizing that they could not hope to escape or defend the walls, they sought a truce for the night, surrendered Adalgar on the spot, and promised meekly to hand over the city without a fight the next day.

While these negotiations were going on, the soldiers, gravely annoyed with the delay of their business and angered because of the exhausting struggles of the night before, began to converge on the town to destroy it. No doubt the place would have been immediately given over to flames and plunder had not Charles himself, moved by compassion for the churches of God as well as for his sister and the Christian people, made great efforts to calm the soldiers down with threats and flattery. After persuading them to give up, he granted his sister's request and withdrew from her city to Samoussy.[18] On the next day Hildegard indeed did homage to him, as she had vowed, and restored the city unharmed and without a fight to his power. Charles received his sister kindly, forgiving her everything she had formerly done against him. He spoke to her with many tender words and graciously promised her all the kindness a brother owes his sister if in the future she would be willing to side with him. Then he let her go wherever she wished. He imposed his rule on the city and having settled these affairs returned to his men, whom he had left near Paris.[19]

Nov./Dec. 841 After receiving Pepin at Sens Lothair was undecided about what to do. Charles had taken part of his army across the Seine and sent it into the forest which is commonly called La Perche.[20] Since Lothair feared that they might interfere with him or his men, he decided to attack them first. By doing so he hoped he could destroy them with ease, frighten the rest into submission, and above all bring Nomenoi, duke of the Bretons, under his control. But Lothair tried to carry out these designs in vain, for every one of them was frustrated. Charles's whole army escaped safely from him, nor did he attract any of Charles's followers to his side; and Nomenoi arrogantly rejected everything that Lothair suggested to him. This was how things stood when Lothair suddenly received news that Louis and Charles, each with an immense army, were seeking to join forces.[21] Seeing himself surrounded by troubles on all sides, Lothair began to withdraw from Tours, after a long and useless diversion, and eventually arrived tired and with worn-out troops in Francia. Pepin now regretted that he had joined Lothair and withdrew to Aquitaine.

Meanwhile, when Charles heard that Bishop Otgar of Mainz and *Feb. 842* others were keeping his brother Louis from crossing the Rhine, he quickly went into Alsace by way of Toul, entering at Saverne. At news of this Otgar and those with him relinquished the bank of the Rhine and retreated, while everybody fled swiftly wherever he could.

[5]

14 Feb. 842 Thus, on the fourteenth of February Louis and Charles met in the city which at one time was called Argentaria but is now commonly called Strasbourg. There they swore the oaths which are recorded below; Louis in the Romance language and Charles in the German.[22] Before the oath one addressed the assembled people in German and the other in Romance. Louis, being the elder spoke first, in this manner:

"You know how often after our father's death Lothair has assaulted my brother and me and has tried to wipe us out. Since neither brotherhood, nor Christian faith, nor any other argument could make for peace with justice among us, we were compelled in the end to submit the matter to the judgment of Almighty God, prepared to be content with what God decided was due to each of us. In this contest, as you know, we had the victory by the mercy of God. Lothair was defeated and fled with his men wherever he could escape. But afterwards, moved by brotherly love and compassion for our Christian people, we did not want to pursue and annihilate our opponents. As before, we asked them only that in the future justice be done to each.

"Yet after all this, Lothair is still not content with the divine judgment and does not stop persecuting my brother and me with armed might. Moreover, he is also ruining our people by fire, plunder, and slaughter. Therefore, we have come together here, driven by dire necessity. And since we believe you doubt that our brotherly love is strong and that our loyalty will last, we have both decided to swear an oath before your eyes.

"We are not doing this out of wicked greed but, if God gives us peace with your help, to safeguard the general welfare. Should I dare, however, which God forbid, to violate the oath that I am going to swear to my brother, I release each of you from his obedience and the oath he has sworn to me."

When Charles had spoken the same words in the Romance language, Louis as the elder first swore to uphold the following in the future:

"For the love of God and for our Christian people's salvation and our own, from this day on, as far as God grants knowledge and power to me, I shall treat my brother with regard to aid and everything else as a man should rightfully treat his brother, on condition that he do the same to me. And I shall not enter into any dealings with Lothair which might with my consent injure this my brother Charles."

When Louis had concluded, Charles swore in the German language by the same words as follows:

"For the love of God and for the Christian people's and our salvation, from this day on, as far as God grants me knowledge and power, I shall treat my brother as a man rightfully should treat his brother, on condition that he do the same to me; and I shall not enter into anything with Lothair that might with my consent injure Louis."

The oath, however, which the followers of the two brothers swore, each in their own language, went like this in Romance:

"If Louis keeps the oath which he swore to his brother Charles, and my Lord Charles does not keep it on his part, and if I am unable to restrain him, I shall not give him any aid against Louis nor will anyone whom I can keep from doing so."

In the German language it went like this:

"If Charles keeps the oath which he swore to his brother Louis, and my Lord Louis breaks the oath he swore to him, and if I am unable to restrain him, I shall not give him any aid against Charles nor will anyone whom I can keep from doing so."

When this was done, Louis went down the Rhine by way of Speyer to Worms, whereas Charles took the route by Wissembourg along the Vosges.[23]

The summer during which the aforementioned battle was fought was extremely cold, and all produce of the field was gathered very late. But fall and winter took their natural course. On the very day on which Louis and Charles and the nobles of the people concluded their treaty a great deal of snow fell, followed by a severe cold spell. A comet appeared in the months of December, January, and February until the time of the conference at Strasbourg, ascended through Pisces at the center, and disappeared after the end of this meeting between the constellation which is called Lyra by some and Andromeda by others and the darker Arcturus. After these brief comments on the progress of the seasons and of a star let us return to the course of our history.

When they arrived at Worms, they selected emissaries and im-
Feb. mediately sent them to Lothair and into Saxony. They decided to wait
842 between Worms and Mainz for their arrival and that of Carloman.[24]

[6]

Here it may not be out of place, since it is a joyous matter and one deserving mention, to say something about the character of these kings and the harmony which prevailed between them.

They were both of medium height, handsome and graceful, and expert in every kind of exercise. Both were bold and generous as well as prudent and well spoken. But every noble quality mentioned was surpassed by the sacred and venerable peace among the brothers. Almost all their meals they took together, and anything of value they possessed they gave each other in great kindness. They ate and slept in the same house. They dealt with public as well as private matters in the same spirit. Neither demanded anything but what he considered useful and agreeable to the other.

For exercise they arranged frequent games in the following way. People would get together in a place suitable for a show and with the whole crowd standing on either side, Saxons, Gascons, Austrasians, and Bretons in teams of equal numbers first rushed forth from both sides and raced at full speed against each other as if they were going to attack.[25] Then one side would turn back, pretending that they wished to escape from their pursuers to their companions under the protection of their shields. But then they would turn round again and try to pursue those from whom they had been fleeing until finally both kings and all the young men with immense clamor rushed forward, swinging their lances and spurring on their horses, pursuing by turns whoever took flight. It was a show worth seeing because of its excellent execution and discipline; not one in such a large crowd and among such different peoples dared to hurt or abuse another, as often happens even when the opponents are few and familiar to each other.

[7]

While this was going on, Carloman joined his father at Mainz[26] with an immense army of Bavarians and Alamanni. Bardo, who had been sent to Saxony, also came there and reported that the Saxons had rejected Lothair's demands and were happy to do whatever Louis and Charles told them.[27] Lothair had been foolish enough to ignore the envoys that had been sent to him.[28] This exasperated Louis and Charles as well as the entire army and they decided to move against him.

7 March So they started after Lothair on March 17, Charles by the difficult
842 route across the Vosges, Louis both on land and on the Rhine by way
of Bingen, and Carloman by way of Einrichi, and they arrived at
Koblenz[29] about the sixth hour of the next day.[30] First they went to
8 March St. Castor's for prayer and heard Mass; then the kings in full armor
842 boarded ship and quickly crossed the Moselle. Seeing this, Bishop
Otgar of Mainz, Count Hatto, Heriold, and everyone Lothair had left there to prevent Louis and Charles from crossing, were seized by fear, relinquished the riverbank, and took to flight.[31] When Lothair at Sinzig learned that his brothers had crossed the Moselle, he fled at once from his kingdom and capital and did not stop until he had reached the bank of the Rhône, accompanied only by the few men who had decided to follow him and leaving everything else behind.[32]

Where Lothair ended his second battle, the third book may end.

[Book IV: March 842–March 843]

Not only would I like to rest from the labor of this history, as I said already,[1] but my mind, filled as it is with all sorts of complaints, tries sorrowfully and unceasingly to withdraw from all public life. But since fortune has tied me first to one event and then to another and unhappily whirls me in violent storms, I cannot imagine how I may enter my haven. In the meantime, though, when I find some leisure, is there any harm in trying, as I have been instructed, to commemorate the deeds of our princes and nobles by writing them down? So I shall take up the fourth book of this history and, if I cannot be useful to posterity in other ways, I will at least by this effort disperse the haze of error about these matters for those who come after us.

[1]

March 842 As soon as Louis and Charles were sure Lothair had left his kingdom, they headed for the palace at Aachen, which at that time was the capital of Francia, and on the day after their arrival considered what might best be done about their brother's abandoned people and kingdom. It seemed to them that first they should submit the matter to bishops and priests, of whom a large number were present. By their counsel, as though by divine command, it would be discovered how these troubles got started in the first place. Since this seemed good advice and rightly so, the matter was put into their hands.

These men examined Lothair's deeds from the very beginning;

how he had driven his father from the kingdom; how often by his greed he had caused Christian people to break their oaths; how often he himself had broken his promises to his father and brothers; how often he had tried after the death of their father to disinherit and destroy his brothers; how much murder, adultery, destruction by fire, and crime of every sort the entire Church had suffered because of his most execrable greed. In addition, they charged that he did not have the knowledge to govern the commonwealth nor could they find a trace of good will in his conduct of the government. In view of this Lothair deserved that the just judgment of Almighty God drove him first from the battlefield and then from his own kingdom.

So it was their unanimous opinion that divine vengeance had cast him out because of his wanton negligence and delivered the kingdom into the hands of his brothers as the better men so that they would rule it in justice. But they did not give the brothers permission to receive it until they had asked them in public whether they intended to rule the kingdom along the same lines as their exiled brother had, or in accordance with the will of God. When Louis and Charles answered that they were willing to govern and rule themselves and their people according to His will, as much as God granted them knowledge and power, the bishops and priests declared: "We ask, admonish, and order you on divine authority to take over this kingdom and to rule it in accordance with the will of God."

Then each of the brothers chose twelve men for this task, of whom I was one; and what seemed to these twelve a fair partition of the kingdom between the brothers satisfied them both. In this division, fertility or equal size of the lands was not considered so much as the fact that they were adjacent and fitted into the territory already held by one or the other of the brothers. Louis received all of Francia and the rest[2] . . . but Charles . . . .[3]

[2]

After this had come to pass each brother received homage from the people who were now under his rule as well as an oath that from now on they would be loyal to him. Charles crossed the Meuse to order the affairs of his kingdom, but Louis went to Cologne on account of the Saxons.

Since I consider the affairs of the Saxons to be very important, I believe that they should not be omitted. Emperor Charles, deservedly called the Great by all peoples, converted the Saxons by much effort, as is known to everyone in Europe. He won them over from the vain adoration of idols to the true Christian religion of God. From the beginning the Saxons have often proved themselves by many examples to be both noble and extremely warlike. This whole tribe is divided into three classes. There are those among them who are called *edhilingi* in their language; those who are called *frilingi*, and those who are called *lazzi;* this is in the Latin language nobles, freemen, and serfs.[4] In the conflict between Lothair and his brothers the nobility among the Saxons was divided into two factions, one following Lothair, the other Louis.

Since this was how matters stood, and Lothair saw that after his brother's victory the people who had been with him wished to defect, he was compelled by various needs to turn for help anywhere he could get it. So he distributed public property for private use; he gave freedom to some and promised it to others after victory; he also sent into Saxony to the immense number of *frilingi* and *lazzi*, promising them, if they should side with him, that he would let them have the same law in the future which their ancestors had observed when they were still worshipping idols. Since they desired this law above all, they adopted a new name, "Stellinga," rallied to a large host, almost drove their lords from the kingdom, and each lived as their ancestors had done according to the law of his choice. But Lothair had also called in the Norsemen to help him, had put some Christians under their lordship, and permitted them to plunder others.[5]

April 842 Louis thus feared that Norsemen and Slavs might unite with the Saxons who called themselves Stellinga, because they are neighbors, and that they might invade the kingdom to revenge themselves and root out the Christian religion in the area. It was especially for this reason, as we noted above, that he went to . . .[6] and at the same time did all he could to avert other hazards to his kingdom lest this most horrible disaster befall the Holy Church of God. When he *May 842* had seen to this matter they went to Verdun, Louis by Thionville and Charles by Reims, to consult on what should be done next.

[3]

At the same time the Norsemen laid waste Quentovic,[7] then crossed the sea from there and ravaged Hamwig[8] and Northunnwig,[9] too. But Lothair, when he had withdrawn as far as the bank of the

Rhône, took up residence there and made use of the shipping on this river. By doing so he drew as many men as he could from all sides for his support. Still, he dispatched an envoy to his brothers, informing them that he was willing, if only he knew how, to send his magnates to them to negotiate about peace.

He received the answer that he should send anyone he wished and that he could easily find out where to come. They themselves, however, continued their march by Chalon[10] to Troyes. When they had come as far as Mellecey,[11] Joseph, Eberhard, Egbert,[12] and others of Lothair's party came to them and declared that Lothair knew he had wronged God and his brothers[13] and that he did not wish the conflict between them and the Christian people to last any longer. If they wished, they might add a little to the third part of the kingdom because of the imperial title which their father had granted to him and because of the dignity of the empire which their grandfather had added to the kingdom of the Franks. But if they did not wish to do that, they should only concede to him the third part of the whole kingdom with the exception of Lombardy, Bavaria, and Aquitaine. Each of them should rule his part of the kingdom with God's help as best he could. Each should enjoy the other's help and good will. To their subjects they should mutually grant peace and justice, and with God's will there should be eternal peace among them.

When Louis and Charles heard this and when it pleased them and their entire people, they met in council with their magnates and considered with grateful hearts what they should do about Lothair's proposals. They declared that this accord was what they had desired right from the very beginning of their quarrel and, although it could not be worked out because of the violations that were committed in the meantime, that they had often proposed it to Lothair. They thanked Almighty God, Whose help finally let them see their brother, through God's grace, ask for that peace and harmony which he had always rejected.

But they submitted the matter as usual to bishops and priests; for no matter where divine authority decided to steer these affairs, they wanted to be ready with joyous hearts for its command. Since everyone thought it best that there should be peace among the brothers, Louis and Charles gave their consent, called for emissaries, and granted Lothair's request.[14] When they had spent more than four days on the partition of the kingdom, they finally decided to offer him as the third part of the kingdom the land between the Rhine and Meuse as far as the source of the Meuse, and from there to the source of the Saône, and then along the Saône as far as its junction with the Rhône, and from there along the Rhône as far as the Tyrrhenian Sea all bishoprics, abbacies, counties, and royal estates on this side of the Alps with the exception of. . . .[15] If he should refuse that, then they should determine by force of arms what belonged to each.

Although this division seemed to some more generous than it should be, it was submitted to Lothair by Conrad, Cobbo, Adalhard,[16] and others. Louis and Charles themselves meanwhile decided to remain at Mellecey until their envoys returned, waiting for Lothair's response.

But when the emissaries came to Lothair, they found him as usual a little less ready for compromise. He said that he was not satisfied with what his brothers had proposed to him as it was not an equal share. He also complained about the fate of his followers, since in the share which had just been offered to him he would not have enough to compensate them for what they had lost. I do not know how they were tricked into doing this, but the emissaries therefore increased Lothair's share beyond the stipulated part, as far as the Charbonnière. Furthermore, if he should accept this within a period of time agreeable to them, they swore that his brothers under oath would then divide the whole kingdom with the exception of Lombardy, Bavaria, and Aquitaine as fairly as possible into three parts, that he would have the choice of the part he wanted, that they would grant him his share for the rest of his life on condition that he did the same to them, and that they would swear to execute this proposal if he wanted them to prove their good faith. Lothair swore that this was what he wanted and that he would carry out his part of the bargain on condition that his brothers did what their emissaries had just sworn to him.

[4]

June 842 Thus, about the middle of June, on a Thursday, Lothair, Louis, and Charles, each with an equal number of their nobles, met near the city of Mâcon on the island called Ansilla and swore each other this oath, namely, that from that day on and in the future they would keep the peace among each other and that in the assembly which their vassals had arranged they would under oath divide the entire kingdom, except Lombardy, Bavaria, and Aquitaine, into three parts as equally as possible, that Lothair should have the choice of the parts of the kingdom, and that each should help his brother all the days of his life to preserve the part which each received on condition that each brother acted toward his brothers in the same way.[17] After settling this business and exchanging words of peace, they departed in peace and returned to their camps to talk over other matters the next day.[18]

Although it was hard to do, they finally reached an agreement that until the assembly to be held on October 1, each should remain peacefully in the part of his choice. Louis then went to Saxony and Charles to Aquitaine to settle their affairs. But Lothair, it seemed, was already sure about the choice of the parts of the kingdom. He went hunting in the Ardennes Mountains and deprived of their benefices all the nobles in his territory who had been obliged to defect from him when he left his kingdom.

Louis, however, distinguished himself by putting down, not without rightful bloodshed, the rebels in Saxony who, as I said before, called themselves Stellinga. Charles, on the other hand, made Pepin flee to Aquitaine.[19] Since Pepin hid there, Charles could do nothing else that deserves to be recorded. But to keep an eye on this land he left behind a certain Duke Warin and others who seemed to be loyal to him. Moreover, Egfrid, count of Toulouse, ambushed some of Pepin's companions who had been sent to murder him and slew others. Charles set out for the assembly which he had convoked with his brother Louis at Worms.

30 Sept. 842 When he arrived at Metz on September 30, he found that Lothair had come to Thionville before the announced assembly met and was living there in defiance of their agreement.[20] To those of Louis' and Charles's party who were to stay at Metz for the division of the kingdom it did not seem quite safe to divide the kingdom at Metz while their lords were at Worms and Lothair at Thionville. The distance from Worms to Metz is, after all, about seventy leagues while from Thionville to Metz it is only about eight leagues.[21] They also remembered that Lothair had often been all too easily inclined and too prompt to deceive his brothers. For this reason they did not dare to put their lives in his hands without any security.

So Charles, who was concerned about their safety, sent to Lothair and told him to give hostages, if he wished Charles's and Louis' emissaries to stay at Metz with Lothair's. Charles wanted to be sure of their safety since Lothair had come to Thionville and was staying there against his word. Otherwise he should send his emissaries to them at Worms and they would give him whomever he wished as hostages. Another proposal was that they should all stay at an equal distance from Metz. But if he did not want this either, their emissaries should meet at a centrally located place of his choice; for Charles said that he would not risk the safety of so many noble men. Eighty men distinguished by their high nobility had been selected from the whole people, and if one did not take precautions against their ruin, he declared, an immense injury could be inflicted on him and his brother.

Then finally they agreed, in fairness to both sides, that their emissaries, one hundred and twenty in all, should meet without hostages at Koblenz and there divide the kingdom as equally as possible.[22]

[5]

Oct. 842 They met there on the nineteenth of October, and to avoid the outbreak among their followers of any strife for any reason those men who had come from Louis and Charles pitched camp on the eastern bank of the Rhine and those who had come from Lothair stayed on the western bank. And every day they went to St. Castor's to confer together. When the emissaries of Louis and Charles took up the division of the kingdom, it was asked with many complaints whether anyone of them was thoroughly familiar with the whole empire. When nobody was found, the question was raised why their emissaries had not in the meantime traveled around the empire trying to make a survey. The emissaries of Charles and Louis replied that Lothair did not want them to do that, and then Lothair's emissaries said it was impossible for one who did not know the whole story to divide anything equally. In the end it was asked, since they were to divide the kingdom under oath as equally and fairly as they knew how, whether they were able to swear to that sincerely, knowing that nobody could do it without proper knowledge. This, too, was submitted to the decision of the bishops.

When the bishops from both sides met in the basilica of St. Castor, those of Lothair's party declared that he who sinned in taking the oath could atone for it, and that it was better for them to sin and atone, than for the Church of God to suffer further from rapine, murder, arson, and adultery. Those of Louis' and Charles's party, on the other hand, asked why they should sin against God since it was not necessary. They said that it was better to make peace among themselves, and at the same time send messengers throughout the entire empire to survey it. Only then, they argued, was it possible to swear that they were dividing safely and fairly something of which they had certain knowledge. In this way, they assured Lothair's party, it was also possible to avoid perjury and other crimes, unless blind cupidity stood in the way. They testified that by making this proposal they wanted to avoid violating their oaths or giving anyone else an excuse to do so. In total disagreement they all went back to their people, whence they had come.

Oct. 842 Then everyone met again in the same building and Lothair's partisans declared that they were ready for their oath and to divide the empire as had been sworn. Louis' and Charles's followers said that they were ready, too, but only if it were possible for them. In the end, since neither side dared to agree to the wishes of the other side without the approval of their lords, they arranged for a peace among themselves until they would be able to know which of these proposals their lords were willing to accept. It seemed that this could be accomplished by the fifth of November. They departed after confirming a truce until this date.

On this day a violent earthquake struck most of Gaul. On the same day the worthy Angilbert was translated to Centulum, and his body, without the help of spices, was found to be incorrupt twenty-nine years after his death. This man was a descendant of a family not unknown in those days. Madhelgaud, Richard, and he came from the same stock, and Charles the Great deservedly held them in high esteem. With Bertha, a daughter of the same great king, Angilbert begot my brother Hartnid and me, Nithard. At Centulum Angilbert constructed a magnificent building in honor of Almighty God and St. Richard and ruled magnificently the monastic family committed to him. Here he ended his life happily and was laid to rest in peace.

Having touched briefly on my own background I want to return to the proper course of my history.[23]

[6]

When all the envoys, as I said before, returned to their kings
Nov. and reported to them what had happened, the brothers agreed that
842 there should be peace among them until the twentieth day after St.
4 July John's Mass. They did so partly because the nobles having once tasted
843 danger did not want any more fighting. To arrange peace the leading men of the people from both sides met at Thionville. They swore that in the meantime the kings would keep the peace among themselves, that they would not fail to divide the kingdom as equally as possible at this assembly, and that Lothair, as had been sworn, should have the choice among the parts. Then each departed wherever he
Nov. wanted to go. Lothair headed for Aachen to spend the winter there,
842 Louis went to Bavaria, and Charles came to Quierzy to take a wife.

At the same time the Moors, on whom Sigenulf, brother of Sigihard, had called for help, invaded Benevento.[24] At the same time too the Stellinga in Saxony rebelled again against their lords. But when it came to battle they were put down in a great bloodbath. And so they who had dared to rise without lawful power perished by it.

4 Dec. Charles, as I said before, took a wife, Hirmentrude, daughter of
842 Odo and Ingeltrud, who was a niece of Adalhard. Charles's father in his time had loved this Adalhard so much that he did anything in his whole empire that Adalhard wanted. Adalhard cared little for the public good and tried to please everyone. Again and again he advised Charles's father to distribute liberties and public property for private use and, since he knew how to manage it so that everyone got what he asked for, he ruined the kingdom altogether. This is how he was easily able at this time to coax the people to do whatever he wanted. It was for this reason above all that Charles married Hirmentrude, because he believed that with Adalhard's help he could win over a large part of the people to himself.[25]

After the wedding had taken place on December 14, he celebrated Christmas at St.-Quentin. At Valenciennes he decided which of his vassals would remain to defend the land between the Meuse and the Seine. He and his wife headed for Aquitaine in the winter of the year of our Lord 843. This winter, however, was excessively cold and long, full of diseases, and rather harmful to agriculture, livestock, and bees.

[7]

From this history, everyone may gather how mad it is to neglect the common good and to follow only private and selfish desires, since both sins insult the Creator so much, in fact, that He turns even the elements against the madness of the sinner. I shall easily prove this by examples still known to almost everyone. In the times of Charles the Great of good memory, who died almost thirty years ago, peace and concord ruled everywhere because our people were treading the one proper way, the way of the common welfare, and thus the way of God.[26] But now since each goes his separate way, dissension and struggle abound. Once there was abundance and happiness everywhere, now everywhere there is want and sadness. Once even the elements smiled on everything and now they threaten, as Scripture which was left to us as the gift of God, testifies: *And the world will wage war against the mad.*[27]

20 March 843 About this time, on March 20, there occurred an eclipse of the moon.[28] Besides, a great deal of snow fell in the same night and the just judgment of God, as I said before, filled every heart with sorrow. I mention this because rapine and wrongs of every sort were rampant on all sides, and now the unseasonable weather killed the last hope of any good to come.[29]

Notes

INTRODUCTION

1. The best guide to the historians of the Carolingian age is W. Wattenbach, W. Levison, H. Löwe, *Deutschlands Geschichtsquellen im Mittelalter. Vorzeit und Karolinger,* II–IV (Weimar, 1953–63).
2. Kurze, p. ix.
3. M. L. W. Laistner, *Thought and Letters in Western Europe A.D. 500 to 900,* rev. ed. (London, 1957), p. 264.
4. Cf. R. L. Poole, *Chronicles and Annals* (Oxford, 1926), pp. 26-36; C. W. Jones, *Saints' Lives and Chronicles in Early England* (New York, 1947), pp. 7-13, on the origins of the annals. On the earlier Carolingian annals, see Wattenbach-Levison-Löwe, II, 180-92; H. Hoffmann, *Untersuchungen zur karolingischen Annalistik. Bonner historische Forschungen,* X (Bonn, 1958), where the earlier literature on the subject is mentioned.
5. Hoffmann, *Karolingische Annalistik,* p. 70.
6. Einhard, ch. 24; W. Braunfels and others, eds., *Karl der Grosse; Lebenswerk und Nachleben,* 4 vols. (Düsseldorf, 1965–67), II, 42–62, 28–41.
7. Wattenbach-Levison-Löwe, II, 246–47.
8. Quoted ibid.; cf. L. von Ranke, *Gesammelte Werke,* 54 vols. (Leipzig, 1868–90), LI, 115.
9. I. Bernays, *Zur Kritik karolingischer Annalen* (Strasbourg, 1883), pp. 169–88, argues against the official character of the RFA.
10. Wattenbach-Levison-Löwe, II, 248, n. 281, 282.
11. *Two of the Saxon Chronicles Parallel,* ed. C. Plummer, 2 vols. (Oxford, 1892–99), II, civ.

12. Wattenbach-Levison-Löwe, II, 248, n. 284.
13. Bernays, pp. 184–88; Wattenbach-Levison-Löwe, II, 249.
14. Wattenbach-Levison-Löwe, II, 250–51, and notes; G. Monod, *Études critiques sur les sources de l'histoire carolingienne,* I. *Bibliothèque de l'école des hautes études. Sciences philologiques et historiques,* CXIX (1898), 102–26.
15. Wattenbach-Levison-Löwe, II, 251–53.
16. Monod, *Études,* pp. 127–42; on Helisachar as author of part of the RFA, see Lina Malbos, "L'Annaliste royal sous Louis le Pieux," *Le Moyen âge,* LXXII (1966), 225–33.
17. Wattenbach-Levison-Löwe, II, 253–54; MGH, *SS,* XV, pt. 1, 379.
18. M. Manitius, *Geschichte der lateinischen Literatur des Mittelalters,* I (Munich, 1910), 646–47; Wattenbach-Levison-Löwe, II, 254–56.
19. Kurze, pp. 3–115 (facing the unrevised annals).
20. Wattenbach-Levison-Löwe, II, 255–56.
21. Kurze, pp. ix-xv. The manuscripts of the RFA have been divided into five classes. The two manuscripts of Class A break off in the years 788 and 749, respectively. Manuscripts belonging to Class B, five altogether, are equally defective and seem to derive from a common source which broke off in the middle of the year 813. Manuscripts of Class C have additions in 773 and 776 at a place different from the other manuscripts and an additional sentence in annal 826. The editors have further subdivided the eight manuscripts of this class into two categories with their own distinctive features. The two manuscripts of Class D have additions for the years 785 and 792 on the conspiracies of Hardrad and Pepin the Hunchback. Seven manuscripts belonging to Class E contain the revised version of the RFA and seem to have spread first from the monastery of Wissembourg in Alsace.
22. Wattenbach-Levison-Löwe, II, 276, 255; III, 337.
23. Ed. B. Simson, MGH, *SrG* (Hanover, 1905); Wattenbach-Levison-Löwe, II, 260–64; Hoffmann, *Karolingische Annalistik,* passim, esp. pp. 13, 26–27, 12.
24. Ed. G. Waitz, MGH, *SrG* (Hanover, 1883); Wattenbach-Levison-Löwe, III, 348–49.
25. Ed. B. Simson, MGH, *SrG* (Hanover, 1909); cf. Hoffmann, *Karolingische Annalistik,* pp. 13–16.
26. Ed. F. Kurze, MGH, *SrG* (Hanover, 1891).
27. Meyer, pp. 90–91.
28. *Die deutsche Literatur des Mittelalters: Verfasserlexikon,* ed. W. Stammler and K. Langosch, V (Berlin, 1955), 735.
29. IV, ch. 5
30. Meyer, p. 123, n. 498.

31. Meyer, p. 90; Nithard, I, Preface; III, ch. 5; Manitius, *Lat. Literatur,* I, 660; *NA,* IX (1884), 617–18 (Virgil); XI (1886), 69–70 (Justin and Sallust).
32. II, ch. 8; III, ch. 3.
33. II, ch. 2, 10; IV, ch. 1.
34. Wattenbach-Levison-Löwe, III, 355–56. His death in a battle against the Normans on May 15, 845, rather than in the battle against Pepin on the Âgout on June 14, 844, was established by F. L. Ganshof, "Note critique sur la biographie de Nithard," *Mélanges Paul Thomas* (Bruges, 1930), pp. 335–44.
35. MGH, *PL,* III, 310–11, no. 33; Mico's entire work, ibid. III, 279–368; cf. Manitius, *Lat. Literatur,* I, 469–76; II, 806; III, 1063; *NA,* IV (1879), 515–21.
36. *Hariulf: Chronique de l'abbaye de St. Riquier,* ed. F. Lot (Paris, 1894), pp. 102, 265.
37. Nithard, I, Preface; II, Preface.
38. III, Preface.
39. II, Preface; Meyer, pp. 81–82.
40. Meyer, pp. 2; 3–18.
41. Nithard, I, Preface, ch. 2, 4, 6; II, Preface; Meyer, pp. 3–4, 7, 13–14.
42. Nithard, I, ch. 2–7; IV, ch. 6; Meyer, pp. 9–13.
43. On these books in general, see Meyer, pp. 18–81.
44. Meyer, p. 79.
45. Nithard, II, ch. 8.
46. IV, ch. 6, 5; III, ch. 5, 6.
47. IV, ch. 2, 5, 7.
48. IV, ch. 6, 7.
49. IV, ch. 7.
50. Meyer, pp. 82–85; for Nithard's verdict on Lothair, see ibid., p. 123, n. 491. Nithard records the negative views which Charles and Louis hold of Lothair: II, ch. 9; III, ch. 5; IV, ch. 1. Nithard personally attacks Lothair: II, ch. 5, 8, 1, 2, 10; III, ch. 3, 7; IV, ch. 3, 4. Nithard comments on Lothair's irresolution: II, ch. 1, 3, 4; III, ch. 3.
51. II, ch. 10; Meyer, pp. 89–90; 124, n. 500.
52. I, ch. 3, 6, 4; Meyer, p. 14.
53. Manitius, *Lat. Literatur,* I, 660; *Verfasserlexikon,* V, 735. In Nithard, III, ch. 5, an entire sentence appears almost word for word as in Bk. IV, ch. 37, of Paul the Deacon's *History of the Lombards.*
54. III, ch. 5; IV, ch. 1; Meyer, p. 126, n. 515.
55. II, ch. 2, 4, 5, 8, 9; IV, ch. 3, 4; I, ch. 6, 3, 5, 7; Meyer, pp. 126, n. 515; 95, n. 68.
56. Manitius, *Lat. Literatur,* I, 659; Meyer, pp. 88–89; 121, n. 474–79.
57. Müller, pp. ix-x; Manitius, *Lat. Literatur,* I, 660. Ch. 59–62 of the

anonymous life of Louis the Pious are based on Nithard, I, ch. 6–8; cf. Meyer, pp. 14–18. Mico: MGH, *PL*, III, 310. Hariulf: *Chronique de St. Riquier*, pp. 79, 102, 265; MGH, *SS*, II, 361.

58. Paris, Bibliothèque nationale, ms. 9768 (s. X); ms. 14663 (s. XV). Cf. Müller, pp. x-xii.
59. Meyer, p. 2.
60. Nithard, I, ch. 5, I; Meyer, pp. 2–3.
61. II, ch. 4, 2, 3.
62. Meyer, p. 88; III, ch. 3; II, ch. 8.
63. Meyer, p. 87; IV, ch. 6, 7; MGH, *PL*, II, 559–64, 653–54. A summary of the available facts and information about Nithard is contained, along with a full bibliography of all editions and translations, in Lauer, pp. xvii-xx.

ROYAL FRANKISH ANNALS

741

1. Charles Martel died at Quierzy on the Oise on October 22 or 15; see *The Fourth Book of the Chronicle of Fredegar and Continuations*, ed. and tr. J. M. Wallace-Hadrill (New York, 1960), p. 97 (*Cont.* ch. 24); *Fredegar, Cont.* ch. 23, p. 97, says that the division of the kingdom had been arranged by Charles Martel, but he does not name Grifo, for whom the late mayor of the palace had a special affection, as one of the heirs; see also BML, pp. 20–21.
2. Cf. Justin, *Historiarum Philippicarum libri* XLIV, XV, 4.
3. Qu. Curtius Rufus, *Historia Alexandri Magni*, IV, 6, 1.
4. Neufchâteau is in Belgian Luxembourg. Swanahilde was relegated to the monastery of Chelles; cf. *Fredegar, Cont.* ch. 25, p. 98.

742

1. Loches: Dép. Indre-et-Loire; Vieux Poitiers: Dép. Vienne.
2. R: "Alamannia which had also defected from the Franks."

743

1. R: "Carloman and Pepin marched with united forces against Odilo"; cf. Livy. XXIII. 28.
2. Odilo's wife Hiltrude was the sister of Pepin and Carloman and had married the duke against their advice; BML, p. 23, see s.a. 748.
3. Apparently, Seeburg near Eisleben, Thuringia; BML, p. 23. In the same year Carloman and Pepin placed Childeric, last of the Merovingians, on the throne which Charles Martel had left unoccupied after the death of the Merovingian king in 737. The narrative sources do not mention this act, which was an admission of weakness; see L. Halphen, *Charlemagne et l'empire carolingien* (Paris, 1947), pp. 18–20; BML, pp. 22–23.

744

1. Pepin did not go along on this campaign but was fighting in Alsace; BML, pp. 24–25.

745

1. Carloman went to Rome after August 15, 747.

746

1. Five miles southeast of Civita Castellana, visible from Rome and offering a magnificent view; LP, I, 170.
2. The move to Monte Cassino occurred about 754. According to Einhard, ch. 2, Carloman withdrew to Monte Cassino because too many noble Frankish pilgrims on their way to Rome tended to pay visits to him. See below s.a. 753.

747

1. Grifo had been released from captivity; cf. BML, p. 29.
2. Schöningen is located between Hildesheim and Magdeburg; the Oker is a tributary of the Aller in the Harz Mountains. Cf. Justin, VI, 7.

748

1. Odilo, duke of Bavaria, died on January 18, 748. Suidger was a count in Bavaria; Lantfrid, who is only mentioned in O, was duke of Alamannia. Tassilo was relieved in 788; see below s.a. 787, 788.
2. Waifar, duke of Aquitaine (744–68).

749

1. Pope Zacharias (742–53); Fulrad, abbot of St.-Denis, died in 784; Burchard, bishop of Würzburg (742–53). The abbot of St.-Denis and the bishop of Würzburg were the highest-ranking ecclesiastics available. The event actually occurred in 750; cf. *Fredegar, Cont.* ch. 33, p. 102; Einhard, ch. 3.

750

1. The events recorded in this annal occurred in November 750; see BML, pp. 32–33.

753

1. Hildegar, bishop of Cologne (750–53).
2. Near Osnabrück.
3. Near Minden.
4. *Fredegar, Cont.* ch. 35, p. 103; BML, p. 35.
5. The palace of Quierzy, often to be mentioned in the RFA, was in Dép. Aisne. The story of Pope Stephen II (752–57) and his coming to Francia is more explicit in *Fredegar, Cont.* ch. 36, p. 104. The king received the news of the pope's coming at Thionville about Christmas; he sent his son Charles to meet the pontiff and accompany him to Ponthiou, where king and pope met on January 6, 754. Pepin then sent an embassy to Aistulf, king of the Lombards, ordering him not to violate Roman territory.

754

1. R: Stephen consecrated him "after he had received assurances from King Pepin as to the defense of the Roman Church." LP, I, 447–48, notes that the king promised the pope under oath to do his best to obey all his orders and to return to the pontiff the exarchate of Ravenna and "the rights and places of the Republic"; see also BML, pp. 36–40.
2. June 5, 754.

755

1. R: "Since the Lombards offered resistance and defended the Alps, the bulwarks of Italy, there was heavy fighting in the *clusae*"; cf. Florus, *Epitome de T. Livio,* I, 38. The *clusae* are the valley of Susa at the foot of Mont Cenis.
2. The true chronology of the events contained in annals 753, 754, 755, 756 seems to be the following:

   753 October 14: Stephen II sets out for Francia.

   754 January 6: Stephen II and Pepin meet at Ponthiou. The pope proceeds to St.-Denis to spend the winter there. An embassy is sent to Aistulf which is to restrain the Lombard king.
   April 14: At a general assembly at Quierzy Pepin promises the pope by charter to return the possessions taken by the Lombards.
   Spring: Pepin is anointed at St.-Denis.
   Summer and fall: Fruitless negotiations are carried on with Aistulf.

   755 Spring: Pepin embarks for Italy.
   Toward the end of the year: Pepin returns from Italy.

   756 January 1: Aistulf appears before Rome.
   Some scholars place the first campaign against Aistulf in the year 754 rather than 755.
3. R: "a not inconsiderable body of Franks." Before long the pope had reason to complain that Aistulf had not "permitted one handful of earth to be restored to blessed Peter and to the Holy Church of God"; see the pope's letter in MGH, *EE,* III, 488–90.
4. See above s.a. 746, n. 2.

756

1. The pope implored the king to undertake this campaign; cf. MGH, *EE,* III, 488–503; BML, pp. 42–43, with further sources; *Fredegar, Cont.* ch. 38, pp. 107–8. Additional information is also in LP, I, 452–53: Not far from Pavia, we are told, emissaries of the emperor approached Pepin and requested the surrender to imperial officials of Ravenna, the castles of the exarchate, and several cities. But Pepin refused to alienate these places from the jurisdiction of the pope. The conquest of Pavia forced Aistulf to hand over the cities listed in the treaty. After taking possession "Pepin had a charter of dona-

tion drawn up for the perpetual possession of these cities by the blessed Peter, the Holy Roman Church, and all the future popes of the Apostolic See. This document is still in the archives of our Holy Church." Fulrad came as the king's representative to Italy, entered every city of the Pentapolis and the Emilia, received hostages from each, and sent these together with the keys of the city gates to Rome. He deposited the keys and the charter of donation on the tomb of St. Peter.

2. Cf. Justin, XXXII, 3.
3. Cf. Livy, XXI, 5.
4. Desiderius (756–74).

757

1. The organ came from Emperor Constantine V Copronymus (741–55). The embassy mentioned here arrived in response to a Frankish embassy; *Fredegar, Cont.* ch. 40, p. 109; MGH, *Cap.,* I, 37–39.

759

1. R: "he was overtaken by a premature death"; cf. Justin, XXXII, 3.
2. Longlier near Neufchâteau in Belgian Luxembourg; Jupille near Liège.

760

1. An unknown place in Auvergne.

761

1. R: "he gathered auxiliary forces from everywhere"; cf. Justin, I, 6. Düren is between Cologne and Aix-la-Chapelle.

762

1. Dép. Deux Sevres.
2. A suburb of Paris.

763

1. R: "he feigned sickness"; for Tassilo's desertion, see BML, p. 50; not much later, perhaps in 764, Tassilo asked for the pope's mediation; MGH, *EE,* III, 545. Einhard, ch. 20.

764

1. R: "There was an eclipse of the sun on June 4, during the sixth hour."

765

1. Where Aisne and Meuse meet.
2. The RFA is silent on a mission which arrived from Constantinople in this year. The popes were much interested in preventing an alliance between Pepin and Constantinople. Pope Paul I (757–67) urged Pepin to insist on the recognition of the Roman primacy and the worship of images and to detain the Byzantine emissaries until a council had been called at Rome; MGH, *EE,* III, 534–35, 548–49, 551; F. W. Buckler, *Harunu'l-Rashid and Charles the Great.* Publications of the Mediaeval Academy of America (Cambridge, Mass., 1931), p. 7.

766

1. Argenton-sur-Creuse: Argantomagus, Dép. Indre.
2. Samoussy: Dép. Aisne; *Fredegar, Cont.* ch. 48, pp. 116–17; BML, p. 52.

767

1. BML, p. 40. Image worship had been officially condemned at Constantinople thirteen years earlier, but the synod of Gentilly approved of it.
2. Albi: Dép. Tarn; Gevaudan is the territory of Dép. Lozère.
3. Ally: Dép. Cantal; Turenne: Dép. Corrèze; Peyrusse: Dép. Aveyron.

768

1. Saintes: *Mediolanum,* Dép. Charente-Inverieure; Mons: apparently, in the area of the River Charente; Sels: now Chantoceaux, Dép. Maine et Loire. Remistagnus, uncle of Waifar, defected, attacked Frankish garrisons, was caught and hanged.
2. R: "which ended the war, as it seemed to him."
3. *Fredegar, Cont.* ch. 53, pp. 120–21, records that at St.-Denis Pepin divided the kingdom; BML, pp. 55–56. According to Einhard, Pepin died of dropsy; he was fifty-four.
4. R: "who was the elder." Time and place of Charles's birth are not entirely certain; Pepin married Bertrada in 749, and Carloman was born in 751. Charles is mentioned for the first time in 754; BML, p. 60; Abel-Simson, I, 9–22.

769

1. Hunald (735–44; 768–69) was the father of Waifar; Einhard, ch. 5; Abel-Simson, I, 43.
2. Now Moncontour de Poitou, Dép. Vienne.
3. Dép. Gironde.
4. Velleius Paterculus, *Factorum dictorumque memorabilium libri novem,* II, 114, 4.
5. Velleius Paterculus, II, 18, 3.
6. Caesar, *De bello Gallico,* VIII, 27.

770

1. Seltz is near Wissembourg in Alsace. Bertrada went first to King Desiderius of Lombardy and arranged for the marriage between Charles and Desiderata, daughter of the Lombard king, a marriage to which the pope was opposed. Charles, who had already an illegitimate son by a noble girl named Himiltrude, sent Desiderata back home after one year of marriage and late in 771 or early in 772 married Hildegard, a lady of aristocratic Bavarian descent. Bertrada's passage through Bavaria, mentioned only by O, may have aimed at a reconciliation with Tassilo; BML, pp. 59, 64, 66.
2. Near Liège.

771

1. Wilchar is called bishop of Sitten in R; but the Wilchar in question was archbishop of Sens (ca. 769–78).

772

1. Preceded in R by "In Rome, after the death of Pope Stephen, Hadrian succeeded to the pontificate"; i.e. Hadrian I (772–95).
2. In the locality of today's Stadtberge on the Diemel River, a western tributary of the River Weser.

773

1. Desiderius offered the pope an alliance directed against the Franks, but occupied simultaneously Faenza, Ferrara, and Comacchio, which Pepin and his sons had given to the Holy See. When Carloman's sons came to his court, he demanded that they be anointed since he wished to divide the Franks, separate the pope from them, and subject Rome and all of Italy to his power. Now the pope sent his embassy to Charles. In the meantime Desiderius and his son Adalgis moved on Rome with Carloman's sons to compel the pope to anoint them, but were prevailed upon to turn back at Viterbo when faced with a papal threat of excommunication. Charles consulted with his magnates and then decided to aid the pope. An embassy was sent to Rome to find out whether the cities had been returned to the pope, as Desiderius had falsely reported to the Franks, and then, together with papal emissaries, on to the Lombards to demand the surrender of the disputed towns. Desiderius refused, and Charles's ambassadors returned, carrying a papal letter which implored the Frankish king to live up to his father's promise. Charles sent one more embassy to Desiderius, offering him a compensation of 14,000 solidi if the cities were surrendered. When the Lombard refused this last offer, the Frankish army was called out; BML, pp. 69–70; LP, I, 487–94.
2. Bernard, a son of Charles Martel, was born before 732 and died in 787; below s.a. 811, 812.
3. R: "The siege of the city was a difficult matter, requiring many efforts, and consumed the entire winter"; cf. Justin, XXXVII, 2. While Pavia was being besieged, Desiderius' son Adalgis fled to Verona with Carloman's widow and her sons. Charles went to Verona, and Gerberga and her sons surrendered voluntarily; BML, p. 72.
4. Charles arrived in Rome on April 2, 774, and renewed the donation of his father. The charter of this donation has not survived, and the pope was never able to obtain all the territories which the papal sources list as included in this gift; BML, pp. 73–74; LP, I, 496–98.
5. This episode is briefly recorded under 774 in R.

774

1. R: "There he grew old holding the office and honor of a patrician."
2. R: "He took Desiderius along with him as a prisoner." BML, pp. 74–76; LP, I, 499. Pavia fell in June 774. Desiderius, his wife Ausa, and a daughter were taken to either Corbie or Liège; Einhard, ch. 6.

3. Ingelheim, now Nieder-Ingelheim, on the Rhine near Mainz, where Charlemagne built a palace between 768 and 774.

775

1. R: "in his first attack"; Florus, *Epitome de T. Livio,* II, 9, II.
2. Hohen-Syburg: where the Lenne flows into the Ruhr; BML, p. 82.
3. Braunsberg in the area of Minden, no longer extant.
4. For the identification of the Austreleudi with the Eastphalians, see BML, p. 82.
5. Angrarii: Germ. *Engern,* a Saxon tribe.
6. The area of Bückeburg, east of Minden.
7. R: "and swore fealty."
8. Between Minden and Osnabrück.
9. Cf. Tacitus, *Annales,* I, 51.
10. Livy, XXIII, 36.
11. R: "and that several cities had already defected to him"; s.a. 776. The story, apparently exaggerated, was that the allies of Hrodgaud, duke of Friuli, were the dukes Hildebrand of Spoleto, Arighis of Benevento, and Reginbald of Chiusi, who planned with Adalgis and a Greek army to capture Rome in the month of March and to restore the kingdom of the Lombards; MGH, *EE,* III, 573–83; BML, pp. 83–85.
12. Near Strasbourg (Sélestat, Bas-Rhin).

776

1. The miracle is not in R; instead we find only a brief record of the Frankish victory.
2. R: "They gave and he accepted their treacherous promises to keep faith." The source of the river is at Lippspringe, near Paderborn.
3. R: "and after leaving a strong garrison"; cf. Livy, XXI, 61.

777

1. R: "whom he had ordered to appear before him; they feigned obedience and submission."
2. R: "Widukind, a Westphalian nobleman, who was aware of his many crimes and out of fear of the king had fled to Sigifrid, king of the Danes." BML, p. 88. Nordmannia is obviously Denmark.
3. R: "submitting himself and the cities over which the king of the Saracens had placed him." Sulaiman ibn Yaqdhanu'l-A'rabi, wali of Barcelona, whose *wilayat* was under Frankish protection, and his son Yusuf were supporters of the Abbasid cause in Spain and opponents of Abd ar-Rahman, the lone survivor of the Umayyads, who had established himself in Spain with the help of the Yamanite party. An attempt of the Abbasid caliph Al-Mansur in 763 to crush the Umayyad ended in failure; but a few years later the Abbasid party in Spain united with revolting Spanish Berbers against Abd ar-Rahman. The rebels intended to obtain aid from African Berbers and would

thus have cut off the Umayyads from the Mediterranean. To strengthen the rebel cause Sulaiman and Yusuf went to Charles at Paderborn in 777 and placed their territories under his protection; Buckler, *Harunu'l-Rashid,* pp. 8–11. Braunfels, *Karl der Grosse,* I, 672–82.

4. Douzy near Sedan and Chasseneuil near Poitiers.

778

1. R: "At that time the assurances of the aforementioned Saracens aroused in him the legitimate hope of capturing several cities in Spain." The conspiracy mentioned in the preceding note failed because of distrust and conflict among the partners in the revolt. Sulaiman in the end faced the whole Umayyad army alone. He therefore sought help from Charles, but this proved to be more of a handicap. Sulaiman took Saragossa and tried to hand the city over to Charles. This outraged Muslim public opinion, and Charles decided to return (not because of the Saxon revolt, news of which reached him only at Autun). Abd ar-Rahman recaptured Saragossa, and Sulaiman was murdered as a traitor to the Muslim cause. Thus, the Umayyads completed the conquest of Spain, with the exception of Asturias and Galicia, and assured the existence of an independent Umayyad caliphate, whose rulers, the emirs of Cordova, used the title "sons of the Caliph"; Buckler, *Harunu'l-Rashid,* pp. 12–14; BML, pp. 89–91. The pope gave his blessing to the campaign; MGH, *EE,* III, 588–589. A crusading motive was added soon; cf. VH, ch. 2.
2. Justin, IX, 2; Tacitus, *Annals,* II, 21.
3. On the report of this event in the RFA, see R. Fawtier, *La Chanson de Roland* (Paris, 1933), pp. 151–80; on Charlemagne's memory in saga and legend, see BML, p. 90; Braunfels, *Karl der Grosse,* IV, 326–36, 337–47, 348–63.
4. R: "They destroyed in like fashion both the sacred and the profane. The wrath of the enemy made no distinction of age or sex"; Tacitus, *Annals,* I, 51; Livy, XXI, 15. Deutz is now part of Cologne, located on the right bank of the Rhine.

779

1. Hildebrand, duke of Spoleto (773–after 788).
2. Near Reims.
3. Where the Lippe flows into the Rhine, near Wesel.
4. Apparently, Bocholt in Westphalia.
5. Probably southwest of Minden.

780

1. R: "although it was all hypocrisy on their part, as usual." Ohrum on the Oker.
2. See above annal 747, n. 1.
3. R: "and his children"; cf. BML, p. 97.

781

1. Pepin was the king's son by his wife Hildegard; he died in 811. Charles was in Rome on April 15.
2. Louis is the later Louis the Pious, the king's son by Hildegard, born in 776. There were no precedents for the offices of king of Italy and king of Aquitaine.
3. Gisela, Charles's daughter by Hildegard, born in 781; Thomas, archbishop of Milan (759–83).
4. Riculf later became archbishop of Mainz (787–813).
5. Sinbert, bishop of Regensburg (756–91).

782

1. R begins: "At the beginning of the summer, when sufficient fodder was available to take the army to Saxony . . ."; cf. Caesar, *De bello Gallico,* II, 2.
2. The Asian empire of the Avars, who were Mongols like Huns and Turks, was destroyed by the Turks in the sixth century. Some of these Turkish tribes acquired their former masters' names and about the middle of the sixth century moved into southern Russia and the Balkans, where most of the Slavs became their subjects or federates. At the end of the century the Avar empire comprised "practically the whole of Central Europe and a great part of the Balkans" and menaced the Byzantine Empire as well as the neighboring Slavic and Germanic tribes. They also constituted a threat to the Frankish kingdom. In the seventh century Slavs, Byzantines, Croats, Bulgars, and Khazars greatly limited the territory ruled by the Avars, but the latter once more consolidated their power in central Europe with the decline of the Merovingian dynasty; cf. F. Dvornik, *The Slavs: Their Early History and Civilization* (Boston, 1956), pp. 25, 36–45, 60–69; on their relations with the Carolingians, see Braunfels, *Karl der Grosse,* I, 719–91; on the titles of their chiefs, see below s.a. 805 n. 1.
3. R: "In the meantime the king was informed that the Slavonic Sorbs, who inhabit the plains between the Elbe and the Saale, had entered the neighboring territories of Saxons and Thuringians to pillage, and by looting and burning had ravaged several places." The descendants of the Sorbs or Lusatian Serbs today live in Upper and Lower Lusatia (Lausitz) in East Germany. R at this point has reminiscences of Livy, XXI, 30; Tacitus, *Germania,* 36; *Annals,* III, 45; Einhard, ch. 11.
4. The land of the Ripuarian Franks west of the Rhine.
5. Cf. Velleius Paterculus, II, 112, 5.
6. The Süntel Mountains are between Hameln and Minden.
7. Cf. Livy, XXI, 59.

8. R: "he believed that he should in no way delay matters"; cf. Florus, *Epitome de T. Livio,* 1, 39.
9. See BML, p. 106; cf. also MGH, *Cap.,* 1, 68–70.
10. R: "All denounced Widukind as the instigator of this wicked rebellion."

783

1. A tributary of the River Ems; the place of battle is not known; BML, p. 108.
2. R: "by whom he begot two daughters"; the daughters were Theoderada and Hiltrude.

784

1. On the Weser near Minden; now Petershagen.
2. Charles (772–811).
3. Steinfurt: (O) once a village on the Ohre; Schöningen: between Hildesheim and Magdeburg.
4. The Emmer is a tributary of the Weser; the village of Lügde is near Piermont. Dreingau: the area north of the River Lippe; Weissgau: the land along the River Emmer.

785

1. On the left bank of the Elbe near Lüneburg.
2. R: "Since the two were well aware of their criminal actions, they were reluctant to place themselves in the king's trust."
3. The conspiracy occurred apparently in 786. Significantly, the original version of the RFA suppresses all information relating to the event; Einhard, ch. 20: "It is supposed that the cruelty of Queen Fastrada was the primary cause of these plots."

786

1. Charles was in Florence in December; cf. his decree to counts and vassals, MGH, *Cap.,* 1, 203–4.

787

1. Arighis, duke of Benevento (758–87); Braunfels, *Karl der Grosse,* 1, 609–71.
2. Charles's daughter Hruodtrude or Rotrude had become engaged to Emperor Constantine VI (780–97) in 781. Charles sent the royal chaplain Witbold to Constantinople in this matter, but eventually did not surrender his daughter into the hands of the Byzantines; BML, pp. 116–17; Abel-Simson, 1, 541–46. In R the Beneventan affairs appear under the year 786.
3. Bishop Arno of Salzburg (785–821); Hunric was abbot of the monastery of Mondsee.
4. R reduces the pope's threat to a single sentence; cf. BML, pp. 117–18.
5. Between Regensburg and Ingolstadt.
6. On Tassilo's submission, cf. Einhard, ch. 11; BML, p. 120. R again shortens this episode; it makes no mention of the fruitless embassy

to Tassilo before the expedition into Bavaria or of a new commendation on Tassilo's part.

788

1. O again is more detailed on this Bavarian episode, but the story in R is substantially the same.
2. Tassilo was tonsured at St. Goar on July 6 and dispatched to the monastery of St. Jumièges; his wife and daughters took the veil; BML, pp. 121–22. He renounced his duchy in 794.
3. Arighis and Romuald of Spoleto had died in 787. In accordance with the pope's wish, Charles at first refused to permit the return of Arighis' surviving son Grimoald. Adalgis, son of Desiderius, and Greek agents were meanwhile scheming in Benevento. Grimoald eventually returned to Benevento after agreeing that the Lombards would shed their beards and place Charles's name on their charters and coins. The king's emissary Winigis, Duke Hildebrand of Spoleto, and Duke Grimoald of Benevento in a battle in Calabria defeated the Greeks who had entered the territory and had been joined by Adalgis; BML, pp. 120–23; MGH, *EE,* III, 615–20.
4. The Huns are the Avars; they had entered Charles's realm as Tassilo's allies; BML, p. 123; s.a. 791, 796, 805, and notes.
5. The original version of the RFA up to this point was compiled as a whole; from now on the RFA were continued annually; see Kurze, p. 84, n. 1.
6. Cf. Livy, XXI, 56.

789

1. The Wilzi or Welatabians were apparently all those Slavs who lived between Sorbs and Obodrites.
2. Witzan, prince of the Wilzi; one Witzin, king of the Obodrites, is slain by the Saxons a few years later; see s.a. 795.
3. Caesar, *De bello Gallico,* I, 26.

790

1. Cf. Livy, I, 57; XXI, 11; 48, 53; XXII, 25, 45.
2. Salz, near Neustadt on the Franconian Saale in Lower Franconia.
3. Cornelius Nepos, *Miltiades,* 7.

791

1. R: "This river is in the middle between the lands of the Bavarians and the Huns and is considered the definite border between the two kingdoms."
2. R: "under the command of Count Theodoric and the chamberlain Meginfrid."
3. Cumeoberg: apparently the Viennese Woods, i.e. the hills west and northwest of Vienna.
4. R mentions a strong bulwark "near the city of Comageni on Mount Cumeoburg" (Kaumberg?), and the return of the king's army by way

of Szombathely and of Theodoric's and Meginfrid's forces by way of Bohemia. Einhard, ch. 13, points out that the war took actually seven years and, "except the Saxon war, was the greatest that he waged." Cf. Abel-Simson, II, 16–25; BML, pp. 131–34; MGH, *EE,* IV, 528–29.

792

1. Felix, bishop of Urgel, and Elipand, bishop of Toledo, were the fathers of the Adoptionist heresy, which claimed that Christ as a man is not the true, but only the adoptive, son of God. At Regensburg, Felix was charged with heresy, defeated in debate, and persuaded to recant. Although he confessed his error before the pope, as the RFA mentions, he later relapsed and was again charged with heresy at the synods of Frankfurt in 794 and Aix-la-Chapelle in 798. Alcuin eventually prevailed on him to recant a second time; his confession is in Migne, PL, XCVI, 881–88; cf. also Migne, PL, CI, 231–300; XCIX, 151–166; Braunfels, *Karl der Grosse,* II, 95–155. Angilbert is mentioned only in O; he was the father of Nithard; Nithard, I, ch. 7; BML, pp. 135–36.
2. Einhard, ch. 20; BML, pp. 136–37. Pepin was put into the monastery of Prüm.
3. Cf. Justin, XVI, 5.

793

1. Traces of this project can be seen in the Karlsgraben near Sand between Treuchtlingen and Weissenburg; Braunfels, *Karl der Grosse,* I, 437–53. The author calculates that no less than six thousand workers were occupied with digging and removing the earth and worked on perhaps as many as fifty-five days.
2. Hisham (788–96), son and successor of Abd ar-Rahman, advanced as far as the River Orbien, captured Gerona, and defeated the Christians under Margrave William; BML, pp. 138–39; Buckler, *Harunu'l Rashid,* p. 18.

794

1. Easter was on March 23.
2. MGH, *Cap.,* I, 73–78; BML, pp. 140–42.
3. St. Alban's in Mainz.
4. Constantine VI (780–97); his mother Irene was the widow of Emperor Leo IV and sole ruler from 797 to 802. The council of Nicaea was held in 787; cf. MGH, *Cap.,* I, 73–74.
5. The Sindfeld is south of Paderborn; BML, p. 143.
6. April 12, 795.

795

1. R: "After he had arrived in the Bardengau he pitched camp near the place called Bardowiek to await the arrival of the Slavs, whom he had

commanded to come to him." Lüne and Bardowiek were villages near Lüneburg in Lower Saxony.

2. The Obodrites were the most westerly outpost of the Slavs and they held at the time of their greatest expansion eastern Holstein and Mecklenburg-Schwerin; Braunfels, *Karl der Grosse,* I, 708–18.
3. With this sentence, according to Kurze, p. 96, n. 4, a different annalist continued the RFA.

796

1. Hadrian d. December 25, 795; Leo III (795–816); for Charles's instructions to Angilbert and his letter to Leo III, see MGH, *EE,* IV, 135, 136–38.
2. The defeat of the Avars in 796 was final; remnants were permitted to settle in southern Pannonia and accepted Christianity, but as a people the Avars disappeared from history. Charles established his sovereignty also over the Slavs of Carinthia, Styria, and Pannonian Croatia and over Byzantine territories in Istria; he thus ruled a vast territory comprising the Alps and Pannonia as far as the Danube and Save and threatened the interests of Byzantium; Dvornik, *The Slavs,* p. 69; BML, p. 148; MGH, *EE,* IV, 153–54, 157–66, 173–74.

797

1. Zatun is probably Zaid, the wali of Barcelona. R adds: "After taking over the city, the king sent his son Louis with an army into Spain to lay siege to Huesca."
2. R: "because it was necessary to crush the arrogance of that faithless tribe."
3. 'Abdallah, son of Abd ar-Rahman and exiled brother of Hisham (d. 796), apparently sought the support of the Frankish king against his nephew; Buckler, *Harunu'l-Rashid,* p. 19.
4. R: "This place is so called by the inhabitants up to the present time." Herstelle is near Minden.
5. R: "He received the ambassador of King Alfonso of Asturias and Galicia, who had brought him gifts." Alfonso II (791–843), king of Galicia and Asturias; BML, p. 154; Einhard, ch. 16.

798

1. Counts Rorih, Had, Richolf, and Garih were killed; BML, p. 153.
2. R: "in the place called Suentana"; now Bornhövde on the Schwentine River.
3. R: "who was in command of the right wing"; cf. Livy, I, 27.
4. R: "because of his shameless ways."
5. Irene's embassy was a result of the military pressure exerted by Harun al-Rashid, caliph since 787. He invaded the Byzantine Empire in 796 and concluded a peace with Irene in 798 which imposed tribute on the Byzantines; cf. Buckler, *Harunu'l-Rashid,* p. 17; BML, p. 154.

799

1. The men responsible for the capture and mistreatment of the pope on the Major Litanies—April 25, 799—were relatives of the previous pope, Hadrian I; MGH, *EE,* IV, 294–96. The pope escaped to St. Peter's at night with the aid of his chamberlain Albinus; cf. BML, p. 155; Abel-Simson, II, 583–87; LP, II, 2–5.
2. They arrived at Rome on November 29, 799. The royal emissaries tried the pope's opponents, determined his innocence, apprehended the slanderers and surrendered them to the king; BML, pp. 156–57; MGH, *EE,* IV, 308–10; LP, II, 5–7.
3. Eric, margrave of Friuli, was killed at the siege of Tarsatika, the modern Rijeka (Fiume), while trying to subjugate the Croats of Dalmatia.
4. Hassan, wali or governor of the city of Huesca.

800

1. The trial of the pope took place on December 1; he purged himself on December 23; BML, p. 164; LP, II, 7.
2. It has been pointed out that the gift of the keys of Calvary was "an ecclesiastical gesture," whereas the gifts of the keys of the city and of the banner imply that Charles achieved some sort of political control, which would mean that Harun conceded it to Charles and thus became the suzerain of the Frankish king; Buckler, *Harunu'l-Rashid,* pp. 29–31.

801

1. For the other versions of this celebrated event, which belongs in the year 800, see LP, II, 7–8; Einhard, ch. 28; BML, pp. 165–66.
2. Although very minor revisions can be detected in the later annals up to 812, O and R from this point on are really identical; Kurze, p. 115.
3. The nomenclator was one of the "justices of the palace," but his duties remain unknown.
4. Harun al-Rashid, emir al Mumenin, i.e., "Prince of the Faithful," appointed Ibrahim ibn al'Aghlab governor of Africa about 800. Fustât, his place of residence, is Abbasiya near Kairwan in southern Tunis. Arabic sources are silent on the relations between Harun al-Rashid and Charlemagne; Buckler, *Harunu'l-Rashid,* p. 46.
5. June 24. Ivrea is north of Turin.
6. Zaid swore allegiance to Charles in 797, but later repented and resumed his allegiance to Cordova; Buckler, *Harunu'l-Rashid,* pp. 38–39; BML, 169; VH, ch. 10, 13.

802

1. On the various Byzantine offices and dignities mentioned in the RFA, see J. B. Bury, *The Imperial Administrative System in the Ninth Century. The British Academy Supplemental Papers,* I (London,

1911), which includes the text of the *Kletorologion* of Philotheus (a. 899), the most instructive document on the grades of officialdom in the Byzantine Empire of the early Middle Ages, especially pp. 22–39. The insignia of the spatarius was a gold-handled sword, of the prothospatarius a jeweled gold collar, and of the candidate a special gold chain. According to the Byzantine historian Theophanes, Charles planned to marry the Greek empress Irene in order to unite the eastern and western empires. His emissaries and those of the pope were sent to Constantinople to negotiate about this project. The empress was prepared to give her consent, but the plan was foiled by the resistance of the patrician Aëtius, who wished to secure the throne for his brother. Irene was deposed before the negotiations led to a definite result; BML, p. 171.

2. Jesse, bishop of Amiens (ca. 799–836); Helmgaud was the count of the palace.
3. March 27.
4. Ortona on the Adriatic near Chieti.
5. Lucera in Apulia.
6. We meet an emissary of that name s.a. 788, a count of Spoleto s.a. 802, 803, and a duke of Spoleto s.a. 799, 815, 822; evidently the same person.

803

1. Cf. MGH, *EE,* IV, 546; BML, pp. 178–79. Nicephorus (802–11). Irene was deposed on October 31, 802.

804

1. East of the Weser near Verden.
2. Einhard, ch. 7, gives the number of Saxons who were taken to Francia as ten thousand; BML, pp. 182–83.
3. The pope spent Christmas with the emperor and left on January 14, 805; BML, pp. 183–84.

805

1. Petronell is in Burgenland, the most eastern province of Austria, south of the Danube; Sabaria, now Szombathely, lies about fifty miles south of Petronell, in western Hungary. It appears that the capcan, as well as the tudun and the canizauci, which are also mentioned in the RFA, were princes of individual Avar tribes, whereas the khagan ruled his own tribe, which was superior to the others, but had a claim to overlordship; Braunfels, *Karl der Grosse, I,* 774–76.
2. East of Épinal in Lorraine.

806

1. Up to that time the Venetians had recognized the supremacy of the Byzantine emperor. Recently, they had tried to annex Dalmatia and had driven out Fortunatus, patriarch of Grado, who enjoyed Charles's favor; BML, p. 187.

2. February 6, 806; MGH, *Cap.*, I, 126–30; BML, pp. 187–89. See s.a. 817.
3. April 12, 806.
4. Navarre and Pamplona had previously succeeded in throwing off the overlordship of Cordova and had accepted the protection of Charles. Since 805 the Spanish March was part of the kingdom of Aquitaine ruled by Louis; Buckler, *Harunu'l-Rashid,* p. 39; BML, p. 191.
5. Nicephorus (802–11); cf. s.a. 812, n. 1.

807

1. This seems to have been a rather complicated Greek water clock or clepsydra.
2. Pantelleria, an island, is about midway between Agrigento in Sicily and Sousse in Tunisia. The Moors, "Mauri," referred to were probably North African pirates in the service of Cordova. Corsica, Sardinia, Sicily, and Italy were being attacked. The headquarters of the Moslem fleet was apparently in Spain, and this discovery may have caused the Frankish campaign against Tortosa, at the mouth of the Ebro, which fell in 811; Buckler, *Harunu'l-Rashid,* p. 39.
3. The duke of Venice had revolted against Constantinople. The expedition of Nicetas was the Byzantine empire's "last serious demonstration against the West"; ibid., p. 37.

808

1. Cf. BML, p. 196; Braunfels, *Karl der Grosse,* I, 699–707.
2. Livy, XXII, 9.
3. Tacitus, *Annals,* II, 1.
4. Livy, XXI, 45.
5. The Wilzi were the traditional enemies of the Obodrites; cf. BML, p. 196.
6. Abel-Simson, II, 389, n. 2; for this defensive bulwark, see the literature in Braunfels, *Karl der Grosse,* I, 701 n. 15.
7. Braunfels, *Karl der Grosse,* I, 683–98. Eardwulf, after the murder of his predecessor Aethelred in 796, placed himself under the protection of Charlemagne; cf. MGH, *EE,* IV, 155, 178–80, 376–78; BML, p. 194. Hruotfrid was abbot of St. Amand (d. 827).
8. April 8, 809.

809

1. The failure of this naval demonstration under Paul and the departure of the Byzantine fleet enabled Pepin, king of Italy, to subdue Venice.
2. Cenwulf, king of Mercia (796–821), had formerly harbored Eardwulf's enemies.
3. *Orobiotae,* "mountain people."
4. Badenfliot was on the lower Stör.
5. Smelding-Connoburg, now Conow, Mecklenburg.
6. The controversy about inserting the *filioque* in the symbolum had first erupted between the monks of Mount Olivet and John, monk of

St. Saba near Jerusalem. Through the mediation of the pope the problem had been brought before the emperor whose chapel used the extended formula; cf. BML, p. 198; Migne, PL, CV, 239–76; XCVIII, 923–29.

7. Bernhar, bishop of Worms (803–23); Adalhard, abbot of Corbie (d. 826).
8. Esesfelth has been discovered on the northern bank of the Stör west of Itzehoe; cf. BML, p. 200, and Braunfels, *Karl der Grosse,* I, 701.
9. Aureolus was the commander of the Spanish March.

810

1. Buckler, *Harunu'l-Rashid,* pp. 39–40. Amorez, Amrus, had been wali of Toledo since 807.
2. Venice had to submit and pay tribute; BML, p. 200.
3. Hruodtrude, born in 775, was one of Charles's three daughters by Hildegard.
4. On all rivers flowing into the ocean, including those of Aquitaine, ships were to be built for the defense against the Normans; BML, p. 200.
5. Cf. Tacitus, *Annals,* II, 7.
6. On this campaign the emperor fell from his horse, which was considered a portent of his impending death; cf. Einhard, ch. 32; MGH, *Cap.,* I, 249; Migne, PL, CIV, 147–58.
7. Charles surrendered Venice to Nicephorus (802–11) in return for Byzantine recognition of his imperial title; BML, p. 202. Al-Hakam, emir of Cordova (796–822), called Abul Aas, now made peace with Charlemagne; Buckler, *Harunu'l-Rashid,* p. 40.
8. Hemming, king of the Danes (810–11).

811

1. Cf. MGH, *EE,* IV, 547; BML, p. 205.
2. Haido, bishop of Basle (d. 836).
3. Unroch was a member of a powerful noble family; on the Carolingian nobility, see Braunfels, *Karl der Grosse,* I, 83–142; on Unroch, ibid., pp. 133–37. His son Eberhard was duke of Friuli, son-in-law of Louis the Pious and father of Emperor Berengar I.
4. Canizauci, see s.a. 805 n. 1.
5. Charles was born in 772 and was to have been Charlemagne's heir and successor; BML, p. 209; MGH, *EE,* IV, 315–16.

812

1. Nicephorus was slain in a battle against the Bulgarian king Krum in July 811. Michael I Rangabe (811–13) was his successor.
2. The embassy of Arsafius and Theognostus delivered the final Byzantine recognition of Charles's imperial title. In return Charles gave up Venice and the Dalmatian maritime cities; cf. BML, pp. 210–11.
3. On Bernard, see s.a. 817, 818, and 817, n. 9; also Nithard, I, ch. 2.

4. Bernard (before 732–87), a son of Charles Martel; Wala (773–836); Nithard, I, n. 16.
5. BML, p. 212. Louis, king of Aquitaine, had ordered an expedition against Huesca under Charles's emissary Heribert, which, however, did not succeed.
6. Grimoald IV (806–18).
7. The eclipse was on May 14.

813

1. Amalhar, bishop of Trier (809–14); Peter, abbot of Nonantola near Modena (804–21). Amalhar or Amalarius of Trier wrote verses on this embassy; MGH, *PL,* I, 426; cf. also MGH, *EE,* IV, 556.
2. See s.a. 817, 818; BML, pp. 231–34.
3. The general assembly took place in March 813; the acts of the councils are in G. D. Mansi, *Sacrorum conciliorum nova et amplissima collectio,* 2d ed., 31 vols. (Florence-Venice, 1759–98), XIV, 57–106.
4. Westarfolda was a place in southern Norway; BML, p. 218; Abel-Simson, II, 520.
5. Leo V the Armenian (813–20).

814

1. A fever forced Charles to take to his sickbed; he first hoped to cure himself by dieting but contracted pleurisy. His illness started apparently on January 22. He was buried in his basilica of Aix-la-Chapelle; cf. Einhard, ch. 31; MGH, *PL,* I, 407–8, 435–36; BML, pp. 224–25; Abel-Simson, II, 528–39.
2. Dép. Maine-et-Loire, arr. Saumur.
3. Emperor Leo V asked for help against the Bulgars; BML, p. 242.
4. Cf. Curtius Rufus, VIII, 2, 27.

815

1. In eastern Schleswig.
2. The island of Fünen.
3. Cf. Tacitus, *Annals,* II, 25.
4. July 1, 815.
5. Three hundred Romans are supposed to have been executed; BML, p. 254.
6. Warden of the Pannonian March from about 811 to 832.
7. See s.a. 813.
8. Cf. Livy, XXIII, 15.
9. Cf. Tacitus, *Annals,* I, 76.

816

1. Pope Stephen IV (June 22, 816–January 24/25, 817) crowned Louis on October 5, 816; Ermoldus Nigellus, *In honorem Hludowici christianissimi Caesaris Augusti,* MGH, *PL,* II, 36–37; Simson, I, 73–74; BML, pp. 260, 264–65. The negotiations between pope and emperor

were concerned with "the needs of the Church"; the pact between the emperor and the Roman Church was renewed; Stephen received an estate and obtained the release of Roman prisoners who were held because of crimes committed against Pope Leo III.

817

1. Apparently, in February 817; Kurze, p. 145.
2. Cf. Einhard, ch. 17.
3. Cf. s.a. 816, n.
4. The treaty that was returned to Pope Paschal I (817–24) by the nomenclator Theodore is in MGH, *Cap.*, I, 352–55; cf. BML, p. 268. The emperor confirmed to the pope and his successors the city of Rome and its duchy, several cities of Tuscany and Campania, the exarchate of Ravenna, the Pentapolis, Sabinia, several places in Lombard Tuscany, the islands of Corsica, Sardinia, and Sicily, the patrimonies in Benevento, Salerno, Calabria, and Naples, the voluntary donations of his father and grandfather, and certain revenues of the former kings of Lombardy. The emperor promised to defend these properties, but never to intervene without papal consent. He granted the Romans free election and canonical consecration of the pope and reaffirmed the papal obligation, as in the days of Pepin and Charlemagne, to send ambassadors to the emperor in order to fasten the bonds of friendship, love, and peace among them.
5. For the *Ordinatio imperii,* see MGH, *Cap.*, I, 270–73; BML, pp. 270–72; E. Mühlbacher, *Deutsche Geschichte unter den Karolingern* (Stuttgart, 1896), p. 334.
6. Cf. Justin, XLIII, 3.
7. Cf. Velleius Paterculus, II, 20, 4.
8. Chalon-sur-Saône.
9. Bernard wanted to dethrone the emperor because he had been disregarded entirely when earlier in the year Lothair was made co-emperor and the empire divided. Bishop Rathald of Verona and Count Suppo of Brescia informed the emperor of the conspiracy. Bernard and his followers submitted in December of 817, confessed their guilt, and were taken to Aix-la-Chapelle.
10. See s.a. 785.
11. Anshelm, archbishop of Milan (?–818); Wolfold, bishop of Cremona (816–18); Theodulf, bishop of Orléans (before 798–818).

818

1. Cf. Livy, XXII, 43.
2. The conspirators were blinded on April 15, 818; Bernard and Reginhar offered resistance, and Bernard died two days later. Nithard, Bk. I, ch. 2; Simson, I, 120–28; BML, pp. 233–34.
3. July 7.
4. BML, p. 277. Sigo, duke of Benevento (818–33).

5. The Timociani were a Slavic tribe on the River Timok, a tributary of the Danube, in Yugoslavia.
6. By the peace of Königshofen (812) the Franks received Istria and Dalmatia, i.e., the entire territory of Slovenes and Croats. They also intended, so it seems, to conquer the lands of Serbs and other Slavs. This attempt was thwarted by the revolt of Ljudovit, ruler of the Pannonian Croats, against the Franks in 819 and his plan to create a Yugoslav empire. Ljudovit rallied many tribes: the Slovenes of Carinthia, Styria, Isonzo, the Slavs on the river Timok in Moesia, and, after defeating their duke Borna, the Croats of Dalmatia. Ljudovit was encouraged by the Byzantines. Sisak, near the modern Zagreb, became his capital. When he was murdered, the attempt to establish a Yugoslav empire failed. The Franks again ruled the Croats, although they permitted the Croats of Dalmatia to elect their own prince; Dvornik, *The Slavs,* p. 70.

819

1. The events relating to Sclaomir, king of the Obodrites, Ceadrag, and Lupus belong in the year 818.
2. Cf. BML, pp. 278–82; VH, ch. 32; MGH, *Cap.,* I, 273–75; 275–80; 280–85; 285–88; 288–91. The wedding was in February 819.
3. Cf. Justin, XXXVIII, 7.
4. Here the annalist is wrong; see s.a. 821.

820

1. See s.a. 818, n. 6.
2. Caesar, *De bello Gallico,* II, 2.
3. The treaty had been made in 817; BML, p. 293.
4. Arabic sources report that the Frankish fleet was beaten by the Moors off Sardinia and lost eight ships; Simson, I, 161.
5. Dép. Vendée, arr. Les Sables d'Olonne.
6. Cf. Tacitus, *Annals,* I, 76.

821

1. March 24, 821.
2. At Nijmegen in May 821.
3. Leo V died on December 24, 820; Michael II the Amorian (821–29).
4. Hugo, count of Tours (d. 826).
5. Cf. s.a. 812, n. 4. Adalhard was a brother of Wala and cousin of Charlemagne; he was intermittently abbot of Corbie, advised King Pepin in Italy after 796, and served as Bernard's guardian in Italy from 810 to 814.
6. Cf. Justin, XLIII, 1.

822

1. Arendsee in the Altmark north of Magdeburg.
2. Cf. BML, pp. 301–2; MGH, *Cap.,* I, 357–58; Nithard, I, ch. 2.
3. Cf. s.a. 818, n. 6.

4. Delbende on the Delvenau in Lauenburg.
5. Simson, I, 182, n. 5; VH, ch. 35; Thegan, ch. 29; Paschasius Radbertus, *Epitaphium Arsenii,* ed. E. Dümmler, *Abhandlungen der königlich-preussischen Akademie der Wissenschaften zu Berlin* (Berlin, 1900), Bk. I, ch. 25–26.
6. This was not a special mission; Lothair was already in charge of the government of Italy; BML, p. 303.
7. The Praedenecenti were a branch of the Obodrites.

823

1. Lothair had held the title of emperor since his elevation to co-emperor in 817; the papal coronation now had only the character of an ecclesiastical sanction; BML, p. 305.
2. Drogo was ordained a priest on June 12, 823; he was bishop of Metz until his death in 855.
3. Adalung, abbot of St. Vaast (809–39).
4. Ebbo, archbishop of Reims (816–35, 840–47); Wattenbach-Levison-Löwe, III, 333–35.

824

1. Under their khagan Krum (803–14) the Bulgars extended their domination over many Slavic tribes in Thrace and Macedonia, and after Charlemagne's defeat of the Avars they incorporated part of modern Hungary into their empire and pushed as far as modern Serbia. They secured this territory against the Byzantines (cf. s.a. 811). Krum's successor Omortag (814–31) prevented the Franks from exploiting their success over Ljudovit; he restored Bulgarian authority over the Slavs on the Timok and over other territories formerly under Bulgarian control; he also attacked Pannonian Croatia. Later, the Bulgars obtained part of the Friulian March. The Bulgars thus prevented the Franks from establishing their control over major parts of the Balkans; Dvornik, *The Slavs,* pp. 70–71.
2. Pope Eugenius II (824–27); LP, II, 69; BML, p. 311.
3. The Byzantine emperor was Michael II (820–29); for the embassy's message on image worship, see Mansi, XIV, 419.

825

1. Cf. Einhard, ch. 5.
2. Lambert, count of Nantes (d. 837); Nithard, I, ch. 4; II, ch. 5.
3. Louis the German (806–76) was crowned and put in charge of Bavaria in 817. He ruled the eastern part of the Frankish empire after the treaty of Verdun (843); BML, pp. 317, 561–62. The event referred to in this annal belongs in the year 826.

826

1. It was probably concerned with image worship; BML, p. 325.
2. BML, p. 326; Simson, I, 256–62. Heriold was baptized on June 24, 826.

3. Cf. s.a. 757.
4. The envoys apparently came to complain about Sigo of Benevento's aggression; BML, p. 326.
5. Abd ar-Rahman II (822–52), successor to his father Al-Hakam, emir of Cordova.
6. Hilduin, abbot of St.-Denis (806–42) and archchaplain of the empire (818–30). He has been considered as the possible author of the RFA from 820 to 829; Kurze, p. 171, n. 1; see the Introduction and Nithard, I, ch. 6, II, ch. 3.
7. Cf. Justin, XXIX, 1.
8. Cf. Velleius Paterculus, II, 50, 1; 56, 1.

827

1. Helisachar, chancellor of Louis the Pious (808–19); see Nithard, I, n. 16.
2. Hugo, count of Tours, and Mathfrid, count of Orléans.
3. Cf. s.a. 824, n. 1.
4. Pope Valentine (827) and Pope Gregory IV (827–44); LP, II, 71–72; 73–83.
5. Einhard inspired his notary Ratleic to obtain the relics in Rome. They were eventually translated to Seligenstadt on the River Main, but parts of them were taken temporarily to St.-Médard near Soissons, where even in the tenth and eleventh centuries the possession of these relics was fraudulently asserted; cf. MGH, *SS,* XV, pt. 1, 391–95; 238–64.

828

1. Hugo and Mathfrid; see above s.a. 827, n. 2; BML, p. 331.
2. Haltigar, bishop of Cambrai (817–31).
3. Cf. Florus, *Epitome de T. Livio* II, 8.
4. Cf. Justin, IV, 2.
5. November 11, 828.
6. MGH, *Cap.,* II, 4.

829

1. BML, p. 338.
2. Bernard, count of Barcelona and commander of the Spanish March, ruler of Septimania, i.e., the coastal region from the Rhône to the Pyrenees.

Nithard

BOOK I

1. Nithard addresses Charles II, nicknamed "the Bald," son of Louis the Pious by his second wife Judith, grandson of Charlemagne, born in 823 and king of the western part of the Carolingian empire from 843 to 877. Charles entered the city of Châlons-sur-Marne about the

middle of May, 841; see Nithard, II, ch. 9; Meyer, p. 128, Appendix I.

2. There had been a party at court which opposed Louis' succession but which now collapsed; BML, pp. 239–40. Louis arrived at Aix-la-Chapelle on February 27, 814; see RFA, s.a. 814.
3. The division of the treasure also included gifts for the poor, for widows and orphans, for churches and for the pope; see e.g., Einhard, ch. 33; Ermoldus Nigellus, MGH, *PL,* II, 29; VH, ch. 22.
4. The sisters were Gisela and Bertha, Nithard's mother, who took the veil at St.-Riquier. The three sons mentioned here were illegitimate sons; Drogo became abbot of Luxeuil in 820 and bishop of Metz in 823 (see RFA, s.a. 823); he died in 855. Hugo became abbot of St.-Quentin and died in 844. Theodoric was born in 810. All were tonsured in 818.
5. See RFA, s.a. 810, 813, 817, 818, and notes; BML, pp. 232–33. Nithard is the only source to mention Bertmund as the official who executed the punishment.
6. BML, pp. 270–72, 295; RFA, s.a. 817. The division was decided on at Aix-la-Chapelle in July 817 and ratified at Nijmegen on 1 May 821. Lothair married in 821, Pepin in 822, Louis in 827.
7. Lothair was born about 795, governed Bavaria from 814 to 817, and in 817 was made heir, emperor, co-regent, and future overlord of his brothers Pepin and Louis. In 822 he took Bernard's place as king of Italy, and Italy was in the future the nucleus of his territory; Meyer, p. 53; BML, pp. 412–13, 419. Irmengardis died on 30 October 818; Louis married Judith in February 819. Charles the Bald was born on June 13, 823.
8. Lothair married Irmengarda, daughter of Count Hugo of Tours, in 821; RFA, s.a. 821. Hugo and Mathfrid, count of Orléans, supported Lothair and the party of unity; their fall in February of 828 was Judith's work; BML, pp. 331–32; Simson, I, 288–90. By picturing them as wicked intriguers and disturbers of the peace Nithard reveals his partiality; Meyer, p. 8.
9. The appointment was in August 829; cf. RFA s.a. 829, n. 2. He wavered between Charles and the youthful Pepin of Aquitaine and was obviously aiming at the creation of some kind of autonomous rule. In 844 Charles was able to lure him to the court and had him sentenced to death. Bernard was the son of William, count of Toulouse (d. 806); BML, p. 342; Meyer, pp. 33, 94, n. 51.
10. Cf. *Annals of Metz,* s.a. 830.
11. The revolt started among the magnates. The objectives of the conspiracy were, according to the old emperor's party (cf. Thegan, ch. 36; *Annals of St. Bertin,* s.a. 830), to dethrone Louis the Pious, to remove the empress and her son Charles, and to kill Bernard, Louis' powerful confidant; according to the opposition (cf. Radbert's

Epitaphium, II, ch. 9), to save the emperor from the disastrous influence of those who dominated him, to maintain the unity of the empire, and to uphold the sworn order of succession. The leaders of the conspiracy recalled the army bound for Brittany and called on Pepin and Lothair to join them with their forces. Nithard's charge that Lothair was the instigator of the rebellion is false; the young emperor was in Italy at the beginning of the uprising, but he joined the conspirators on his return to Francia at the beginning of May 830, although Einhard attempted to dissuade him. Louis of Bavaria had already before him arrived in the rebel camp; cf. BML, pp. 343–46; for Judith see VH, ch. 32, 37, 44, 52, 54, 59, 61, 62, 63, and Simson, I, 145–48. The daughter of Count Welf and a Saxon mother, Judith, young, beautiful, and learned, became a powerful influence at the court where her favorites and relatives soon filled important positions.

12. At a general assembly at Compiègne in May 830, which was dominated by Lothair, Louis the Pious admitted his guilt, consigned his controversial spouse to the nunnery of Saint-Croix at Poitiers, and promised to rule in the future with the better counsel of his vassals. Louis remained emperor in name only; Lothair was again co-emperor and now the real ruler. Louis was held in honorable captivity, probably in St.-Médard's at Soissons, but was able to influence affairs. Cf. BML, pp. 346, 563; Meyer, pp. 4–5; the most extensive source for the assembly at Compiègne is Radbert's *Epitaphium*, II, ch. 10.
13. Only after he was deposed in 833 was Louis urged to forsake a secular life; see Lauer, p. 11, n. 8.
14. The ordinance concerning the succession of 817 was annulled, Lothair's position as heir to the entire empire eliminated, he himself excluded from any share in the empire except Italy, and the empire newly partitioned among Louis, Pepin, and Charles. Meyer, p. 53; BML, pp. 420–21, 350–52; MGH, *Cap.*, II, 21. The partition was never carried out since at the general assembly of Ingelheim on May 1, 831, Louis the Pious again changed his policy, pardoned those condemned at Aix-la-Chapelle in February, and received Lothair with honors; BML, pp. 421, 353.
15. Pepin fled the court on December 27, 831, "because he had not been received honorably by his father," VH, ch. 46. He finally met his father again at Jouac near Limoges, probably in September of 832, but Nithard's laconic report that he was dispatched into Francia meant that Louis the Pious had deprived him of Aquitaine. At Doué Pepin escaped from his father shortly afterward. Louis' campaign against the rebellious son late in 832 was a failure; BML, pp. 355, 359, 360. For substantially similar reasons the emperor's son Louis

revolted in the spring of 832 and attacked Alamannia. In April the father crossed the Rhine and Louis' revolt collapsed; the son submitted to his father at Augsburg in May 832; Meyer, p. 69; BML, pp. 356, 565.

16. Wala through his father Bernard (d. 787) was a grandson of Charles Martel and thus a cousin of Charlemagne. His brother was Adalhard and his wife Rothlindis, a sister of Bernard of Septimania. Wala (773–836) served the Carolingians as count and later as abbot of Corbie (826–36) and Bobbio, but was four times banished in the course of his career; RFA, s.a. 811, 812, 822. Helisachar, a Goth from Septimania, served as the chancellor of Louis the Pious from 808 to 819 and was one of the leading men at the court until he was banished in 830. He returned in 833 but then is no longer mentioned in the sources. Louis the Pious heard about the revolt early in 833. The reasons for the joint action of the sons were obviously Judith's renewed ascendancy and its sinister consequences as revealed, for example, by the transfer of Aquitaine to Charles; cf. BML, p. 363.

17. Pope Gregory IV (827–44) arrived from Rome with Lothair to help restore the unity of the empire and preserve the original agreement on the succession. The party of the old emperor looked upon the pope as a tool of the rebels, and the bishops loyal to Louis the Pious received the head of the Church with undisguised hostility; BML, pp. 365–66; Migne, PL, CIV, 296, 302, 301. The place where the two hostile armies met on June 24, 833, was called Rothfels (now Sigolsheim northwest of Colmar) and soon referred to as "the field of lies"; BML, pp. 366–67.

18. He kept his father in the monastery of St.-Médard at Soissons and his brother Charles in the monastery of Prüm. At the general assembly of Compiègne in October 833 many swore loyalty to Lothair; see MGH, *Cap.*, II, 51; a public trial of the old emperor was conducted and Louis the Pious submitted to public penance at Soissons; BML, pp. 368–71; VH, ch. 51. After the revolt Lothair received, in addition to Italy, Provence, Burgundy, the Frankish lands on the left bank of the Rhine, and Frisia. The unity of the empire was not preserved but Lothair acted as emperor in the palaces of Compiègne and Aix-la-Chapelle; Meyer, p. 53; BML, p. 368.

19. The younger Louis intervened for his captive father already in 833, first by way of messengers, in December by a personal meeting with Lothair at Mainz. In January he sent an embassy to Aix-la-Chapelle which was permitted to speak to Louis the Pious in the presence of his guards. In February Louis and Pepin, who resented Lothair's attempt to expand his power at their expense, set out for Aix-la-Chapelle with armed might. Then Lothair took his father to St.-Denis; BML, pp. 371–73.

20. Hugo and Mathfrid have been mentioned already; Lambert was apparently the count of Nantes who died in 837. Lothair fled from Paris on February 28, 834; BML, p. 373.
21. Louis the Pious was restored at St.-Denis on March 1, 834; BML, pp. 374, 381.
22. This is not correct; Lothair was offered pardon if he returned in peace; Thegan, ch. 53; *Annals of St. Bertin,* s.a. 834; BML, pp. 374–75.
23. Judith was brought back to Francia not by her guards but by supporters of Louis the Pious; Simson, II, 101–2. Judith purged herself after the general assembly of Aix-la-Chapelle in 831; there had been no further charges of this kind in 833; BML, pp. 350–51, 375; Meyer, pp. 10–12.
24. Odo was count of Orléans; on Vivian, perhaps an error for William, see Lauer, p. 21, n. 4; Fulbert cannot be identified.
25. Gerberga was a nun, the sister of Bernard of Septimania; Lothair had her put in a barrel and drowned in the Saône as a witch. Her brother had been charged with using magic in his control of the emperor; Thegan, ch. 52; VH, ch. 44; *Annals of St. Bertin,* s.a. 834; BML, p. 377.
26. Dép. Loir-et-Cher.
27. The next event in Nithard's history, the grant of part of the kingdom to Charles, falls in the year 837. The major events touching on the conflict between father and sons during the preceding two years were the following: At a general assembly at Thionville in February 835 a declaration of loyalty signed by all present was issued in the form of a book for the information of the people; the bishops wrote and signed individual declarations. On February 28, 835, the solemn reconciliation of the emperor with clergy and people took place; on March 4 Ebbo, archbishop of Reims and standard-bearer of the hostile party, confessed and resigned. Lothair's relations with the emperor remained unsettled. He had left for Italy with his closest supporters in 834. In 835 and 836 the emperor sent embassies to him. In May 836 finally Wala appeared at the general assembly of Thionville and arranged a safe-conduct for Lothair. But the son used an epidemic in Italy during the summer of the same year (which killed Wala, Hugo, Mathfrid, and Jesse of Amiens among many others) as a pretext not to come across the Alps. The emperor then dispatched an embassy to Italy to find out whether his son would come to him at a later date. He also commanded him to return the Italian possessions of Frankish churches and to restore their positions to those men who had left Italy with the empress in 834. Lothair refused and next year, 837, Louis the Pious announced a journey to Italy and demanded from Lothair an honorable reception and ade-

quate provisions. The attacks of the Norsemen prevented the Italian expedition, and Lothair now closed and fortified the Alpine passes; BML, pp. 380–82, 385–86, 389–90, 391–92.

28. As for the location of the areas not readily identifiable, Moilla: upper valley of the Niers; Haettra: north of the latter between Rhine and Meuse; Hammolant: on the right bank of the lower Rhine between Yssel and the Saxon border; Ornois: the valley of the Ornain; Blasois: the area of the Blaise; Bar: Bar-sur-Aube in Burgundy and Bar-le-Duc in Lorraine; cf. Lauer, p. 25, notes.

29. The meeting between the younger Louis and Lothair took place in the valley of Trent probably in March 838. The reason for the meeting was obviously the recent grant to Charles. Louis the Pious suspected a new conspiracy and told his followers to be prepared. The emperor ordered Louis to come before the general assembly at Nijmegen in June 838. On that occasion a violent argument broke out between father and son. With the exception of Bavaria Louis had to surrender all his lands on either side of the Rhine; Meyer, pp. 54, 69, 9–10; BML, pp. 568, 394, 396, 397.

30. Louis submitted again to his father in April of 839; BML, pp. 400, 402.

31. Other sources claim he returned to Frankfurt; see BML, p. 401.

32. Book I, ch. 3.

33. The new division was, of course, at the expense of Louis, who would retain only Bavaria. Lothair chose the part of the empire east of the Meuse. Louis, the son, was required to swear not to leave Bavaria, otherwise the emperor would take an army to Augsburg in September; BML, pp. 403–5; 429, 570; MGH, *Cap.*, II, 58.

34. Cf. Luke 15:21.

35. Cf. John 13:34.

36. Pepin had died on December 13, 838. In the fall of 839 an expedition of the emperor attempted to break the resistance the Aquitanians put up to Charles; VH, ch. 61; BML, pp. 405, 407. Simson, II, 191, n. 2.

37. Chalon-sur-Saône.

38. By the middle of February 840 Louis the Pious at Poitiers received the news that his son Louis had revolted again and had occupied all lands east of the Rhine. A general assembly at Worms on July 1, 840, was to concern itself with the rebellious son, but a fortnight earlier the old emperor died; Meyer, p. 70; BML, pp. 570, 409.

39. Louis actually died in his sixty-third year, ruled Aquitaine for almost thirty-three years, and was emperor for twenty-six years and nine months. The island on which he died was Petersaue in the Rhine; BML, pp. 411–12, 431.

Notes

Nithard

BOOK II

1. Lothair's march was not delayed; he was in Italy on June 20 and in Strasbourg on July 24. The unexpected meeting was at Kostheim near Mainz; Nithard is obviously less familiar with these localities. Lothair was at Mainz on August 13, 840; Meyer, pp. 55–56, 149; BML, pp. 433–35.
2. The emissary Nithard was our author; Adalgar was a count of Charles's party; see below Bk. III, ch. 4.
3. His purpose was to secure the territories assigned to him by the treaty of Worms; Meyer, pp. 20, 96, n. 83.
4. The *carbonariae,* la forêt Charbonnière, were the area between Sambre and Scheldt in the present Belgian province of Hainaut. "This side" is southwest and "on the other side" northwest of it; Meyer, pp. 20, 96, n. 82; Lauer, p. 43, n. 3. It constituted the frontier between Neustria and Austrasia.
5. Of the men mentioned here Odulf was the lay abbot of St.-Josse (Dép. Pas de Calais), cf. Meyer, p. 112, n. 317; Gislebert is mentioned below Bk. III, ch. 2.
6. This Hugo could be the illegitimate son of Charlemagne and abbot of St.-Quentin; Meyer, p. 102, n. 172.
7. Charles was in Aquitaine after October 10, 840. In the meantime Lothair was punishing those who resisted him by confiscating their benefices; BML, p. 435. The Meuse was the border of Charles's land.
8. Pepin is the son of Charlemagne's grandson Bernard who had been blinded in 818.
9. On 10 October 840 Lothair was at Ver near Senlis; BML, pp. 435, 436.
10. Of the lands assigned to Charles at Worms in 839 one-third, which included Burgundy, was now left out; BML, p. 436; Meyer, pp. 21, 56–57.
11. Charles was at Nevers until the end of December 840; Meyer, p. 22. On Bernard see Bk. I, ch. 3, and note.
12. Lambert was first a supporter of Charles but then seized the county of Nantes, allied himself with the Bretons, and thus became a dangerous opponent to Charles. See above Bk. I, n. 20, and Lauer, p. 52, n. 1.
13. 8 May 841; Bk. II, ch. 4.
14. Warnar was the brother of Count Lambert; Lauer, p. 55, n. 1.
15. Cf. Bk. II, ch. 3.
16. *Aeneid* 2. 20.
17. Cf. *Aeneid* 2. 28.
18. Warin: above Bk. I, ch. 5.
19. Saint-Germain-des-Prés near Paris.

20. Charles left the monastery of St. Germain-des-Prés on the evening of April 12, 841. The mouth of the Loing is near Moret.
21. La forêt d'Othe is located between Sens and Troyes and surrounded by the rivers Armance, Armancon, Yonne, Vanne. This was probably the night from April 12 to 13; Meyer, p. 98, n. 109.
22. Lothair by his indecisive and devious actions was driving Charles and Louis into an alliance; Meyer, pp. 57–58. In the meantime Louis had secured the lands east of the Rhine, received homage from Franks, Alamanni, Saxons, and Thuringians, and occupied and fortified the towns on the left bank of the Rhine. Lothair did not come to the meeting with Louis arranged for November 11, 840, and moved against Louis in March 841; BML, pp. 438, 571–72; Meyer, pp. 71–72; Mühlbacher, *Deutsche Geschichte,* pp. 429–30.
23. Otgar had been archbishop of Mainz since 826 and had been a loyal follower of Lothair in the days of Louis the Pious. He died on June 21, 847. Count Adalbert of Metz had waged the campaigns of Louis the Pious against the younger Louis; Meyer, pp. 58, 113, n. 226. The *Annals of Fulda,* s.a. 841, call the count an "instigator of quarrels."
24. *Aeneid* 10. 770.
25. The borders referred to are those on which they agreed at Orléans; Bk. II, ch. 4; BML, p. 436; for the emissaries, see Bk. II, 7.
26. It cannot be established who sought help first, but there was now a natural community of interest between the two brothers; Meyer, pp. 25–26; BML, p. 572; E. Dümmler, *Geschichte des ostfränkischen Reichs,* I, 2d ed. (Leipzig, 1887), p. 146, n. 43.
27. Châlons-sur-Marne.
28. The place of battle was not far from Donauwörth in Bavaria. Adalbert was slain, and Louis was finally able to establish his control over the tribes of southern Germany; Meyer, p. 73; BML, pp. 440, 572; Mühlbacher, *Deutsche Geschichte,* p. 432.
29. Near Châlons-sur-Marne.
30. Lothair's movements between Easter 841, when he was at Aix-la-Chapelle, and the beginning of June are uncertain.
31. About Fontenoy en Puisaye as the place of battle, see E. Müller, "Der Schlachtort Fontaneum (Fontanetum) von 841," NA, XXXIII (1907), 201–24; Lauer, p. 72, n. 2.
32. Whether this Hugo is the uncle of the brothers is not certain.
33. Hegibert, Hirmenald, and Frederic remain obscure figures.
34. Seven o'clock in the morning.
35. St. Cloud on the Seine is meant.
36. Six o'clock in the morning.
37. The "brook of the Burgundians" was east of Fontenoy; cf. Lauer, p. 77, n. 3.

38. Of the places mentioned here "Brittas" was probably Bois-des-Briottes, "Solemnat" Soleme; "Fagit" was between the other two places.
39. The sources for the battle are named in BML, pp. 442–44. The battle was a cavalry battle and its military aspects have been examined by Meyer, pp. 136–41, Appendix VI. All sources stress the magnitude of the losses on both sides; cf. Lot/Halphen, I, 35–36; MGH, *PL,* II, 138–39. The flower of the Frankish nobility died, and Hugh of Fleury later noted the permanent division of the empire as the result of the battle. The battle, nevertheless, as Nithard's later books show, was not decisive; cf. Mühlbacher, *Deutsche Geschichte,* p. 437. Nithard's assertion that there was no pursuit of the enemy whatsoever is incorrect; see *Annals of St. Bertin,* s.a. 841.

Nithard

BOOK III

1. Cf. Ps. 27:7, 32:20, 39:18, 113:9–11; Eccli. 51:2.
2. These observations Nithard wrote down in the fall of 841; they indicate that the military effect of the battle of Fontenoy was nullified; Meyer, pp. 32–33.
3. Dép. Seine-et-Oise.
4. The passage relating to Soissons in its entirety was considered a later insertion by Müller, pp. 30–31, note.
5. *Berniacum,* Berny, arr. Soissons.
6. Charles left Reims late in August and was in Corbény on Sept. 1; BML, p. 445; Lot/Halphen, p. 42.
7. Hugo apparently is again the abbot of St.- Quentin, who died as Charles's loyal supporter in the battle on the Âgout on June 14, 844; Meyer, pp. 34–35. Gislebert or Gilbert was count of the Maasgau, the land on the lower Meuse; cf. Bk. I, ch. 6. Lothair's movements at this time can be reconstructed from the *Annals of St. Bertin* and the *Annals of Fulda,* s.a. 841. After the battle of Fontenoy Lothair went to Aix-la-Chapelle, where he spent the entire month of July 841. He distributed crown property and tried to secure Saxons and Normans as allies. After gathering troops he went to Mainz (August 20), crossed the river near Worms, apparently in pursuit of Louis. Suddenly, he broke off his campaign, returned to Worms, where he attended his daughter's wedding, and was at Thionville on September 1. Charles's advance into the Meuse area, the nucleus of the Carolingian domain, probably caused this retreat. Charles now withdrew towards the Seine, reaching the river before Lothair. Lothair followed him and in the last days of September made his headquarters at St.- Denis. Late in October he went up the Seine and Yonne to Sens, turned in vain against Charles at the forest of Perche, and

proceeded to Le Mans, where he permitted his troops to plunder and forced even monks and nuns to swear oaths of fealty to him. From Le Mans he went south toward the Loire and reached Tours. When he heard that Charles planned to unite his forces again with those of Louis, Lothair began to retreat, crossed the Seine early in 842, and was at Aix-la-Chapelle in February. His campaigns had been a failure; Meyer, pp. 59, 63–65; BML, pp. 444–47.

8. *Wasiticum* has been identified with both Visé, on the Meuse between Liège and Maastricht, and with Wasseiges, arr. Waremme, on the Méhaigne; BML, p. 445; Meyer, p. 34; Appendix VII, pp. 141–43; Lauer, pp. 90–91, n. 6.
9. Hugo may be the abbot of St.-Quentin; Meyer, pp. 102, n. 172; 101, n. 163.
10. Bishop Emmon of Noyon (840–59).
11. Meulan on the right bank of the Seine below Paris.
12. Charles was still at St.-Cloud on October 18, 841, when Nithard was writing his *Histories* there, but Lothair had left his headquarters at St.-Denis by November 6; Meyer, p. 35.
13. Apparently, piles of wood to be lit at the appropriate moment; BML, pp. 445–46; Meyer, p. 102, n. 178, 179.
14. Hildegard was a daughter of Louis the Pious by his first wife Irmengardis and served as abbess of the monastery of St. Mary at Laon.
15. Cf. Bk. II, ch. 2.
16. *Aeneid* 4. 466.
17. Ten o'clock in the morning.
18. Five miles from Laon.
19. Charles was at St.-Denis on 6 November 841; Lot/Halphen, I, 46.
20. North of Mortagne-sur-Huine, Dép. Orne.
21. After the battle of Fontenoy Louis pressed his advantage and used the fall of 841 to recover his strength. By threats and special favors he subjugated the majority of Saxons and all East Franks, Thuringians, and Alamanni. About the middle of August 841 Louis stayed first at Salz near Neustadt in Lower Franconia and then in Frankish Swabia; Meyer, pp. 74–75; BML, p. 573.
22. The oaths exchanged at Strasbourg were a reconfirmation of the alliance between Louis and Charles, which was now about nine months old. The oaths are of supreme significance because Nithard preserved the texts in the vernacular, thus providing us with some of the most ancient examples of the French and German languages. It has been suggested that Nithard was the author of the texts of the oaths, or that the Romance oaths were influenced by the style of the Carolingian chancery and that Nithard altered the texts. For the extensive literature on this point, see Wattenbach-Levison-Löwe, III, 356, n. 204. Cf. also A. Tabachovitz, "Les Serments de Strasbourg et

le ms. B.N. lat. 9768," *Vox Romanica,* XVIII (1958), 36–61; Lauer, pp. 104, n. 1–4, 106, n. 1–3, 108, n. 1.

23. *Wasagus,* Germ. *Wasgau,* the Hunsrück mountains, on the left bank of the Rhine, between Rhine and Moselle. The monastery of Wissembourg, Alsace, belonged to Otgar, archbishop of Mainz.
24. Carloman (ca. 830–80), son of Louis.
25. *Aeneid* I. 313.
26. February to March 842; BML, p. 574.
27. Bardo was a count who died in 856; Meyer, pp. 75, 104, n. 213.
28. Dümmler, *Ostfränk. Reich,* I, 133, n. 4; 151, n. 3; 177, n. 2. Lothair was in Aix-la-Chapelle in February of 842. There he heard that his brothers had united their forces on February 14. Lothair now chose the Moselle as his line of defense, and in March he went himself to Sinzig, a few miles north of the Moselle where the Ahr flows into the Rhine. Louis and Charles appeared on the right bank of the Moselle on March 18, 842; Meyer, p. 65; BML, p. 447.
29. Bingen is on the left bank of the Rhine about forty miles from Koblenz. Einrichi was the name of a district on the right side of the Rhine. The speed implied here is extraordinary—they left in the morning and arrived about noon—and would have been possible only for mounted troops; BML, p. 447; Meyer, pp. 40, 104, n. 217.
30. One o'clock in the afternoon.
31. Cf. Dümmler, *Ostfränk. Reich,* I, 174, n. 2.
32. Lothair withdrew from Sinzig to Aix-la-Chapelle on March 19. Toward the end of the month he left his capital and headed in a southerly direction, thus giving rise to the rumor that he was forsaking the imperial crown and the Carolingian heartland and fleeing to Italy. But at Easter, on April 2, he was at Troyes and soon appeared in the neighborhood of Lyons where he had supporters. After replenishing his forces he eventually turned north again and reached Mâcon on June 15, 842; Meyer, pp. 65–66; BML, pp. 447–50.

Nithard

BOOK IV

1. Bk. III, Preface.
2. Three lines were left empty in the manuscript at this point. The new division apparently attempted to limit Lothair to Italy. Nithard names the principle of division—contiguous territory—but apparently left spaces in his manuscript where he later intended to insert the names of the lands assigned to each of the brothers; Meyer, pp. 41–42; BML, pp. 448–49, 574; Lauer, p. 120.
3. Four lines were left blank; then the same hand corrected *Karolo* into *Karolus* and added :"He received the western kingdoms, from the

British ocean to the River Moselle, in which part the name of Francia has remained ever since."

4. The Saxons had been especially loyal to Louis the Pious, and a Saxon army had helped in 839 to defeat his rebellious son Louis. Since 840 there was, however, a Saxon party which supported the son. Some sources associate the rebellion with a simultaneous relapse into heathenism and note the spread and ferocity of the revolt. Lothair's pact with the rebels, who were driving their "legitimate lords," as one annalist says, out of the country, may indicate that Lothair was not discriminate in the choice of his means. The threat of the Saxon revolt to Louis' position was particularly serious, since Saxony comprised a territory twice as large as the original Frankish lands east of the Rhine. The name of the Stellinga remains obscure but may have meant associates or allies; Meyer, pp. 59–62, 76.
5. Lothair gave the Frisian island of Walcheren and some neighboring places to Heriold. The *Annals of St. Bertin,* s.a. 841, castigate such measures because of their disastrous consequences. Heriold appears first in 814 and disappears after 842. The Normans had been entering the mouths of the Rhine, Meuse, Scheldt, Seine, and Loire since 834.
6. A lacuna of ca. twenty letters; Meyer, p. 120, n. 463.
7. Étaples on the Canche (Pas-de-Calais).
8. Hamblehaven in Hampshire or Harwich in Essex.
9. Norwich? cf. *Annals of St. Bertin,* s.a. 842.
10. Chalon-sur-Saône.
11. Arr. Chalon-sur-Saône.
12. Iosippus, Joseph, Bk. I, ch. 7; Egbert: Hegibert? Bk. II, ch. 10. Eberhard, margrave of Friuli, husband of Charles's sister Gisela. He was also a patron of Sedulius Scottus and Gottschalk.
13. Cf. Luke 15:21.
14. By way of diplomacy Lothair had at least partly made up for his military and moral disaster in March; Meyer, pp. 45–46, 67; BML, p. 449.
15. For various attempts to supplement the text in this lacuna of about twelve letters, see Meyer, p. 107, n. 248; Lauer, p. 128, n. b.
16. Conrad is Judith's brother of Bk. I, ch. 3; Cobbo was a Saxon count, Meyer, pp. 44–45; Adalhard is the same as above in Bk. II, ch. 2. He was lay abbot of St. Maximin in Trier in 838.
17. The meeting on the island of Ansilla, located nine miles south of Mâcon in Saint-Symphorien d'Ancelles, took place on June 15 and 16, 842. Lothair went into the Ardennes; before August 29 he came to Trier; during the last days of September he went, against the agreement with his brothers, to Thionville. He left Thionville in February

843 and was in Aix-la-Chapelle in March; BML, p. 450; Meyer, pp. 46–48, 67–68.

18. In August 842 Louis held a general assembly at Salz; subsequently, he turned against the Stellinga from whom Lothair now dissociated himself; cf. *Annals of St. Bertin,* s.a. 842; Meyer, pp. 77–78; BML, pp. 576–77.
19. Pepin was about fifteen years old when his father died in 838. He caused Charles much trouble and defeated his forces in the battle on the Âgout in June 844. He eventually apostatized and joined the Normans in their attacks on Aquitaine. In 864 he was taken prisoner, sentenced to death, but pardoned and permitted to die in a monastery at Senlis; Meyer, pp. 48–50.
20. Nithard complains about Lothair being at Thionville and thus close to Metz, but does not criticize Charles for passing through Metz; Meyer, pp. 47–48, 109, n. 278.
21. Metz is less than twenty miles from Thionville and more than one hundred and twenty from Worms.
22. The manuscript says one hundred and ten, an obvious error; Meyer, p. 109, n. 272.
23. Angilbert died on February 18, 814. The earthquake occurred on October 24; this is consequently the day of Angilbert's translation.
24. Sigihard, duke of the Lombards, was killed in 839. Sigenulf, the Lombard prince of Salerno, ruled from 839 to 849. The fleets of the Saracens advanced as far north as the mouth of the Po. Their growing pressure was soon blamed on the wars among the sons of Louis the Pious; BML, p. 452.
25. Hirmentrude died in 869 after giving birth to many children; Odo was the count of Orléans who replaced Mathfrid; cf. Bk. 1, ch. 5.
26. Osea 14:10; Ezech. 33:20; Acts 13:10; II Kings 15:23.
27. Wisdom 5:21.
28. The correct date is March 19.
29. The outcome of the events described in Nithard's work was the division of the empire at Verdun in August 843; the sources and the arrangements of the treaty are dealt with in detail in BML, pp. 454–55.

Bibliography

The revised *Royal Frankish Annals* were first printed at Cologne in 1521, the original annals at Ingolstadt in 1601. Both texts were reprinted in the 17th- and 18th-century collections of A. Duchesne and M. Bouquet, R also in those of M. Freher and R. Reuber. The first critical edition of both O and R by G. J. Pertz in MGH, *SS,* I (1826), 134–218, was the basis for the standard edition by

F. Kurze, *Annales regni Francorum 741–829 qui dicuntur Annales Laurissenses maiores et Einhardi.* MGH, *SrG* (Hanover, 1895). The earlier editions are listed on pp. xv and xvi.

There are both German and French translations of the RFA:

O. Abel, *Einhards Jahrbücher. Die Geschichtsschreiber der deutschen Vorzeit,* II (Berlin, 1850); rev. ed. W. Wattenbach. *Die Geschichtsschreiber der deutschen Vorzeit,* 2d ed., XVII (Leipzig, 1888; repr. 1940). A revised version of this translation was printed together with Kurze's text in: R. Rau, *Quellen zur karolingischen Reichsgeschichte,* 3 vols. (Darmstadt, 1955–60), I, 10–155.

F. P. G. Guizot, *Collection des mémoires relatifs à l'histoire de France* (Paris, 1823–35), III, 1–16.

A. Teulet, *Einhardi Opera,* 2 vols. (Paris, 1840–43), I, 118–401.

An excellent modern analysis of the work with an extensive bibliography is in W. Wattenbach-W. Levison-H. Löwe, *Deutschlands Geschichtsquellen im Mittelalter. Vorzeit und Karolinger,* II (Weimar, 1953), pp. 245–56.

Among the other general works on medieval literature, see: M. Manitius, *Geschichte der lateinischen Literatur des Mittelalters,* 3 vols.;

Handbuch der klassischen Altertumswissenschaft, IX, Abteilung 2 (Munich, 1911–31), I, 646–47.

R. L. Poole, *Chronicles and Annals* (Oxford, 1926), pp. 33–34.

M. L. W. Laistner, *Thought and Letters in Western Europe:* A.D. 500 *to* 900, rev. ed. (London, 1957), pp. 262–64.

The following studies are specifically devoted to the *Royal Frankish Annals:*

L. von Ranke, "Zur Kritik fränkisch-deutscher Reichsannalisten," *Abhandlungen der preussischen Akademie in Berlin* (1854), pp. 415–435; repr. in *Gesammelte Werke,* LI (Leipzig, 1888), 95–121.

G. Waitz, "Zu den Lorscher und Einhards Annalen," *Nachrichten von der Göttinger Universität* (1857), pp. 46–52.

B. Simson, *De statu questionis: sintne Einhardi necne sint quos ei ascribunt, Annales imperii* (Königsberg, 1860).

———. "Zur Frage nach der Entstehung der *Annales Laurissenses maiores,*" *Forschungen zur deutschen Geschichte,* XX (1880), 205–14.

———. *Jahrbücher des fränkischen Reichs unter Karl dem Grossen,* II (Leipzig, 1883), 604–11; I, rev. ed. (Leipzig, 1888), 1–5, 657–64.

W. Giesebrecht, "Die fränkischen Königsannalen und ihr Ursprung," *Historisches Jahrbuch,* I (1865), 189–229.

F. Ebrard, "Die fränkischen Reichsannalen und ihre Umarbeitung," *Forschungen zur deutschen Geschichte,* XIII (1873), 425–72.

E. Dünzelmann, "Beiträge zur Kritik der karolingischen Annalen," *NA,* II (1877), 475–537.

R. Arnold, *Beiträge zur Kritik karolingischer Annalen* (Leipzig, 1878).

M. Manitius, "Einhards Werke und ihr Stil," NA, VII (1882), 517–68.

———. "Zu den *Annales Laurissenses maiores,*" *Mitteilungen des Instituts für österreichische Geschichtsforschung,* X (1889), 419–27.

———. "Zur Sprache und Entstehung der älteren *Annales Laurissenses maiores,*" ibid., XIII (1892), 225–38.

I. Bernays, *Zur Kritik karolingischer Annalen* (Strasbourg, 1883).

G. Kaufmann, "Die karolingischen Reichsannalen," *Historische Zeitschrift,* LIV (1885), 55–70.

R. Dörr, "Beiträge zur Einhardsfrage," *NA,* X (1885), 241–305.

F. Kurze, "Über die karolingischen Reichsannalen von 741–829," *NA,* XIX (1894), 295–329; XX (1895), 9–49; XXI (1896), 9–82.

———. "Zur Überlieferung der karolingischen Reichsannalen und ihrer Überarbeitung," NA, XXVIII (1903), 619–69.

———. *Die karolingischen Annalen bis zum Tode Einhards. Beilage zum Jahresbericht des Luisengymnasiums zu Berlin* (1913).

E. Bernheim, "Das Verhältnis der *Vita Caroli Magni* zu den

sogenannten *Annales Einhardi,*" *Historische Vierteljahresschrift,* I (1898), 161–80.

G. Monod, *Études critiques sur les sources de l'histoire carolingienne. Bibliothèque de l'Ecole des Haute Etudes,* CXIX (1898).

H. Wibel, *Beiträge zur Kritik der Annales regni Francorum* (Strasbourg, 1902).

———. "Zur Überlieferung der karolingischen Reichsannalen und ihrer Überarbeitung," *NA,* XXVIII (1903), 670–86.

L. Halphen, *Études critiques sur l'histoire de Charlemagne* (Paris, 1921).

H. Hoffmann, *Untersuchungen zur karolingischen Annalistik. Bonner historische Forschungen,* X (Bonn, 1958).

L. Malbos, "L'Annaliste royal sous Louis le Pieux," *Le Moyen âge,* LXXII (1966), 225–33.

Nithard's *Histories* were first printed in Paris in 1588 and then reprinted in various major collections. There are two modern critical texts:

Nithardi historiarum libri iv. ed. K. Pertz (1839); rev. W. Arndt (1870); 3rd ed. E. Müller. MGH, *SrG* (Hanover-Leipzig, 1907).

P. Lauer, *Nithard: Histoire des fils de Louis le Pieux,* ed. P. Lauer. *Les classiques de l'histoire de France au moyen âge,* VII (Paris, 1926).

Nithard has been translated into German by J. von Jasmund, *Nithards vier Bücher Geschichten. Die Geschichtsschreiber der deutschen Vorzeit,* VI (Berlin, 1851); 3d ed. W. Wattenbach. *Die Geschichtsschreiber der deutschen Vorzeit,* 2d ed., XX (Leipzig, 1889); 5th ed. E. Müller (Leipzig, 1912); and R. Rau, *Quellen zur karolingischen Reichsgeschichte,* I (Darmstadt, 1955), pp. 386–461 (which reprints Müller's Latin text on pages opposite the translation).

French translations are in Guizot, *Collection,* III, 425–97, and Lauer, *Nithard,* where the translation faces the Latin text.

Nithard's life and work are briefly discussed in Müller's and Lauer's introductions to the Latin text and in a number of general works of reference, especially:

A. Ebert, *Allgemeine Geschichte der Literatur des Mittelalters im Abendlande,* 2 vols. (Leipzig, 1880), II, 370–74.

M. Manitius, *Geschichte der lateinischen Literatur des Mittelalters* (Munich, 1910) I, 657–60.

W. Stammler-K. Langosch, *Die deutsche Literatur des Mittelalters: Verfasserlexikon* (Berlin, 1933–55), V, 733–35 (M. L. Bulst).

Wattenbach-Levison-Löwe, *Deutschlands Geschichtsquellen im Mittelalter. Vorzeit und Karolinger,* III, 353–57.

Important modern works on Nithard are:

G. Meyer von Knonau, *Über Nithards vier Bücher Geschichten: Der Bruderkrieg der Söhne Ludwigs des Frommen und sein Geschichtsschreiber* (Leipzig, 1866).

M. Manitius, "Zu deutschen Geschichtsquellen des 9. bis 12. Jahrhunderts," *NA,* IX (1884), 618; XI (1886), 69, 70, 73.

U. Berliere, "Nithard, Abt von Centula (St. Riquier)," *Studien und Mitteilungen des Benediktinerordens,* VIII (1887), 175–81.

E. Müller, "Die Nithard-Interpolation des Klosters St. Medardus bei Soissons," *NA,* XXXIV (1909), 681–722.

H. Prümm, *Sprachliche Untersuchung zu Nithardi Historiarum libri* IV (Diss. Greifswald, 1910).

F. L. Ganshof, "Note critique sur la biographie de Nithard," *Mélanges Paul Thomas* (Bruges, 1930), pp. 335–44.

Index

Ann Arbor Paperbacks

Waddell, *The Desert Fathers*
Chinard, *Thomas Jefferson*
Erasmus, *The Praise of Folly*
Donne, *Devotions*
Malthus, *Population: The First Essay*
Roland, *The Song of Roland*
Berdyaev, *The Origin of Russian Communism*
Einhard, *The Life of Charlemagne*
Edwards, *The Nature of True Virtue*
Gilson, *Héloïse and Abélard*
Taylor, *The Mind of Plato*
Aristotle, *Metaphysics*
Kant, *Education*
Boulding, *The Image*
Duckett, *The Gateway to the Middle Ages* (3 vols.): *Italy; France and Britain; Monasticism*
Bowditch and Ramsland, *Voices of the Industrial Revolution*
Luxemburg, *The Russian Revolution and Leninism or Marxism?*
Rexroth, *Poems from the Greek Anthology*
Hook, *From Hegel to Marx*
Zoshchenko, *Scenes from the Bathhouse*
Thrupp, *The Merchant Class of Medieval London*
Procopius, *Secret History*
Fine, *Laissez Faire and the General-Welfare State*
Adcock, *Roman Political Ideas and Practice*
Swanson, *The Birth of the Gods*
Xenophon, *The March Up Country*
Trotsky, *The New Course*
Buchanan and Tullock, *The Calculus of Consent*
Hobson, *Imperialism*
Pobedonostsev, *Reflections of a Russian Statesman*
Kinietz, *The Indians of the Western Great Lakes 1615–1760*
Bromage, *Writing for Business*
Lurie, *Mountain Wolf Woman, Sister of Crashing Thunder*
Leonard, *Baroque Times in Old Mexico*
Bukharin and Preobrazhensky, *The ABC of Communism*
Meier, *Negro Thought in America, 1880–1915*
Burke, *The Philosophy of Edmund Burke*
Michelet, *Joan of Arc*
Conze, *Buddhist Thought in India*
Trotsky, *Problems of the Chinese Revolution*
Chesnutt, *The Wife of His Youth and Other Stories*
Gross, *Sound and Form in Modern Poetry*
Zola, *The Masterpiece*
Chesnutt, *The Marrow of Tradition*
Aristophanes, *Four Comedies*
Aristophanes, *Three Comedies*
Chesnutt, *The Conjure Woman*
Duckett, *Carolingian Portraits*
Rapoport and Chammah, *Prisoner's Dilemma*
Aristotle, *Poetics*
Boulding, *Beyond Economics*
Peattie, *The View from the Barrio*
U.S. Department of HEW, *Toward a Social Report*
Duckett, *Death and Life in the Tenth Century*
Langford, *Galileo, Science and the Church*
McNaughton, *The Taoist Vision*
Anderson, *Matthew Arnold and the Classical Tradition*
Milio, *9226 Kercheval*
Weisheipl, *The Development of Physical Theory in the Middle Ages*
Breton, *Manifestoes of Surrealism*
Burt, *Mammals of the Great Lakes Region*
Lester, *Theravada Buddhism in Southeast Asia*
Scholz, *Carolingian Chronicles*
Marković, *From Affluence to Praxis*
Eden, *Crisis in Watertown*
Wik, *Henry Ford and Grass-roots America*
Sahlins and Service, *Evolution and Culture*
Wickham, *Early Medieval Italy*
Waddell, *The Wandering Scholars*
Rosenberg, *Bolshevik Visions* (2 parts in 2 vols.)
Mannoni, *Prospero and Caliban*
Aron, *Democracy and Totalitarianism*
Shy, *A People Numerous and Armed*
Taylor, *Roman Voting Assemblies*
Goodfield, *An Imagined World*